CHILDREN'S LANGUAGE AND THE LANGUAGE ARTS

McGRAW-HILL BOOK COMPANY

New York St. Louis San Francisco Auckland Bogotá Düsseldorf
Johannesburg London Madrid Mexico Montreal New Delhi
Panama Paris São Paulo Singapore Sydney Tokyo Toronto

CAROL J. FISHER
University of Georgia

C. ANN TERRY
University of Houston
Clear Lake City

Children's Language and the Language Arts

Library of Congress Cataloging in Publication Data

Fisher, Carol J.
  Children's language and the language arts.

  Includes bibliographies and index.
  1. Language arts (Elementary) I. Terry, Ann,
joint author. II. Title.
LB1576.F44   372.6   76-23294
ISBN 0-07-021107-8

CHILDREN'S LANGUAGE
AND THE LANGUAGE ARTS

1 2 3 4 5 6 7 8 9 0 D O D O 7 8 3 2 1 0 9 8 7 6

This book was set in Primer by Monotype Composition Company, Inc.
The editors were Stephen D. Dragin, Janis M. Yates, and Phyllis T. Dulan;
the designer was Anne Canevari Green;
the production supervisor was Leroy A. Young.
The drawings were done by J & R Services, Inc.
R. R. Donnelley & Sons Company was printer and binder.

Thomas England conceived and took all chapter-opening photographs except
the Chapter 7 opening photograph, credited to Juanita Skelton.

See Acknowledgments on pages 357–359.
Copyright included on this page by reference.

Contents

10. Written Discourse—Self-Expression and Communication 203

Preface

The program of instruction that is presented in *Children's Language and the Language Arts* is based directly on two theories: Piaget's views of learning and the psycholinguistic view of language acquisition and development. Throughout this text, language and intellectual development are related to children's activities. The more knowledgeable teachers are about how children learn and how language develops, the more able they are to use experiences that offer extensive learning opportunities to develop a stronger language arts program. The teacher becomes a decision maker in curriculum planning rather than a dispenser of knowledge and isolated activities which may be meaningless. Selected experiences, based on an understanding of children's abilities and needs at particular stages of development, are given as examples of appropriate language arts activities. Instead of presenting extensive lists of activities that are often ends in themselves instead of means to an end, this text suggests those which can be extended and molded into a progression that ultimately leads to established learning objectives.

Actual samples of children's oral and written language are included—not only for illustrative purposes, but to develop proficiency in diagnosing and evaluating the learning needs of children. For example, stories written by children of different ages are included for practice in writing comments focused on their positive qualities or for analyzing various mechanical aspects. Samples of children's manuscript and cursive handwriting are shown for practice in diagnosis of their strengths and weaknesses. This text, then, incorporates children's work for practice activities as well as for illustration.

There are three principal parts to *Children's Language and the Language Arts*. The first part, "Perspectives: Language Arts, Language, and Learning," presents the theoretical background for the rest of the book. The introductory chapter illustrates in words and pictures the rich classroom environment and the types of activities that should be the core of the language arts program. This overview is followed by chapters on learning theory, language acquisition, and a descriptive chapter on the English language.

The second part, "Language Skills: Substance and Strategies," includes chapters on all the oral and written skills of communication. Chapter 5 discusses the development of vocabulary and thinking skills while various approaches to grammar and usage are presented in Chapter 6. The areas of listening, oral discussion, and dramatization receive special attention in Chapters 7, 8, and 9, followed by an extensive exploration of children's writing in Chapter 10. The discussion of children's writing ranges from the recording of direct observations and experiences to writing imaginative stories and poetry. The final chapter in this part suggests methods of teaching the various supportive writing skills—capitalization, punctuation, spelling, and handwriting.

Part Three is called "Components: A Comprehensive Language Arts Program" and explains the interrelationship of children's literature and reading to the other parts of the language arts. Chapter 12 shows the integration of language and literature while Chapter 13 suggests the importance of using children's language to teach reading. The last chapter describes a fully integrated language arts program and how parental involvement can help promote children's learning.

Children's Language and the Language Arts is intended for use as a textbook in a basic course in language arts methods or as a guide for in-service teachers who wish to have a classroom more like the one envisioned in the text. As mentioned earlier, the text contains information for developing a language arts program that considers children's linguistic and cognitive abilities. The opening chapters on learning theory, language, and language acquisition each have a concluding section entitled "Understanding through Involvement" which has activities for the learners to do which will enhance their understanding of the theoretical material.

Many pre-service teacher education programs provide field-based experience so that these students have access to children in a classroom situation. In-service teachers have that same opportunity for immediately trying out new ways of working. For these reasons, and because we believe that adults, like children, learn best when they are active participants in their learning, we have included two groups of activities at the end of each of the chapters in Part Two, "Language Skills: Substance and Strategies." The first group of activities is called "Preliminary Learning Activities" and does not require a classroom setting or a group of children. It is intended to give the student appropriate experiences that are preliminary to working with children. The second group of activities is "Participation Activities." It contains activities to be done with children in or as a result of classroom experience.

The authors wish to thank and acknowledge the many special people who have helped to make *Children's Language and the Language Arts* a published reality. Unfortunately, space limits us to mentioning only a few names. We first extend our sincere appreciation to Charlotte S. Huck and Martha L. King, the two persons who inspired us to write a text for the language arts. Second, we feel the photographs included in the book are exceptional because of the contributions made by Charles Jones, Thomas England, Juanita Skelton, and Barbara Friedburg, the staff and children at the Martin Luther King, Jr., Laboratory School, Evanston, Illinois, the preschool of the University of Houston at Clear Lake City, and the Clarke County Schools, Georgia. Finally, but certainly not least, we are grateful to our family, friends, and colleagues who have given us help and encouragement throughout the writing experience.

Carol J. Fisher
C. Ann Terry

PART ONE

Perspectives: Language Arts, Language, and Learning

There are many theories that deal with how children learn and how language is acquired and developed. Each theory has its own implications for specific instructional practices in the classroom. Behaviorist theory, closely associated with B. F. Skinner, regards learning as a conditioning process. Students are assigned a task and they are rewarded in some way when it is successfully completed. If children are unsuccessful, they may be given a negative reward. Behavior modification and language programs, such as Bereiter-Engelmann, are founded on these learning principles. However, because we firmly believe that developmental theory best explains children's linguistic and cognitive growth, we have chosen to present a language arts program that is based on the work of Jean Piaget and current psycholinguistic theory. The two go hand-in-hand, suggesting a definite sequence to children's development that can be facilitated by a rich and active learning environment.

The discussion in Chapter One focuses on a classroom setting where all the language arts are integrated, instruction is individualized, and children are actively involved in their learning. Listening, speaking, writing, and reading are shown to be interrelated language processes that occur naturally throughout the school day. The total language arts program reflects a teacher's awareness and understanding of developmental theory.

Chapter Two provides the learning theory on which the classroom environment in Chapter One is based. According to Piaget, children learn best when they themselves are actively involved in their own learning. This suggests that children be given direct experiences and concrete objects that can be seen, handled, and touched. Children also need to talk and write about their activities. Recording their observations of the classroom guinea pig, measuring and talking about the growth of their bean plant, writing a poem about something brought back from a nature walk, all represent opportunities to put experiences into words.

An understanding of how the English language has developed both historically and linguistically provides us with important insights into the uniqueness of our language. Therefore, through the discussion in Chapter Three we learn how vocabulary develops, is often borrowed, and sometimes changes. Because dialects are also a part of our linguistic heritage, a portion of the chapter is devoted to geographical and social language variations.

The final chapter in Part One, Chapter Four, presents a detailed discussion of how children acquire and develop language. The emphasis is on children's ability to process from their linguistic environment the language around them, and to develop, test, and revise "rules" about how language operates. Linguistic research is cited to show a developmental sequence in children's language acquisition, and major implications for teaching are discussed.

CHAPTER ONE

The Language Arts Defined

PREVIEW QUESTIONS

1 What topics or subjects are included in the language arts?

2 What are the key characteristics of a language arts program in operation?

3 What might a classroom conducive to such a program be like?

4 What role does the teacher play in the language arts program?

If you are not exactly sure what a language arts course includes, it may be because when you were in elementary school the term *language arts* was not used. You might remember, instead, English, reading, handwriting, and spelling. Today, with a renewed emphasis on using language to communicate accurately with others and to express ideas and feelings through creative language, the term *language arts* has come into use to describe all the language-related activities in the elementary school program.

In the past, the various language arts—reading, writing, speaking, spelling, handwriting—have been taught separately as independent subject areas, but the trend is now toward an integrated language arts program. For example, how can spelling instruction occur separately from functional writing? It is because we wish to communicate effectively with others in writing that the need to spell words correctly arises. Writing, putting letters together to make words, and stringing words together to make sentences, provide the child with personalized reading material. Essential to this process is legible handwriting. Children are continually practicing letter formations, attending to spacing, differentiating between letters that are similar and, in general, attempting to make their writing readable. At the very heart of each of the language arts is language itself. Reading, writing, and listening are all forms of language processing. Therefore, a good language background is necessary for each and every child. Sharing, conversations, and discussions have real value when it comes to facilitating and improving children's reading, writing, and listening skills.

In addition to integrating the traditional English and reading areas into language arts, there has also been a change in the kinds of language experiences included in the overall program. Experiences with literature written expressly for children have become a part of the language arts as have increased amounts of listening and oral language activities. There has been a shift from the English program that stressed only written communication to one more equally balanced between oral and written learning experiences. The oral components include dramatization, storytelling, listening, and discussions.

To get a better idea about the language arts program, suppose we look at some elementary school classrooms where the children are actively involved in such an approach to learning.

AN OVERVIEW OF A LANGUAGE ARTS PROGRAM

The students in this classroom are not all doing the same things at the same time. The language arts experiences have been planned around their interests and needs. Not only are the children pictured on these pages engaged in reading, writing, and meaningful conversations, they are active participants in their own learning—choosing and selecting their own books, listening while another child reads a story aloud, and asking friends for help when they need it.

The pictures and activities described indicate three of the most important aspects of a language arts program based on current theory about how children learn and how they acquire and develop their language. Such a program is characterized by (1) *individualization* of the experiences children encounter, (2) active *involvement* in their learning activities, and (3) *integration* of communicative or creative language arts skills with one another as well as other areas of the curriculum.

Individualization

When you observe children in the classroom, you notice almost immediately that some excel in one area while others are better in another. Some children have a background of experience or temperament that makes learning easier for them. Some children de-

Children are always anxious to taste some of the pudding they have each helped to make. After discussing the cooking activity with their teacher, they read and followed the recipe making sure each ingredient was measured carefully. (*Photograph by Thomas England*)

These two children are conversing about stories they are writing. They feel free to talk and learn from one another. (*Photograph by Thomas England*)

velop more slowly than others and are not yet ready for increasingly more complex tasks. If an entire class is given a single assignment, some children will quickly complete it while others work methodically along, and still others may not be able to do it at all. Teachers who are concerned about developing each child to the fullest need to vary children's assignments, and thus individualize children's learning.

Involvement

We find that children in the elementary school learn best when they are actively involved in each learning situation. What they are doing must seem important to them in a very personal way. Active involvement means working with specific, concrete materials and experiences instead of abstract ideas or materials from a textbook or some other secondary source. Children need things to touch and examine, build and construct, collect, observe, and categorize before they move into reading about more distant ideas or places. As fantasy must be grounded in reality, abstractions must touch experience.

Integration

Instead of setting up a whole series of small blocks of time for each of the curricular areas—8:00–8:10 for handwriting, 8:10–9:00 for reading groups, 9:00–9:15 for spelling, 9:15–10:00 for library on Monday, creative writing on Tuesday and Friday, and so on—the various areas of the language arts need to be integrated with each other and with other content areas such as science, math, and social studies. Reporting on a science experiment or role playing various occupations develops language arts skills and at the same time promotes basic understanding in other content areas. This type of integrated study provides for large blocks of time and allows the teacher to capitalize on teachable moments instead of letting the clock dictate when a learning experience is to end.

A friend has offered Darin some help with his story. He wanted to know how to spell one word in particular—*crocodile. (Photograph by Thomas England)*

The classroom library area is a comfortable place for children to read and share books. These students chose to read during this time, rather than write stories or cook. (*Photograph by Thomas England*)

Each child in the classroom has a reading partner. Every day they choose a book to read and share with one another. (*Photograph by Thomas England*)

This student has chosen a special place to read and concentrate on his book. (*Photograph by Thomas England*)

These are the characteristics of the language arts program you will find described in this book. The basis for such a program is found in current linguistic theory which describes how children acquire and develop language and in cognitive psychology which describes a developmental learning process. It values both communicative and creative language and recommends a classroom environment in which 1) learning is individualized, 2) children are actively involved in what they are doing, and 3) content and skills are integrated. It emphasizes both written and oral aspects of the language arts, allowing time for discussions, listening experiences, dramatizations of stories and situations, an oral sharing of ideas and experiences as well as the development of skill in reading, spelling, handwriting, conventional punctuation, and capitalization. There are skills to be learned and imaginative ideas to be shared. Perhaps most important of all, each child feels good about what he or she can do and about attempting new things.

A LANGUAGE ARTS CLASSROOM

To illustrate, let's look at a class where a variety of learning experiences are occurring simultaneously. The drawing of the physical classroom arrangement, in Figure 1, may help you visualize the setting as you read.

When we glance around the room, we see a small group of children seated in the listening area. They have chosen to listen to some Curious George[1] stories and afterward write their own stories about him. Across the room, six children are seated in pairs reading to one another. One child reads several pages while the other listens —then it is time for the other to read. The writing area is a busy place today, too. A small group of students is dictating an experience story to their teacher. They listen as one student reads the story from the large sheet of chart paper. A discussion follows and results in a unanimous decision to change the ending of their story.

Figure 1

A classroom plan

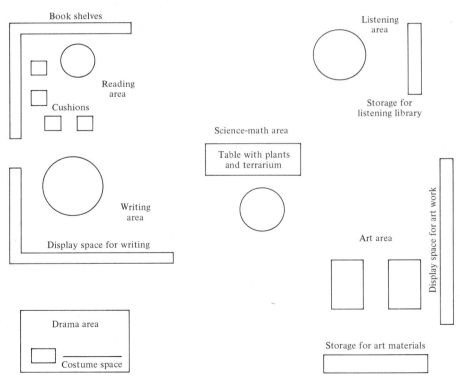

Leaving the writing area, we pass a science table filled with plants that the children are growing. A cassette tape player has been placed on the table and a sign reads, "Play me and learn about our plant collection." We next see four students standing at the art tables, conversing occasionally as they paint with large swooping strokes. Their pictures, rich and colorful, will soon be added to the display space in the art area. Finally, we walk to the drama area where two children have decided to dramatize the Yugoslavian folktale, *Nail Soup*.[2] Both have searched through the costume trunk and selected some appropriate clothing and props. The girl, taking the role of the old woman, is dressed in a long apron with a scarf tied around her head. Slowly she begins to hobble around the make-believe kitchen. The boy, wearing a soldier's cap, knocks on the old woman's kitchen door. The drama then begins to unfold as the hungry soldier starts his trickery—convincing the old woman that her hidden vegetables would make delicious nail soup.

A LOOK AT LANGUAGE IN THE LANGUAGE ARTS

Humans developed language in order to communicate more effectively with others. Essentially then, the purpose of language may be viewed as one of communication. Besides enabling you to converse with a friend or read a long-awaited letter or the day's newspaper, language has a creative side. Creative language may be observed in novels, plays, musical lyrics, and in your own speech and writing.

If we look at language from a technical point of view, there are two phases: productive and receptive. The model in Figure 2 illustrates the relationship between productive and receptive language.

When we produce an idea or thought, we use primarily speaking or writing as means of communication. These represent the *productive* phases of language. In turn, if we receive an idea or thought

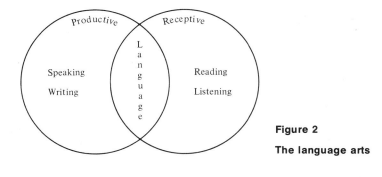

Figure 2

The language arts

from someone, we are usually involved in reading or listening. These, then, are the *receptive* phases of language. In order to become adept at producing or receiving ideas and information from others, an individual must be able to understand and use language effectively. It is for this reason that a good language arts program includes many opportunities for children to hear, read, and use language.

THE TEACHER AND THE LANGUAGE ARTS PROGRAM

Planning an individualized language arts program that includes the integration of language related activities and considers that children's growth occurs when they are actively involved requires a special kind of teacher. A program such as this is administered by a facilitator of learning, not a dictator of learning. The desks that traditionally are placed in straight rows are now grouped together in order to facilitate talk. Children move freely about the room working on projects, choosing books to read, and writing stories or recording observations. The teacher also moves about the room working with groups of children or individual students. The teacher's desk that appeared at one time in front of the room has been moved to the side and serves as a base from which to operate.

The bulletin boards and even the walls spill over with children's work—stories, poems, paintings, charts of observations, and displays of things they have collected and mounted. Each is carefully prepared for display and the collection reflects the children's varying abilities and interests. There are large cushions or perhaps a sofa or rocking chair to curl up on while listening to a story. There are easels and paints ready to use, and a bin full of clay for modeling. There is a box of fabric remnants, yarns, laces and trims, buttons, sequins, aluminum foil, magazines, pieces of cork, and many other things to use for collages or costumes. There is an area for writing that has a variety of pens and papers to use, and it is a quiet area where children may work undisturbed. There may not be a chair and desk for every child, but there are chairs at the writing center, at a large table used for making projects, and at a smaller table used for group work. There is also a large carpeted area where all the children can sit and listen to a story or meet for a planning session. Each child has a private storage area for those things traditionally stored in desks.

Teachers who work in this kind of classroom need to structure learning situations just as traditional teachers do; they simply do it in a different way. Structure comes from the questions asked, from the materials made available in the classroom, and from the teacher's knowledge of each child's interests and abilities. It is not a matter of doing anything at all and having students learn; it is allowing them to meet challenging and purposeful situations from which they learn best.

The teacher keeps careful records of each child's progress. There may be weekly charts to ensure that children participate in all areas of the curriculum: math, reading, writing, science, oral speaking, social studies, and so on. Although children may choose when they work on math and writing, or what particular math and writing activities they complete, they may not choose not to do it. At the center of it all, is the informed teacher who is continually providing the learning choices.

Children are constantly involved in activities that reflect an understanding of their learning needs and abilities. Work on skills is balanced with more imaginative activities. Oral experiences are part of the classroom as are writing and reading. Children have experiences with productive language as well as with receptive language experiences. In essence, the environment is one in which children participate actively in their own learning, and school is an enjoyable place to be.

REFERENCES

[1] Hans Angusto Rey, Curious George, Houghton Mifflin, Boston, 1941.
[2] Harve Zemach. *Nail Soup*, Chicago: Follett, 1964.

CHAPTER TWO

Learning through Active Participation

PREVIEW QUESTIONS

1 What stages of development do elementary school children go through, and what behavior is typical of these stages?

2 In what kind of learning environment does the greatest growth take place?

3 What kinds of activities foster children's development?

4 How can one assess children's abilities and needs, and how often should one do so?

Throughout the history of education various theories have been advanced to explain how children learn, and these have been interpreted in many ways in actual classroom practices. A major theorist in developmental cognitive learning is Jean Piaget, a Swiss psychologist, whose interest in how children's thought processes develop has led to the view of learning on which the language arts program presented in this text is based.

Piaget became interested in intellectual development through observations of his own two children. He was intrigued with their comments, questions, and errors—seeing them all as clues to their thinking. He began to give them tasks to determine how well they were able to reason and think logically. His research, first with his own children and later with other children at different age levels, has long been known. Many educators are now applying his theories realizing they have something important to say about how children learn.

An earlier practitioner who made a lasting contribution to education in this country is John Dewey, an educator whose philosophy of education is being rediscovered in some educational circles. Dewey sought to reform traditional education of the 1930s. He and his followers began the progressive education movement (founded on the belief that children learn by doing) because they were dissatisfied with what they saw happening in the schools of that day. Dewey interpreted the traditional educator's view of learning as the "acquisition of what is incorporated in books and in the heads of elders."[1] Drill, memorization of factual material, and the teacher as an authoritarian figure characterized the traditional school in Dewey's mind; whereas freedom of activity, learning through experience, and the teacher as a director of children's learning were typical of the progressive school.

As one looks at Piaget's investigations and what Dewey was saying in the 1930s, it seems that Piaget's findings support Dewey's educational philosophy. That is, the research Piaget has done concerning children's cognitive or intellectual development substantiates Dewey's theory that children learn by doing. Learning is an active process, not a passive one. Workbooks, ditto sheets, and "pencil and paper curriculums" are not effective means for stimulating children's learning and thinking; yet they persist and live on in many of today's elementary school classrooms.

To gain a better understanding of a learning environment that incorporates everything that we know about children and learning, let's look more closely at Piaget's research on cognitive development. A review of some of his theories may be helpful in seeing how they can be applied to the elementary school classroom and language arts program.

COGNITIVE ORGANIZATION AND ADAPTATION

According to Piaget, mental development occurs through a process of organization and adaptation. To more clearly explain this process, let's use an example.

Mark is 2½ years old and very interested in learning about the world around him. He is busy tasting, touching, hearing, and observing all things in his immediate environment. As he is doing this, he is mentally processing a variety of stimuli. Mark does this by developing categories or *schemata* for organizing the stimuli. What he takes in through his various senses is mentally organized into newly developed or already established categories. These categories essentially become his frames of reference. For instance, Mark has observed and petted his dog Charley. When he plays in the yard, he frequently sees the neighbor's dog Ralph. From his observations and experiences with Charley and Ralph, Mark develops a "dog" *schema* or category. A dog to Mark may mean having a head, four legs, and a tail, and whatever external stimuli fit in his category or *schema* must be a dog. When driving out in the country one day with his parents, Mark sees an animal that has a head, four legs, and a tail. To Mark, it is a large dog. Thus, he calls the pony a dog as he assimilates this new animal into his dog *schema* because it has all the proper characteristics. Piaget refers to this last cognitive process as assimilation. This means Mark took the new stimulus, the pony, and related it to his existing "dog" *schema*. As Mark has more experiences with ponies, cows, and various kinds of dogs, he will refine his "dog" *schema* and will develop new categories for animals that are not dogs.

Leo Lionni's book for children, *Fish Is Fish*,[2] illustrates this process in a very meaningful but humorous way. A frog and fish become friends. The frog leaves the pond one day to explore the world. He returns much later to visit his friend and tell him about the "extraordinary things" he has seen. He explains to the fish that he has seen cows. "They have four legs, horns, eat grass, and carry pink bags of milk." The fish pictures a cow in his mind, and sees a fishlike creature with four legs, horns, and a pink bag. The fish has assimilated what the frog has told him about cows into his own existing *schema*. Until the fish has more experience outside his marine environment, he cannot refine his categories.

To illustrate further, let's take the story on beyond the book. Suppose the fish was caught one day and placed in a glass tank where it could see the world as the frog did. Its *schemata* would change. It would take in new information and stimuli that would alter or modify its existing ones; or certain external stimuli might cause the fish to create entirely new *schemata* or categories. When this process occurs, Piaget refers to it as *accommodation*.

In differentiating between the cognitive processes of assimilation and accommodation, Wadsworth explains that in assimilation the stimuli are forced to fit the person's existing structure while in accommodation the reverse is true. The person changes the *schema* to fit the new stimuli.[3]

How can we apply this to children's learning? Essentially it means that children need many experiences in order to develop new *schemata* and refine others. Good preschool or primary programs are conceived and organized around this concept. In them, children become a part of a learning environment that is rich in new and varied experiences. A school week might include a visit to a neighborhood shopping center, a morning at the children's zoo where animals can be petted, a walk through a large grocery store, lunch in a park, and a tour of a nearby treefarm or nursery. When in the classroom, the children have a wealth of materials at their reach—blocks for building, concrete objects to manipulate, puzzles to put together, dress-up clothes for costumes, small animals to feed and observe, and books for browsing and reading. There is time to paint or dramatize highlights of their experiences and time to talk about them.

For older children whose learning is still grounded in concrete experiences, the learning environment involves firsthand observations and direct participation in ongoing classroom activities. The school week might include a visit by someone from the local police department to explain and demonstrate fingerprinting and voice-printing, a trip to a local florist for a display of traditional flower arrangements, time to build and use a greenhouse to start seeds for early planting, an interview of a local author of children's books, or a hike along a nature trail or nearby river to check on soil or water erosion. The classroom is supplied with an abundance of books—books for recreational reading, books with taped readings, informational books for resources, and homemade books. There are materials to experiment with—jawbones of horses, batteries and wire, light bulbs, electric bells, etc. There are opportunities to work alone, with a partner, or with a large group.

FURTHER IMPLICATIONS FOR TEACHING AND LEARNING

According to Piaget, the processes of assimilation and accommodation continue throughout our adult lives. The cognitive structures become more numerous and complex as an individual grows and

---

develops mentally. However, the same cognitive processes continue to function for the three-year-old, the eight-year-old, and the twenty-five-year-old. The older individual is better at differentiating across stimuli and has a more complex network of *schemata*.

When we consider how a child develops intellectually, the number and quality of the educational experiences becomes very important. What kind of stimuli are children assimilating and accommodating when they are given worksheet after worksheet to complete? If a child listens to her teacher 75 percent of the school day, what is the quality of the experience? What happens to the intellectual climate when children's curiosities, questions, and conversations do not have as high a value as that of a "quiet" classroom.

If we accept Piaget's theories of cognitive development, then the classroom environment cannot be a passive one. Rather, the child is active in the learning environment, constantly exploring, hypothesizing, experimenting, conversing, and questioning. Convergent experiences limit and stifle children's intellectual development. The teacher is therefore concerned about offering students divergent experiences that extend their thinking and learning processes. Memorization of facts and emphasis on learning content that soon may be out of date do not help children develop new cognitive structures or ways of thinking and discovering.

STAGES OF INTELLECTUAL DEVELOPMENT

As mentioned earlier, the intellectual process is the same for the adult as the child. Assimilation, accommodation, and a striving for a balance between the two continues throughout one's life, but mental structures become increasingly complex with age. It is the continuing development and change in cognitive structures that have caused Piaget to say there are stages of intellectual development. According to Piaget, all children go through identifiable stages or periods of cognitive development:

Period of sensorimotor intelligence (birth to approximately two years)
Period of preoperational thought (approximately two to seven years)
Period of concrete operations (approximately seven to eleven years)
Period of formal operations (approximately eleven to fifteen years)

Educators frequently misunderstand what is meant by the cognitive stages and the ages given for each, and thus misinterpret them. This has long been a concern to Piaget, and he warns that they should not be viewed as a set of limitations. As a child moves from one stage to the next, a new potential is reached. The ages represent averages, says Piaget, and cannot be considered static. It is possible for a nine-year-old to be in the preoperational stage of development, whereas a six-year-old may have advanced to concrete operations. However, the development is continuous and children move from one stage to the next, building an increasingly complex network of cognitive structures. One stage grows out of the other, and children become more and more adept at dealing with abstractions. The important point is that children go through these stages in this sequence or order even though there may be differences in their ages when in a given stage.

The child in the period of concrete operations thinks best with something to manipulate, whereas the child who has moved into the period of formal operations may reason logically without the help of tangible or concrete experiences. It seems necessary for teachers to know and understand the changes that occur from one stage to another if they are to plan an appropriate learning environment for children. Piaget suggests "it is essential for teachers to know why particular operations are difficult for children, and to understand that these difficulties must be surmounted by each child in passing from one level to the next. It is not the stages that are important; it is rather what happens in the transition."[4]

Period of Sensorimotor Intelligence (birth to Approximately Two Years)

Why should you be concerned about the first stage described by Piaget? Teachers do not usually work with children this age. However, when we consider that each new stage incorporates the previous stage, the period of sensorimotor intelligence is significant and cannot be omitted.

This stage or period of development begins at birth and progresses sequentially through what might be called substages. From birth through about the first month of life, children's behavior and actions are completely reflexive. They are born with such reflexes as sucking, grasping, crying, and moving various parts of the body. Newly born infants are also totally egocentric, meaning that they are aware only of themselves and their basic needs. From one to four months young children begin to suck their thumbs. The thumb-sucking is intentional and demonstrates accommodation to the environment. It is habitual and therefore cannot be considered reflexive action. Between four and eight months of age children become less egocentric and begin to notice the world around them. They handle objects, move them around, and if they find something of significant interest, will repeat a behavior. For example, if children shake a rattle and enjoy the sound, they will shake it again and again. From eight to twelve months intentional behavior definitely emerges; this involves using specific means to obtain an end. Children may move a stuffed animal aside to reach a favored toy. During this period the children also develop the concept of object constancy. They know an object exists and when it is taken away or out of sight, they look for it. Before, when an object was moved out of view or hidden, they would make no effort to search for it. Games such as "peekaboo" or "hide-and-seek" are good for children this age to play because they help establish the notion of object constancy or permanence. The attainment of object constancy is a major achievement of the sensorimotor period."

The next period, occurring between twelve and eighteen months, is characterized by "experimentation." Instead of simply repeating or practicing interesting behaviors, the infant begins applying behaviors to new situations. Problem solving can be observed as the child finds new means to an end. In essence, the young child is demonstrating a kind of intelligent functioning for the first time.

The sixth and last substage of the sensorimotor period begins at eighteen months and continues through the age of about two years. During this time, mental actions begin to replace physical ones. Problems are solved internally rather than in some physical way. Children arrive at a solution by thinking or reasoning about a situation first. They are not able to visualize something, however, without actually doing it.

Period of Preoperational Thought (Approximately Two to Seven Years of Age)

Following the sensorimotor period, the child moves into what Piaget calls the preoperational period. Children are usually in this stage of cognitive development when they first enter a school setting. Therefore, it is especially important that the changes that occur during this period are understood by individuals who are interested in working with preschool, kindergarten, or primary age children. Characteristics which children display during this stage of development are egocentrism, lack of conservation, and animism.

Egocentrism of the preoperational child   During this period the child is very egocentric. The egocentrism demonstrated throughout this stage is unlike that of the newborn infant. Preoperational children are cognizant of others and the world around them, but they experience difficulty in seeing or understanding another's point of view. To them, everyone else sees and thinks just as they do. A teacher will discover that children in the preoperational stage will need and want to be at the center of all activity. As an example, a kindergarten teacher asked if someone would help her five-year-olds learn to work with puppets. She had tried to emphasize the importance of letting the puppet do the actions and talking, but the children insisted on participating, too. "The puppet may begin the story," she said, "but the child inevitably finishes it. They just can't seem to keep themselves out of it!" The response to her request was that little could be done to keep them from taking the part of the puppet; her children's behavior was quite typical. They simply are unable to remove themselves from the situation. This does not mean that puppetry should not be continued in the classroom. Children enjoy puppets and the experience is certainly worthwhile. Puppetry enables them to use their language creatively and organize their view of reality. Children can identify with the puppets and test out what they know with what others know.

Children's egocentrism is also evidenced through their oral language communication with others. They always think that the other person must know what they already know. If one child is attempting to give information to another, significant parts are often left out and the speaker becomes exasperated when the other person does not understand. To illustrate, Suzanne was asked to build a simple construction with large red and blue blocks. Her friend Juan was placed on the other side of a partition and given an identical set of blocks. When she had completed her block construction, she was asked to tell Juan how to place his blocks to make the same construction. She began, "You put this red block here and this blue block over here and this other block on top of this one." Needless to say, he had difficulty duplicating the construction and began to ask many questions. Finally, becoming frustrated with Juan's apparent lack of understanding, Suzanne put her hands on her hips, looked intensely at her block construction, and said, "Why can't you do it? It's right in front of you!" Elkind suggests this behavior can "be explained by saying that the child assumes words carry much more information than they actually do, because he believes that even the indefinite 'thing' somehow conveys the properties of the object it is used to represent."[6] Children seem unable to separate the object from the word that refers to it. When

Suzanne says, "Put the blue one here," she doesn't understand why Juan cannot do it because it seems very clear to her. This, in part, is due to her egocentrism; she can only visualize it from her point of view.

Teachers of young children can readily observe the egocentrism that exists in their play, conversations, and overt behavior. Rather than becoming annoyed with children because they persist in telling about an experience they have had over the weekend instead of talking about a prescribed topic, the teacher who understands children in this stage of development is interested in what they have to say. Egocentrism can also be observed in children's written compositions. For example, when given a choice between dictating a story about a selection of pictures or their own experiences, a group of kindergarten children unanimously decided to dictate a story about something that had actually happened to them.

Conservation The ability to conserve involves perceptual constancy, reversibility of thought, and the ability to reason logically. Children's thinking is dominated by their perception, thus "seeing is believing." For example, if a child sees the following, he will tell you that there are the same number of blocks in each row as in Figure 3.

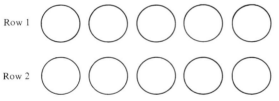

Figure 3   Rows of equal length

However, if the blocks in row 1 are spread apart, thus making a longer row, the child will say there are more blocks in row 1 as in Figure 4.

Figure 4   Rows of unequal length

Because the row is longer, he believes that it contains more blocks. For the child in this stage of development, the rows contain the same number of blocks only as long as there is visual correspondence. The child is not able to reason that there are the same number of blocks in each row when they are just rearranged. Preoperational children have not attained perceptual constancy.

Children during this stage of development also have difficulty in doing tasks that require reversibility of thought. It is not until about age seven that a child can reverse operations. Piaget tells about presenting children with three different colored balls—A, B, and C—on a wire. They were told to watch as the three balls were inserted into a tube. The correct expectation was that the balls—A, B, and C—would come out of the other end of the tube in the order in which they were inserted. However, when the tube was rotated 180° before the balls reappeared, the children did not expect the order to be that of C, B, A. They were in fact astonished at the outcome.[7]

The preoperational child does not conserve. Bound by their perceptions and lacking reversibility of thought, these children are unable to conceptualize that regardless of any changes in its shape or position, the amount or quantity of matter always remains the same. We observed the child's inability to conserve in the example using blocks. A child who is not conserving can also look at two glasses containing the same amount of water, but because one is taller, believes it contains the most. They are focusing on one aspect —tallness—and to them, a tall glass must contain more than a shorter one. It is not until about age seven that children begin to conserve.

Childhood animism The child in the period of preoperational thought believes inanimate objects have life. The clouds are alive because they move, an automobile is alive because it runs, and a river is alive because it flows. At this age children interpret reality using themselves as models. It is not until later that children can distinguish between reality and fantasy in the way adults do.

Characteristics of children in preoperational period How can this knowledge about the preoperational child be applied in the classroom? Remember the following when establishing the learning environment for preoperational children.

1. They are active. Children move about within the classroom setting. Sitting all day is not natural for these children.
2. They are egocentric. They are interested in themselves and will not be interested in their neighbor until later. These children need to be made to feel as though they have something to say and contribute and be allowed to carry out their own ideas.

3. They have their own world of fantasy. Children's imaginative play should be encouraged; they need to listen to both fantasy and realistic books and talk about them.
4. They are beginners. They learn through mistakes, and trial and error is a learning process. The teacher needs to be patient and understanding, giving children time to learn at their own rates.
5. They want stimulation. They have the desire to explore and experiment. Naturally curious, they may ask question after question. The teacher must provide a rich learning environment—things to observe, touch, handle, taste, explore, and so on.
6. They are talkative. They learn by talking and working actively; therefore, conversation is a natural part of the learning environment.
7. They are individuals. All children are different and have neither the same interests nor the same backgrounds of experience. They may be at different levels of development and therefore need choices; they should not be expected to be all together on the same page on the same day.
8. They need to be successful. Encouragement and praise should be continuous within the learning environment.
9. Children are bound by their perceptions. They are unable to conserve until they are in the concrete operational period of cognitive development. The teacher should assess children's developmental levels and understand their capabilities.

Period of Concrete Operations (Approximately Seven to Eleven Years of Age)

This period of intellectual development extends through the elementary school years. The child during this time makes noticeable advances in cognitive organization. In contrast to children in the preoperational stage of development, children in this period are able to reason and no longer is their thinking dominated by their perceptions. General characteristics of children in this stage of development include the ability to conserve, the continuing need for concrete experiences, and the development of social awareness and interaction.

Concrete operational children have the ability to reverse their concepts, a reasoning capacity necessary in order to conserve. Children who have attained reversibility of thought, for example, can look at two balls of clay, identical in size, shape, and weight, and when the appearance of one is changed, tell you the amount is still the same. They are no longer bound by their perceptions. Children are able to reason that the balls of clay contained equal amounts in the beginning and that changing the shape or appearance of one does not alter the quantity.

The concrete operational child still has difficulty in understanding many verbal and symbolic abstractions. Because of this, students in this stage of development do best when a variety of direct and concrete experiences are provided for them—listening walks, fieldtrips, visiting speakers, and so on. Classroom materials should also be concrete and plentiful—geoboards; measuring cups; cubes and blocks for counting; scrap materials for making puppets, collage pictures, and other art constructions; and models that can be taken apart and put back together.

When children reach the concrete stage of development, they become less egocentric. They are able to take another's point of view and engage in meaningful conversations. It is at this time that assimilation to the peer culture occurs. There is true interaction—children are interested in playing and talking with other children. Games become popular, from checkers to tic-tac-toe, and children have the desire and the ability to follow the rules.

Egocentricity diminishes and children develop a social awareness not seen in the previous stage. They understand and discuss another's point of view; and it is through interaction with peers that children attempt to validate their own thoughts. Social interaction is important for these children because it promotes cognitive development. Actually, it is through such social exchange that accommodation occurs.

While the children in the concrete stage of development have advanced beyond the thinking of the preoperational period, they have not yet attained the highest level of thought. Therefore, they cannot yet mentally handle verbal abstractions without the help of concrete or tangible experiences. That is, the concrete operational children can only solve problems using real objects and events. Their thinking is grounded in the concrete. Like the preoperational child, they need direct concrete experiences—excursions around the neighborhood, fieldtrips within the community, and conversations about what is observed. There should be materials in the classroom that can be manipulated, touched, and talked about. In reality, this stage may be considered as a transition period between preoperational thought and the last stage of cognitive development when formal thought finally appears.

Characteristics of children in concrete operational period   A knowledge and understanding of the concrete operational child essentially dictates the type of learning environment that is provided.

You will want to remember the following about children who are approximately seven to eleven years of age.

1. They require an abundance of concrete materials and experiences. Children during this period are still partially bound by their perceptions and, according to Piaget, think best with something in their hands. Therefore, the classroom is filled with a wide assortment of materials to manipulate and handle, small animals and plants are available for observation, fieldtrips and environmental excursions are provided, writing grows out of real experiences, and so on.

2. They need a rich language environment. Their oral language is developing throughout the period of concrete operations. The teacher encourages conversation and discussion, makes a wide variety of books available to children, reads stories aloud, and provides a listening center with records and tapes.

3. They are active. Concrete operational children can sit for longer periods of time than preoperational children; however, they still need opportunities to move about and become actively involved in their learning.

4. They have individual interests. Learning can and should grow out of children's interests. The teacher recognizes this and encourages individual pursuits through reading, constructing models, discussion, record keeping, and so on.

5. They want adult approval. Thus, encouragement and praise can stimulate and foster children's learning.

6. They are individuals. They have different interests and learn at different rates. They will be at different levels of development. Teachers provide for these differences by offering learning choices and experiences that meet personal needs. The children have opportunities to decide about what they learn.

7. They are socially aware of others. Children this age want to communicate and exchange ideas with others. The classroom environment encourages and facilitates children's communication.

Period of Formal Operations (Approximately Eleven to Fifteen Years of Age)

Children during this period develop formal operational thought. They differ from the concrete operational child in that purely verbal tasks are no longer difficult for them. They can now perform cognitive tasks without the help of manipulative materials or concrete experiences. Therefore, the student is capable of solving all classes of problems. A fifteen-year-old's thinking may not be equivalent to an adult's, but the cognitive structures necessary for such thought have been attained. The development until this time has been qualitative, and any changes in thought hereafter are quantitative. Assimilation and accommodation continue throughout adulthood altering one's thinking, but the potential for mature thought is reached at the end of the formal operational period.

IMPLICATIONS FOR TEACHING

In talking about education Piaget refers to the "traditional school" and the "active school." For our purposes let's borrow and use these terms throughout this section to contrast the two types of learning settings.

Considering what has been said about children's cognitive development, the thinking and reasoning abilities of the elementary school age child are not the same as an adult's. Therefore, we as educators cannot expect a young child to perform as an adult. However, Piaget suggests "traditional school theory has always treated the child, in effect, as a small being who reasons and feels just as we do while merely lacking our knowledge and experience."[8] Viewing the child in this manner, some educators have attempted to supply the content or subject matter necessary for children to function on an adult level. Elementary school curriculums have been developed stating what content shall be taught with little attention given to children's developmental levels (this includes physical, social, linguistic, and cognitive development of the child). The teacher dictates what content is to be learned next by the child and how it is to be acquired. Learning is structured according to what the teacher wants, rather than allowing children to use their own organizational patterns. This acquisition of knowledge usually takes the form of completing workbook or ditto pages, answering questions, or doing written exercises assigned from a commercially produced textbook.

In contrasting the traditional with the active school, Piaget indicates the latter type of learning environment "appeals to real activity, to spontaneous work based upon personal need and interest."[9] This does not imply, however, that children can do whatever they want; it means that learning takes place through a child's inherent interests and natural curiosity. The teacher in the active school considers students' social, physical, cognitive, and linguistic development when structuring the learning environment. Rather than the curriculum being built around content, it is built around the child. More specifically, children are active participants in their own learning. Reading, writing, and listening grow out of meaningful experiences. Conversation with peers is regarded as a significant part of a child's mental, social, and linguistic development. Concrete or real objects and events are always present in the learning environment. The child acts on his environment, rather than being acted upon, and thus internally organizes experiences (assimilation and accommodation). This is the learning climate of the active school.

The teacher is responsible for establishing the learning environment. The physical organization, concrete materials, and experiences are planned by the teacher. It is the teacher who is the knowledgeable source in the active classroom, not the textbook materials spelling out areas of content. The teacher understands how children learn best and is aware of each child's needs, abilities, interests, background of experience, and level of development.

The teacher who forms the classroom curriculum around the child's needs, interests, and abilities becomes a facilitator or director of learning. The teacher in the active school is not in the role of the dispenser of knowledge. Through a teacher's intervention at the appropriate time, a child's learning may be extended or the quality of an experience raised. Questions, comments, words of encouragement, or suggestions can all act as learning stimulants. A question at the right moment may extend a child's thinking or cause that child to study a problem in greater depth.

Trust is important in this type of learning setting. That is, a teacher must learn to trust children with their own learning. Trial and error are integral parts of the learning process. Children need to be given time to work out solutions to problems. As they explore and experiment within their environment, assimilation and accommodation occur. Teacher intervention throughout this process can be significant; however, intervention can become interference if it is not presented appropriately when the child needs the help.

It is important for the teacher to listen to children. Their questions, comments, and conversations can reveal their thinking. Much can be learned about a child's level of development if one listens carefully and knowledgeably. Children's errors reveal their thinking; in fact, it probably is more beneficial for the teacher to look closely at children's mistakes than at what they say or do correctly. Piaget states, "Above all, teachers should see the reasons behind errors. Very often a child's errors are valuable clues to his thinking."[10]

The language arts program is based upon sound theory about how children learn. The teacher's knowledge about children's cognitive development helps in planning activities and experiences that promote language and thinking skills. In the active school, reading and writing take place within a meaningful context, and students listen and talk because they are involved and interested in what they are doing. An understanding of students' needs, abilities, and level of development is used as a basis for planning all classroom experiences.

Understanding through Involvement

1. Administer the following Piagetian task to a group of five- or six-year-olds and a group of eight- or nine-year-olds. Compare the two age groups according to the children's verbal responses and explanations, each child's ability to succeed at a task, individual children's level or stage of cognitive development, children's observed behavior as they do the tests.
   Piagetian task: Conservation of continuous quantity—Liquid
   a.) Materials
      1) Two glasses the same size

      2) One tall, narrow glass or container

      3) Colored liquid
   b.) Getting ready: Pour equal amounts of colored liquid into the two glasses that are the same size. Have the tall, narrow glass or container within reach.
   c.) What to do and say: Place one short glass of liquid in front of the child and the other in front of you.
      Teacher: (Name), *do you have more to drink, do I have more to drink, or do we each have the same amount to drink?*
      Child's response:
      (Pour liquid from your short glass into the tall, narrow glass)
      Teacher: *If I pour my drink into this glass, do I have more, do you have more, or do we each have the same amount?*
      Child's response:
      If a child has reversibility of thought and is able to conserve,

---

the response will reveal that the amount of liquid in the tall, narrow glass is equal to the amount of liquid in the shorter glass. When this is the child's reply, ask: "How do you know they are the same?"

2. Select a five- or six-year-old child and a seven- or eight-year-old child. Conduct the following activity *separately* with the two children, assessing each child's ability to take another's point of view.

    If the children do not remember the story *Goldilocks and the Three Bears*, you will want to read it aloud to them. Ask them to first retell the story from the bears' point of view. Afterward, have the children retell the story from Goldilock's point of view.

    The story is written from the point of view of the bears; therefore, retelling the story as Goldilocks might, requires reversibility of thought and the ability to take another's point of view.

3. In Leo Lionni's story, *Fish Is Fish*, the frog tells the fish about his experiences since leaving the pond. As he describes the birds, cows, and people that he has seen, the fish mentally sees each of them with fishlike characteristics, that is, birds are colorful fish with wings.

    Read the story first to a group of preoperational children. Ask them to draw a picture of what a dog would see if the frog told him the story about the world outside of the pond. Afterward, read the story to a group of concrete operational children and ask them to draw the same picture showing how a dog would visualize the birds, cow, and people. Now compare the two sets of drawings—you should find them quite different.

4. Children's questions are clues to their thinking. Record, either in writing or on tape, young children's questions and analyze them using your present knowledge of developmental theory. This may be done in a school setting or with young children you know.

    Answers to questions will also provide insights to children's thinking. To illustrate, try asking the following questions and record young preoperational children's responses. Conduct the same activity with concrete operational children and then compare the two sets of responses. *Where does the sun go at night? During the day, where does the moon go? Are trees alive?— flowers?—rocks? Why does the rain fall?*

REFERENCES

[1] John Dewey. *Experience and Education.* New York: Collier, 1939, p. 19.

[2] Leo Lionni. *Fish Is Fish.* New York: Pantheon, 1970.

[3] Barry J. Wadsworth. *Piaget's Theory of Cognitive Development.* New York: McKay, 1971, p. 16.

[4] Eleanor Duckworth. "Piaget Takes a Teacher's Look," *Learning,* October 1973, p. 25.

[5] Mary Ann Spencer Pulaski. *Understanding Piaget.* New York: Harper & Row, 1971, pp. 19–20.

[6] David Elkind. *Children and Adolescents, Interpretive Essays on Jean Piaget.* New York: Oxford University Press, 1970, p. 52.

[7] Jean Piaget. *Six Psychological Studies.* New York: Vintage Books, 1967, p. 31.

[8] Jean Piaget. *Science of Education and the Psychology of the Child.* New York: Viking, 1970, p. 159.

[9] Ibid., p. 152.

[10] Eleanor Duckworth. "Piaget Takes a Teacher's Look," p. 24.

CHAPTER THREE
Describing Our Linguistic Heritage

PREVIEW QUESTIONS

1 How do historical or political events affect a language?
2 How does our language develop and change?
3 What effect does nonverbal communication have on teacher-pupil relationships?
4 How do dialects differ?
5 What kind of program is appropriate for students whose home language is not English?

The English language has had a fascinating history since its arrival on the British Isles with the Anglo-Saxon invasion in the fifth century. It has been affected by political events such as the peace treaty made by King Alfred the Great in 886, the Norman conquest of England under William the Conqueror in 1066, and the ascension to the throne of England in 1714 of George I, a German who never learned to speak English. English has absorbed a tremendous number of borrowed words from other languages—especially Latin and French—yet still retains some vocabulary stemming directly from the Angles and Saxons. It has undergone considerable changes in the sound system and accommodated great changes in the ways we relate one word to another. English lasted some 1,000 years without a dictionary which included common words, and it has survived all attempts to Latinize its grammar.

Perhaps a pair of related words, *deer* and *venison*, will illustrate some of the historical developments in our language. *Deer* comes from an Old English word *dēor* which meant *beast* while *venison* comes from the Old French word *veneison* which meant *hunting or game*. The association of the original English word with the animal and the French word for the meat product of the animal occurs frequently in our vocabulary, for example:

From Old English	*From French*
cow	*beef/veal*
pig	*pork*

These pairs might make one consider the relation of the native Englishman who apparently dealt more with the living animals and less with their table products than did the French. Not only do we see reflections of the historical events in the pair—*deer/venison* —the word *deer* also illustrates one of the ways that word meanings shift through the years. *Deer*, which used to mean any wild animal, has now come to mean only one particular kind of wild animal. This is an example of how words shift meanings and, in this case, specialize.

THE HISTORY OF ENGLISH

English was not the native language in the British Isles. When Julius Caesar explored the island in 55 and 54 B.C. it was inhabited by Celts. About one hundred years later the Roman legions came and conquered the southern two-thirds of the island and remained there until the early 400s. There were raids from the northern Germanic tribes and these tribesmen settled in what is now England. When the legionnaires withdrew, the Celts were unable to stop the invaders and so the Germanic peoples were able to make permanent settlements. These three tribes all spoke Low West German dialects which became fused into what we call Old English. Since there are very few Celtic words which were borrowed or retained in Old English, the Angles, Saxons, and Jutes probably had little contact with the Celts. The latter retreated to what is now Scotland, Wales, Ireland, and Cornwall.

There was a means of writing at this time—the Runic alphabet—but it was used only for magic spells and inscriptions; there were no written histories and the literature was transmitted in oral form. Extended writing was introduced by the Roman missionaries who came to convert England to Christianity beginning in 597 A.D. The development of written literature and history was slowed down by the Viking raids and invasions from 787 until 886 when King Alfred the Great of West Saxony made a treaty which gave the Vikings the northeastern part of the island. It was also King Alfred the Great who had many books translated into English, and the Anglo-Saxon Chronicle was begun during his reign.

The next major influences on written English take place in the 1400s. At this time education was extended to the middle classes and both men and women learned to read and write. These skills were no longer the province of just the nobility, the religious orders, and clerks. Then in 1476 Caxton set up a printing press in London and books became available to many more people. The existence of printing established certain conventions of writing—especially spelling—and also established the English of the London area as a standard.

In the 1700s there were several important influences on the written language. In 1706 the Kersey edition of *The New World of English Words* was published, the first dictionary to include basic words as well as more unusual ones. Samuel Johnson's dictionary was published in 1755. It derived its words from the language actually used and included word meanings and dated references indicating when particular words appeared. The 1762 publication of Lowth's *Short Introduction to English Grammar* had a significant influence on written language. In contrast to Priestly's grammar published the year before, Lowth was more concerned with regularity than actual usage, and his grammar reflected how he thought English *should* be spoken and written based on the concept of a universal and Latinate grammar.

One of the interesting features of the English language is the astounding number of non-Germanic-based words, or borrowed words, in our language. These are primarily Latin, Greek, French, and Scandinavian in origin. The latter entered the language at the time of the Viking raids and were easily absorbed by the Anglo-Saxons who had come from neighboring areas. Latin words entered English primarily at two time periods. Many were brought by the Roman missionaries who by 700 A.D. had made England a center of learning and scholarship in which most writing was in Latin. Another period of borrowing occurred in the 1500s at the time of the English Renaissance. At this time another group of Latin words was borrowed in addition to many Greek ones. The borrowings from French also occurred at two main times. Many French words came into the language along with the Norman conquest in 1066. Frenchmen were put in the important secular and religious positions; they saw no reason to change their language, and so the English were almost forced to learn some French to get along. Many of these words became an integral part of the language. Then in 1216 Henry III became King of England and again imported many Frenchmen. Thus a new group of French words entered the English language along with this new ruling group.

Words are still being borrowed from other languages, but the vocabulary of a language changes in other ways, too. New inventions, places, and phenomena have to be named (*space shuttle, astronaut,* and *cosmonaut*). This may be done by making compound words from other words or word parts, or by blending two words together as in *smog* or *brunch*. Proper names and brand names may become generally used. Word meanings may also shift by becoming specialized or generalized, elevated or degenerated. Thus *hūswif* became contracted to *hussy* and was so uncomplimentary that the original elements were later recombined to *housewife*. Some usages become common and accepted and others drop out of ordinary usage.

The development of the English language has not been just a series of borrowings from other languages along with the development of a written language. A third series of changes has taken place in the pronunciation and syntax of English. Since English was a blend of three German dialects, it originally had many of the characteristics of that language. There were word endings or inflections to indicate gender, tense, case, and so on. These inflectional endings began to disappear as an established word order developed in the 1300s and 1400s. More recent changes in syntax are the development of the past and progressive verb tenses such as *have been being treated* and an increase in verb-adverb combinations such as *put down, put off,* and so on.

The most significant of the sound changes occurred between about 1450 and 1650 and is called either the Great Vowel Shift or the Fifteenth-Century Vowel Shift. Before the shift the pairs of short and long vowels had about the same general sound; the difference was simply the length of time they were held. The vowels were similar to those in modern Spanish or Italian. After the vowel shift occurred the sound /a/ as in *papa* changed to /e/ as in *place;* the /e/ changed to /i/ as in *feet;* the /i/ became dipthonigized to /ai/ as in *bite;* the /ɔ/ of *off* changed to /o/ as in *stone;* the /o/ changed to /u/ as in *fool;* and the /u/ became dipthonigized to /au/ as in *mouse* (slash marks indicate sounds or phonemes). The vowel shift occurred after many of the spelling conventions had been established, and so today we have the situation of using the same letters to represent phonetically unrelated sounds. In fact, the sound shift accounts for most of our inconsistency in spelling vowel sounds.

The chart which follows indicates the major historical events which affected the English language and the progression of changes in the language. Information for the chart comes primarily from L. M. Myers's *Roots of Modern English.*[1] The samples of Old English from *Beowulf,* of Middle English from Chaucer, and of Early Modern English from Shakespeare may illustrate the changes which have taken place in the language throughout the last twelve centuries.

DATES	HISTORICAL EVENTS	INFLUENCE ON LANGUAGE
55–54 B.C.	Britain inhabited by Celts Julius Caesar invades Britain	No English language Celtic languages and Latin spoken
43 A.D.	Roman conquest of Britain	in geographic area of Britain
409	Roman legions withdrawn Celtic inhabitants must resist Pict raids from the north and Germanic raids along east coast	
450–650	Anglo-Saxon invasion Angles from Denmark occupy the northern two-thirds of what is now England; the Saxons from northern Germany occupy most of the southern third; a third group (Jutes?) occupies the southwest corner	OLD ENGLISH PERIOD (400–1100) All three Germanic tribes speak Low West German dialects that are mutually understandable; these fuse into what we call Old English; very little borrowing or use of Celtic Probably no written histories of this period; Runic alphabet used for magic spells and inscriptions; literature transmitted orally
597	Roman missionaries begin converting England; St. Augustine	Although people illiterate, the missionaries introduce extended

DATES	HISTORICAL EVENTS	INFLUENCE ON LANGUAGE
	of Canterbury sent by Gregory the Great with 40 companions	writing; within one hundred years England becomes one of the centers of learning and scholarship; much of writing in Latin as Bede's (ca. 731) *Ecclesiastical History of the English People,* but from 650 on some poetry in English, especially in Anglian dialect
787–886	Danish Viking raids begin in northern England; from 850 or so Danes begin to make permanent settlements. In 886 King Alfred the Great, king of Wessex (West Saxony) stops them and by a treaty gives them the northeastern part of England leaving the southern part free. The Danes are gradually absorbed into the English population. More Danish raids in 900s and early 1000s	The Vikings destroy books which are useless to them and which they fear might contain magic spells their enemies could use against them King Alfred the Great has many books translated into English; there is an English translation of Bede's *Ecclesiastical History* and *The Anglo-Saxon Chronicle* is begun

---

SAMPLE OF OLD ENGLISH

"þu eart endelaf   usses cynnes, Wægmund inga;   ealle wyrd
thou art last remnant of our kin   of-Waegumundings; all   fate

forsweop   mine magas   to metodsceafte, eorlas   on elne;
swept away my   kinsmen to destiny   earls   in valor

ic him   æfter sceal."
I them after must."

c. 700 A.D. *Beowulf*, lines 2813–2816

DATES	HISTORICAL EVENTS	INFLUENCE ON LANGUAGE
1066	Norman conquest of England by William the Conqueror who defeats King Harold at the Battle of Hastings; William gains control of all of England and organizes it into one country instead of numerous semi-independent earldoms; redivides land holdings and puts Normans and other Frenchmen in most of the important positions, both secular and religious	Norman rulers speak French and see no reason to change; some English learn French as a way to get ahead; a great many more learn at least some French words and these become a part of English

DATES	HISTORICAL EVENTS	INFLUENCE ON LANGUAGE
1100s	Kings and nobles consider themselves Frenchmen who have lands in England	
1204	Normandy lost to the English crown; nobles must choose between English and French holdings	**MIDDLE ENGLISH PERIOD (1100–1500)**
1216–1272	Henry III is King of England and imports Frenchmen from areas outside Normandy whose speech is more like Central French and unlike Norman French, especially that spoken at that time in England	The Norman English begin to feel quite English in contrast to the new French in power; more and different French words enter the language By the late 1200s French begins to disappear as the primary language, even with the nobility
1250s	Oxford and Cambridge well established	
1350	English is used in schools	
1362	English required to be used in all lawsuits	English of this period is not a unified language, but a variety of dialects which must be translated to be understood; there is no book of grammar, no dictionary, no spelling book, and not even agreement on the alphabet Many sound changes take place; perhaps more important is the beginning of the loss of inflectional endings (to indicate gender, tense, case . . .) and the development of a standard word order
1387–1400	Chaucer's *Canterbury Tales*	Tremendous number of French words added to English vocabulary from 1200–1400; some are Norman French and some Central French

---

SAMPLE OF MIDDLE ENGLISH

At nyght was come into that hostelrye
Wel nyne and twenty in a compaignye
Of Sondry folk, by aventure yfalle   (*aventure* = chance)
In felaweshipe, and pilgrimes were they alle,
That toward Caunterbury wolden ryde.

c. 1390 A.D. Chaucer, *Prologue to the Canterbury Tales*, lines 23–27

DATES	HISTORICAL EVENTS	INFLUENCE ON LANGUAGE
1400–1500	Extension of education and more secular education; by 1500 many middle-class men and women learn to read and write English	**MODERN ENGLISH PERIOD (1500–Present)**
1476	William Caxton sets up first printing press, and London becomes the center of printing	Careers as authors encouraged Establishment of conventions of writing, especially spelling London English established as the standard, except for Scottish dialect
1500–1660	English Renaissance	
1642–1660	First Civil War Restoration	Many changes in pronunciation (the Great Vowel Shift) although spelling set Tremendous increase in vocabulary; borrowings from Latin, borrowings from other modern languages, revivals from middle English. This gives English many synonyms to express exact shades of meaning and words that express an idea that might take four or more "native" words to express (e.g., *conflagration:* a number of fires burning at the same time and adding to each other)

SAMPLE OF MODERN ENGLISH—ENGLISH RENAISSANCE PERIOD

But that the dread of something after death—
The undiscovered country from whose bourn
No traveller returns—puzzles the will,
And makes us rather bear those ills we have
Than fly to others that we know not of?

             c. 1600 A.D. Shakespeare, *Hamlet,* Act III

DATES	HISTORICAL EVENTS	INFLUENCE ON LANGUAGE
1660–1800	The authoritarian period	Throughout this period in America new vocabulary from borrowed Indian words and new things (*squash, bluff*) Development of the great difference between how people actually speak and school theory of how they should speak based on concept of a universal grammar

DATES	HISTORICAL EVENTS	INFLUENCE ON LANGUAGE
1670–1713	Unsuccessful attempt by Dryden and Swift to set up something in England comparable to the French Academy	
1706	Kersey edition of *The New World of English Words*	First dictionary to include basic vocabulary as well as "hard" words
1714	George I succeeds Queen Anne; he is German and does not even learn to speak English	Movement to set up an English Academy dies
1747–1755	Samuel Johnson's Dictionary	Derived from language actually used and includes meaning, dated references, and a grammatical introduction
1762	Lowth writes *Short Introduction to English Grammar*	Becomes *the* authority on what is correct; authoritarian attitude and concern for regularity rather than actual usage
1800s	Trade with the world and the establishment of the British Empire	Only about two-thirds of the population of the British Isles speak English; others are the Irish, Scottish, and Welsh Vocabulary is growing from 50,000 words in Johnson's dictionary to 450,000 in *Webster's Third New International Dictionary*
1840	Population of U.S.A. surpasses that of England and its individual characteristics affect the English language	Borrowed words from other settlers (*cookie* and *sleigh* from the Dutch) as well as from Indians
1900s	Industrial Revolution	Modern technology adds new words; compound words; acronyms like NATO; brand names like Kodak or Stetson Great changes in the meaning of older words such as *nice* which once meant *silly* and *deer* which once meant any *wild animal* The main structural changes in English since the 1700s are: simplification of inflections stopped, further development of the past and progressive verbs, and an increase in verb-adverb combinations such as *put down, put off, put out*
1932	*Current English Usage* by Leonard completed by National Council of Teachers of English	Revival of interest and acceptability in basing grammar on usage (a theory advanced by Priestly in 1761 but not accepted then); usage classified as literary, colloquial, or popular/illiterate

DATES	HISTORICAL EVENTS	INFLUENCE ON LANGUAGE
1952	Fries's *Structure of English*	Grammars developed which *describe* how English operates instead of *prescribing* what is correct or incorrect Structural grammar
1957–1965	Chomsky's *Syntactic Structures* and *Aspects of the Theory of Syntax*	Transformational Generative grammar
1970s		Emphasis on sociolinguistics

Many children in the upper elementary grades enjoy working with the history of words. They may like collecting words based on new inventions or other newly invented words. They may even enjoy inventing some of their own by compounding or combining other word parts. They might interview older people to find out what the slang words were when they were young and make up a list of new and old slang expressions. They can also write to children in another part of the country to find out what words they use for certain things.

Children might like to trace the origins of words connected with particular sports, foods, or fashions. This can be one activity as a part of a larger unit of study. In working with modern historical events, children might make a list of words new to our language between 1900 and 1940 and another list containing new words from 1941 until the present. These would be words related to events which took place during those time periods. Exact dating can be checked in *Webster's Third New International Dictionary*, Springfield, Massachusetts, 1961.

CONCEPTS OF LANGUAGE

The nature of language becomes somewhat apparent from examining its historical development. We can observe the systematic traits of the language. The changes which have occurred are not haphazard; they occur in recognizable patterns. Languages are based on conventional patterns that permit communication. Certainly language is symbolic. There is nothing about a particular word or pattern of words that has to be; other languages use other words and other patterns. We use a word or words to represent an idea and that word or group of words then symbolizes the idea. When the symbol is accepted by others it becomes useful as a means of communicating through language. This is also a reflection of the arbitrary nature of languages. There are a few onomatopoetic words such as *swoosh* or *ping,* but for example, there is nothing "card-like" about the word *card.* The words we use and the ways we show their interrelationships are purely arbitrary.

English, like other languages, is ever changing and evolving. It is not static. This is particularly evident in the words or lexicon of the language. New words are being added, meanings shift, and some words virtually disappear. English is a redundant language. There are many indicators of particular relationships which enable us to grasp quite easily a speaker's idea even if we don't notice each inflection. For example, in *Jim and Paul go to their jobs right after school,* there are four indications of plurality—the *and,* the verb *go* which would be *goes* in the singular, *their* which is plural, and *jobs* which is also plural. These characteristics of language—that it is systematic, conventional, symbolic, arbitrary, evolving, and redundant—should help us see more clearly the nature of language and view more accurately the process of communicating through language.

LINGUISTIC TERMS

Linguistics, or the study of language, has given us some new and accurate means of describing our language. Although the terminology may at first glance appear to be difficult, it is actually easier because it does not involve overlapping descriptions or numerous exceptions. Linguistics has contributed new ways of looking at language and its relationship to psychology and to sociology in the branches of psycholinguistics and sociolinguistics.

There are three main areas of contrast in discussing language: the sounds of the language or its *phonology,* the study of word meanings or *semantics,* and the way word relationships are indicated through word order or endings and so give meaning to an utterance which is called *syntax.*

Some linguistic terms which may be helpful are defined in the following ways.[2]

Phoneme. A basic, indivisible, minimal unit of sound. The smallest usable unit of speech sound in a language.
Grapheme. A graphic symbol used in writing; a basic unit of the writing system of a language—refers to letters of the alphabet, punctuation marks, and so forth.

Morpheme. A single, basic, meaning-bearing unit of a language. A morpheme can be a word or part of a word. For example, *cats* consists of two morphemes; *cat,* a "free" morpheme that can stand alone and *-s,* a "bound" morpheme that must occur with at least one other morpheme.

Grammar. The internal structure of language; the rules by which a language operates.

Deep structure. A concept from transformational grammar, indicating that the underlying structural relationships of a sentence contain information necessary for deriving meaning from that sentence.

Surface structure. The superficial or observed structural relationships of parts of a sentence.

Because our language is so intertwined with thought or cognition and because it is influenced by a number of sociological factors, modern linguists, psychologists, and sociologists are exploring the relationships of psychology and sociology to language. Their insights into how language operates in the communication process have helped us understand language as communication.

FUNCTIONS OF LANGUAGE

Children's experiences with language, even from the very early stages of acquisition, help determine their view of how language is used and what it is for. A child's view of the uses of language may be quite different from the teacher's who sees language primarily as a means of conveying information. For the child sees many uses for language: it may create a new world through make-believe and sound and rhythm play, it may be highly personal as it helps to develop personality, or it may be used to control behavior.

In discussing the functions of language, Halliday[3] suggests that language is defined for the child by its uses and summarizes the models of language in terms of the child's intentions. The *instrumental function* occurs when children use language to get something they want—to satisfy material needs. In its *regulatory function* language is used to control behavior as the child hears "do as I tell you." Language also has an *interactional function* when language is used to mediate and maintain personal relationships, to define who is "one of us" and who is not. A fourth model of language is the *personal function* in which language is a facet of the child's individuality. Here language is a means of making public the self—the self as a speaker. The *heuristic function* of language includes language as a way of finding out about things by asking questions. Children also use language to find out about language so that by school age they know what a "question" is, what an "answer" is, and what "knowing" and "understanding" mean. In its *imaginative function*, language can be used to create a whole new world, a linguistically created environment focused on sounds. The final model is the *representational function* that adults are so aware of. Here, language is a means of communicating information or ideas; it is "I've got something to tell you" in use.

Children's image of language is very broad in terms of the possible functions it serves. Teachers need to be aware of the multiple functions of language for they are all equally real to the child. Teachers who fail to recognize that the imaginative function is as valid for children as the representational function may fail to see the needs and opportunities inherent in a given experience. Some children may not meet the demands that school makes because they are not meeting the demands of school language. The teacher must help children develop their language in all its models or functions, not just concentrate on the representational function. For we always encounter language in use—language functioning.

NONVERBAL LANGUAGE

Communication involves both being understood and understanding others. Verbal language is part of this, but nonverbal language also communicates. In fact, nonverbal cues are most often accepted as "the real thing" when they contradict verbal language.

Nonverbal language consists of virtually everything that communicates meaning except for verbal language. It may involve the tone of voice, facial expressions, body stance or posture, gestures, the expressions of the eyes, physical distance, dress, or even the omission of words or deeds. A brief aversion of the eyes or body shift can indicate disagreement or boredom. A lift of the chin and opening of the eyes may show a spark of interest. Some nonverbal language—a gesture of the finger meaning to *come* or a narrowing of the eyes to say *no*—is used intentionally. Other nonverbal cues are given without our awareness. This often happens as we try to mask our real feelings with verbal language. Our unawareness of the cue is no indication at all, however, that the cue is not being noticed and responded to.

An understanding of nonverbal language is terribly important because teachers often work with children whose nonverbal language system may differ from the teacher's. Where the systems differ there may be a serious lack of communication. Teachers who are aware of nonverbal cues may use these cues to change the personal interrelationships in the classroom and encourage communication from children.

Teachers who work with children of various cultural groups need to understand what meanings their own nonverbal cues project and how to interpret the nonverbal messages they receive from their students. An obvious illustration of this is eye contact. Suburban children habitually maintain eye contact with the teacher to project attention and respect. In Southwestern Indian cultures, however, children lower their heads and eyes to show deference and respect. Nonverbal behavior of children in inner city schools may be interpreted as "smarty" or insolent when it is not intended that way at all. The more aware a teacher is of the nonverbal behavior of students, the more effective the communication between teacher and students.

Teachers may use their knowledge of nonverbal communication to enhance the communication and interaction in their classrooms. To illustrate, let's consider space and distance—two areas of obvious importance in the classroom. In the traditional classroom the teacher's desk is at the front of the class with the students' desks in rows. The teacher's territory is that area around the desk and from the desk to the board and to the first row of pupils. Galloway comments, "More imaginative, fluid arrangements of desks and furniture influence the potential meaning of a learning context."[4] Distance is often maintained by staying in one's own territory or by setting up a table or some other object to maintain distance. Intentionally removing these can establish a closeness, a rapport, and more interaction. Physical arrangement of the room, therefore, reveals how a teacher feels about interaction and communication in the classroom. There are a number of other nonverbal cues which will encourage communication: a smile or nod to show enjoyment or agreement, a warm greeting or praise, vocal intonation and inflection patterns which indicate approval and support, a spontaneous attempt to help a pupil, maintaining eye contact when listening, and a stance of alert attention. All these are suggestive of interest and enthusiasm on the part of the teacher and tend to motivate. They set up the situation for success.

Nonverbal language is not something to be taken lightly. Because it is so subtle, it is terribly difficult to fake. Perhaps the most important factor in nonverbal communication is that it must be congruent with verbal behavior and with other aspects of nonverbal communication. Just saying, "Good!" or "That's fine" is not communicating success unless the voice and the facial expression are also saying good!

DIALECTS OF ENGLISH

Dialects are variations of the language. Speaking a dialect other than the one most frequently used in a particular place or situation means differences in language—but only differences, not deficiencies. The English language is composed of a group of dialects which overlap, and so the dialect spoken in one area is understandable to speakers of a neighboring dialect. Speakers of a dialect several regions away, however, may experience some difficulty in understanding. Ashley and Malmstrom suggest that a language is a composite structure of overlapping idiolects, or speech patterns of an individual at a particular time of life.[5]

The dialects are usually determined by geographic regions or areas, although social factors also affect dialects. This is particularly evident when a group of people from one region come to live within a different geographic area but continue to associate mostly with each other for various social or economic reasons.

We tend to think that the way we ourselves speak is the right way, and that others are either "affected" or are "ignorant." This is partly because we don't really have a clear understanding of dialect variation and partly because the way we speak is such an intrinsic part of ourselves. Somehow we just wouldn't be the same people if we spoke quite differently. Would you be you if you didn't sound like yourself?

In discussing whether one dialect is better than another, we have to further define *better*. Better in what way? For the general purposes of communication, no one dialect is better than another. Each dialect is capable of expressing the thoughts of the speaker as well as another. Each particular dialect is also the best way of communicating with other speakers of that dialect. There are, however, some dialects which have greater social acceptability than others. Right or wrong, this is the situation today; and many who wish to become accepted by a different group must alter their language to be accepted. Liza of *My Fair Lady* must still change her language to be accepted as a duchess instead of being marked as a flower girl. Perhaps this will change; perhaps it is already changing. Certainly we had several distinct dialects reflected in the language of three consecutive presidents during the 1950s and 1960s

Figure 5   The five major dialect regions in the United States.

in Presidents Eisenhower, Kennedy, and Johnson. There is also a trend in radio and television to drop the single-style national network English for more individualistic language in announcers and performers.

Before discussing the teacher's role in working with children who speak less socially acceptable dialects, let's examine some of the causes for dialect variation in the United States and the kinds of variation which exist in dialects. There are five major dialect regions in this country: the coastal New England region, the northern region, the north midland region, the south midland region, and the southern region. The dialect regions do not follow state boundaries since those boundaries do not reflect two of the basic reasons for dialect divergence—patterns of original settlement and migration patterns. Examine the map in Figure 5 which illustrates the major dialect regions.

The dialect regions indicate that a person from northern Georgia or Alabama has a dialect more similar to someone from southern Ohio or Indiana than to someone from Florida. Someone from upper New York State would sound more like someone from Wisconsin than someone from southern New Jersey. In today's highly mobile society, however, many individuals have a unique dialect which is the result of having lived in several areas or having participated in several social contexts. If you examine a map that shows physical features, the division of regions begins to look quite sensible. If you add to it the original settlement areas and trace the migrations westward, the dialect regions actually look reasonable. Another great influence on the dialect patterns has been the impact of major cities on the surrounding area. Cities such as New York, Philadelphia, Charleston, Chicago, St. Louis, New Orleans, and San Francisco were important cultural centers as well as the focus of later immigrations.

Just as there are three major areas of contrast in describing a language, the same contrasts are used in describing dialects. There may be *phonological* differences or differences in pronunciation, *lexical* or *semantic* differences which involve the particular vocabulary item used, and *syntactic* differences which may involve the addition or omission of words or inflections and changes in the order of words.

The most frequent differences are the phonological ones. These differences in pronunciation are very obvious even to a casual listener. They seldom cause real difficulty in understanding, but they may cause difficulties in reading—particularly in the area of phonics instruction. Two words that are pronounced differently in one dialect may be homonyms in another dialect. *Pin* and *pen* may be pronounced the same or distinctly differently; *merry, Mary,* and *marry* can be homonyms, or only the first two may be pronounced the same, or none of the three may sound alike.

The next most frequent dialect difference occurs in the lexical items used. A carbonated beverage is called many different things: in Rochester, New York—*pop;* in Queens, New York—*soda;* in Boston—*tonic;* or in Georgia—*Coke.* A small river may be called any of the following: *creek, stream, brook, run, branch, fork, prong, gulf, binnekill, binacle, rivulet, gutter, kill, bayou,* or *burn.*[6] These differences in words used for particular things will not usually cause difficulties in understanding.

The least frequent difference is in the syntactic area. When syntactic differences do occur, though, they usually cause real difficulty in comprehension. In Spanish-influenced English *no* is used before a verb if the verb is followed by a negative word as in *Sarah no talk to no one.* In Afro-American English the inverted word order is used for indirect as well as direct questions as in *I want to know is he going somewhere.*[7] The apparent absence of the possessive *-'s* in this same dialect as in *My aunt house* may be a syntactic difference or it may be, as some linguists suggest, simply a difference in pronunciation. The addition of words is exemplified in some dialects by *I might could give you that* in the South or by *The Mr. Smith is here* or *on the Grand Avenue* in Spanish-influenced English.[8]

There is no problem in dealing with children who speak a dialect divergent from the teacher's own if the dialect they speak is equally socially acceptable. Thus, a teacher from the Midwest who teaches in suburban Boston or Providence does not feel any need to alter the dialect patterns of children in the class even though their dialect is quite different. The problem arises when the teacher is faced with children who speak a different dialect which is not as socially acceptable.

There are three factors to be considered in deciding what to do with dialect differences in such a situation. First, teachers need to remember that for purposes of communication no dialect is better than any other and that each is best for communicating with its own speakers. Secondly, the way one speaks and the dialect one uses is an integral part of each person. This is particularly true of young children who do not have much knowledge and understanding of the world outside their own family and neighborhood. Teachers who try to change the language used by elementary school children are in essence saying that the way they talk is right and the way the children and their parents talk is wrong. Finally, although some dialects are less acceptable universally in business or social contexts, an individual can add a second dialect or change a present dialect when that person makes a rational and conscious effort to do so. When children or young adults indicate they want to change their dialect or learn another dialect, then the teacher can be of help.

This does not mean that a teacher doesn't need to know about dialects or doesn't have to deal with dialect differences. The teacher needs to be able to determine exactly what differences exist and how these differences will affect the child's understanding of reading instruction or instruction in writing. Just as most of us have learned to write the k in knot that we don't pronounce, some children will have to learn to write the 's on my aunt's house. Phonic programs for reading instruction based on one dialect may not fit the pronunciation patterns of another dialect. Most important of all, teachers need to accept the idea both at the intellectual and the action level that differences in dialect are only that—differences— and not ignorant or immature or defective speech.

ENGLISH AS A FOREIGN LANGUAGE

In many parts of the United States there are children in our schools whose native language is not English and whose cultural traditions are not American. They must be helped to live in an English-speaking society, but not at the price of alienation from their family and native culture. These children need many of the experiences with language that all children need—opportunities to do or see or hear something and talk about it. They need an environment rich in English language structures and vocabulary and opportunities to use language in various ways.

Education for children who are bilingual—those who have some language abilities in two languages—usually necessitates recognizing biculturalism. A bicultural component[9] would involve a teacher knowledgeable in the history and culture of the pupil's home language, recognition of the contributions of the child's home culture in all subject areas, and material dealing with that culture and history included in the curriculum.

In elementary schools children who are not yet proficient in English language skills should be taught within their native language to attain literacy while instruction in English oral skills is begun. The final goal of the program is literacy in English. Such an approach values the child's home language and culture while developing the skills to progress in the English language community also.

SUMMARY

The history of English has a rich and long tradition of change and variation. That same pattern of language change continues today as new words are added to our language and as we accept more individualistic kinds of expression. We are becoming more interested in preserving children's abilities to speak other languages and other dialects without restricting them from also being accepted within the framework of the American culture and English language. The main objective in elementary schools is developing confidence in expressing ideas in both oral and written language.

Understanding through Involvement

1. Have several people who come from different areas of the United States read several paragraphs aloud and try to pinpoint both similarities and differences in pronunciation.
2. One of the most interesting aspects of dialectical differences lies in the words we select to express a particular idea. Following

is a checklist that may be used to survey people about the words they use for particular things.

a.) To be absent from school: *lay out, lie out, play hookey, play truant, skip, skip school, ditch, flick, flake school, blow school, absent*

b.) End of school day: *school lets out, turns out, breaks up, breaks, leaves out, goes out, is out, is over, closes*

c.) Teacher writes with chalk on the: *board, blackboard, chalkboard, writing board, eraser board.*

d.) Missed the school bus: *got bus-left, got left, missed the bus*

e.) Said when promoted in school: *passed, got promoted, made my grade, made my pass, was moved up, was put up*

f.) Got ahead of you in line: *cut line, jumped line, broke in line, broke up, scrounged, pulled up, butted in line, ditched*

g.) General name for a carbonated drink: *Coke, soda, soda pop, pop, drink, soft drink, tonic, dope*

h.) Sleeveless undershirt worn by men: *undershirt, gall shift, T-shirt*

i.) A boy who is aggressive toward girls: *forward, getting fresh, being mannish, fast*

j.) Paper container for groceries: *bag, poke, sack, toot*

k.) Others related by blood: *family, folks, kind, kinfolks, people, relation, relatives, relations, kin*

l.) Dog of no special kind: *common dog, cur, cur dog, face, feist, mongrel, no-count, heinz, sooner, mixed dog, mutt*

Additional items may be found in the two sources from which these were selected.[6,10]

3. Since it is often hard to recognize dialect variations with which we are in constant contact, one person may tape-record short interviews with each member of your class and then play back these interviews for analysis.

4. Divide into groups of three to seven people and assign some new names for ordinary objects (a pencil, chalk, notebook, book, and chalkboard). Practice talking about the classroom using these new names your group has invented. Compare the names your group chose with those chosen by other groups. Are any of the names better than the other? Are they better than the name we ordinarily use for the object? Why is it important to have the same name for any given object?

5. Look through advertisements for newly coined words. These may be found in newspapers, magazines, on television, or on billboards.

REFERENCES

[1] L. M. Myers. *The Roots of Modern English.* Boston: Little, Brown, 1966.

[2] John F. Savage. *Linguistics for Teachers: Selected Readings.* Chicago: Science Research, 1973, pp. xvi–xix.

[3] M. A. K. Halliday. *Explorations in the Functions of Language.* London: Edward Arnold, 1973, pp. 9–21.

[4] Charles M. Galloway. "Nonverbal Language in the Classroom" (mimeographed). Columbus, Ohio: Ohio State University, 1967, p. 14.

[5] Annabel Ashley and Jean Malmstrom. *Dialects USA.* Champaign, Illinois: National Council of Teachers of English, 1967.

[6] Roger W. Shuy. *Discovering American Dialects.* Champaign, Illinois: National Council of Teachers of English, 1967, pp. 17–24.

[7] Jean Malmstrom and Constance Weaver. *Transgrammar.* Glenview, Illinois: Scott, Foresman, 1973, pp. 355–378.

[8] Ibid.

[9] Protase E. Woodford. "Bilingual/Bicultural Education: A Need for Understanding," IN *The Challenge of Communication* (Gilbert A. Jarvis, ed.). Skokie, Illinois: National Textbook, 1974, p. 401.

[10] Hugh Agee. "The Analysis of Student Talk: Classroom Possibilities for Dialect Study," *The English Journal*, September 1972, pp. 878–882.

CHAPTER FOUR

Acquiring Language

PREVIEW QUESTIONS

1 How do children learn to speak their native language?

2 What influence do adults—parents and teachers—have on children's language?

3 Why do children vary in their ability to use language?

4 What can teachers do to help children develop linguistic maturity?

Children's first words bring joy and amazement to their parents. What a thrill and delight—they can talk! At first they may just say, *Mama* or *Dada*, but very soon they can express an entire idea. Telegraphic sentences like *me cookie* or *allgone doggie* become longer as they begin to speak more like the adults with whom they are in contact. Learning to talk seems so natural and children learn so quickly that most adults simply take it for granted. How do such young children do it? Are they born knowing how to speak? Do children imitate what they hear? Is it taught? Children move from saying a two- or three-word sentence to full adult speech. What explains this?

An understanding of how children acquire language is critical to any language arts program. It is especially crucial to a program like the one suggested in this text that aims to build upon each child's ability to use language both communicatively and creatively. The teacher needs to know what factors have been important in the child's development of language because they have implications for classroom practices.

The psycholinguistic view of language acquisition presented here comes from cognitive psychology and linguistics. This view of acquisition suggests that children draw language from their linguistic environment which is then internally processed to develop the common sets of rules used by adult speakers. Thus, language acquisition is similar to the scientific method in which observations are made, hypotheses are formulated, and the hypotheses then tested against the data collected. As they learn to talk, children progressively amend their language until it becomes more and more like that spoken by adults with whom they are in contact. Smith says that "a child learning to talk is systematically trying out alternative rules to see which ones apply—that he is 'testing hypotheses', literally conducting linguistic experiments, to discover specifically what kind of language is talked around him."[1]

Basic to this view of how language is acquired is a consideration of the child's capacity for language, how language is processed, what sequence of development may be expected, and what variations may be involved.

THE BASES OF LANGUAGE ACQUISITION

The source of language acquisition includes both the human capacity for language and the particular linguistic environment of the child. Language acquisition results from a complex combination of biological and environmental factors.

Biological Factors

Linguists do not agree on exactly how biological factors affect language learning, but they do agree that human beings inherit some capacity or facility for a spoken language. One view of the biological factors important to language development is that of Lenneberg who has explored those biological endownments that make language as we know it uniquely possible for human beings. His research suggests that language is a species-specific trait of man.[2] Lenneberg also suggests that language might be expected from the evolutionary processes themselves and that the basis for language capacity might be transmitted genetically.

McNeill agrees that there is a biological basis for language although his view is quite different from Lenneberg's. He suggests that human beings inherit the notion of a sentence as a way of organizing language. He states that virtually everything that occurs in language acquisition depends on prior knowledge of the basic aspects of sentence structure. Thus the concept of a sentence may be part of the human being's innate mental capacity. McNeill's argument is as follows:

> The facts of language acquisition could not be as they are unless the concept of a sentence is available to children at the start of their learning. The concept of a sentence is the main guiding principle in a child's attempts to organize and interpret the linguistic evidence that fluent speakers make available to him. What outside observers see as distorted or 'telegraphic' speech is actually a consistent effort by a child to discover how a more or less fixed concept of a sentence is expressed in the language to which he has, by accident, been exposed.[3]

Others would argue that what the child inherits biologically is the ability to organize the surrounding language and figure out what substitutions can be made, how to indicate plurality or past time, how indeed language works to communicate ideas. There are not sufficient data at present to judge which view of biological factors is correct. There does, however, appear to be adequate data to support the idea that biological factors are involved in language acquisition in some way.

Environmental Factors

In addition to the biological capacity of humans for language, an important factor in language acquisition is the environmental or experiential factor. Central to language acquisition is the verbal

---

contact with adult speakers of the language. Two very early studies (those of McCarthy and Davis) have established the importance of adult language contacts. A more recent investigation by Cazden indicates that within the adult-child interaction a particular kind of verbal stimulation may be important.

McCarthy and Davis, in two separate studies in the 1930s, examined differences in language development among twins, children with brothers or sisters, and only children.[4] Both researchers found that only children are superior in linguistic skill to the other two groups, and that children with siblings are superior to twins. The studies thus indicate that children who associate more with adults and with adult language are more linguistically mature than children who spend more time with other children.

The importance of the adult input in children's linguistic development was evident in a recent experimental study by Cazden.[5] One group received forty minutes a day of extensive and deliberate expansions of their telegraphic sentences. In this treatment the adult repeated in full sentence form what the child had said in telegraphic form. For example, *allgone milk* might be expanded by the adult as, *Yes, your milk is all gone*. A second group was exposed to an equal amount of time spent in focusing attention on the children's ideas; but instead of repeating what they said, the adult continued the conversation with a related sentence. In this group, *allgone milk* might be extended to *Do you want some more?* or perhaps, *Then let's clean up and go outside*. The third group received no special treatment. Contrary to expectations, the second group—which had received responses to their sentences, with the adult extending ideas and introducing different grammatical elements, word meanings, and relationships among ideas—performed better on all the measures of language development than the first group, who received only the simple expansions of the children's sentences into full sentence form. Cazden comments that "semantic extension proved to be slightly more helpful than grammatical expansion" for several reasons that may have a bearing on language development programs for children.[6] In the extension treatment there was a richness of verbal stimulation and the focus was on the child's ideas instead of on grammatical structures. McNeill has also suggested that attempts to expand children's telegraphic sentences into full sentence form may be inaccurate at least part of the time and thus may mislead or interfere with development. Cazden's research seems to indicate that the kind of adult contact that is particularly important involves using mature rather than simplified language to extend children's sentences and ideas.

Piaget's View of Psychological Structures

Language is an intellectual response and, in Piaget's view, particular intellectual responses are not inherited. Instead, children inherit a tendency to organize their intellectual processes and to adapt to their environment.[7] The theoretical framework suggested by Piaget indicates that biological factors affect intelligence in three ways: there are inherited physical structures that set broad limits on intellectual functioning; there are inherited behavioral reactions that influence the first few days of human life; and there are two basic inherited tendencies—organization and adaptation.

Organization Organization is "the tendency common to all forms of life to integrate structures, which may be physical or psychological, into higher-order systems or structure."[8] The process of organization may be clearly seen in language acquisition as children apply their own organization to linguistic rules. In the early stages of language, important content words are employed in the child's speech and only the nonessential words (as far as meaning) are left out. In later stages of acquisition, rule development or organization appears when rules are applied too generally to words which do not follow the overall pattern. This is quite obvious as the child says *catched, runned,* or *holded,* or says *mines* instead of *mine,* adding the /z/ sound used on his, hers, yours, or theirs.

Adaptation Adaptation to the environment takes place through the two complementary processes of assimilation and accommodation. "Broadly speaking, *assimilation* describes the capability of the organism to handle new situations and new problems with its present stock of mechanisms; *accommodation* describes the process of change through which the organism becomes able to manage situations that are at first too difficult for it."[9] After accommodation the individual is able to assimilate increasingly novel situations; these are then accommodated and an increasingly complex and more mature system evolves. Adaptation through these two processes as described by Piaget may account for the way new linguistic structures in the adult language children hear are incorporated into the existing language and how their linguistic rules are revised to fit the new evidence children get from trying out their language.

Piaget's description of how intellectual functioning operates within the child suggests that this functioning is an interaction of inherited abilities and personal experiences. Thus, the psycholinguists who describe the inherited capacity for learning language and the researchers who have found important influences in the child's linguistic environment agree when we consider language to be an intellectual function as described by Piagetian theory.

PROCESSING LANGUAGE FROM THE ENVIRONMENT

How children use the adult language in their environment is a key issue in language acquisition. It has strong implications for what teachers should do to help children develop their language, what methods are most effective, and even what content is appropriate.

Most children sound very much like their parents; they pronounce words the same way their parents do, and they use many of the same lexical items or vocabulary as well as many of the same grammatical or syntactic structures. From this one could easily assume that children learn their language from their parents or other adults with whom they are in close contact. They do, but not merely by imitating the adult language they hear; instead, children incorporate the language surrounding them into their own rules system. If you examine the speech of two-year-olds, you find consistent patterns unlike those used by adults. Parents do not say, *I holded* or *Ask me if I no make mistake*. Imitation or copying of adult speech does not account for differences such as these. Processing and rule development does account for the similarities between children's speech and that of their parents and also for the differences between the two.

Incorporating Adult Language

The psycholinguistic thesis is that children draw language from their linguistic environment and then process this language to discover regularities and induce generalizations or "rules" about its phonology and semantic and syntactic structures. The "errors" that children make are evidence of the rules they have developed. As they gain more experience with language and with mature language, their rules more closely approximate that of the adults'.

An interesting insight into this processing of language comes from a study that asked children to imitate sentences;[10] their inability to do so is most revealing about what language rules they have, and at the same time reveals the ineffectiveness of direct copying or imitation in learning a language. The elicited imitation involved specific sentences in order to see what constructions the children would repeat accurately and which they would change or be unable to repeat at all. One such sentence given to a two-and-a-half-year-old was. *This one is the giant, but this one is little.* It was repeated as, *Dis one little, annat one big.* The researchers comment that evidently the child has comprehended the underlying meaning of the sentence, and is then using that meaning in a new form when imitating. They point out that this process of filtering a sentence through one's own productive system is a process that would be described in Piaget's terminology as, "a sentence, when recognized, is assimilated to an internal schema, and when reproduced, is constructed in terms of that schema."[11] This sort of recasting of sentences to fit one's productive patterns is especially obvious in repetitions such as, *Mozart who cried came to my party* which was repeated as, *Mozart cried and he came to my party,* or *The owl who eats candy runs fast* repeated as *Owl eat a candy and he run fast.* Evidently who-clauses were not part of this child's productive system, and so they were changed as the child tried to repeat them.

Two other studies examined imitations in children's speech as a part of investigating the process of language acquisition. In these studies, unlike Slobin and Welsh's work which specifically asked children to imitate sentences, a whole body of the children's language was examined. Ervin studied grammatical differences between imitated and free utterances of one- and two-year-olds and concluded that there is no evidence that the child's progress toward adult grammar is greatly affected by imitation of adult sentences.[12] This same general conclusion may be drawn from a longitudinal study of two children, Adam and Eve. A part of this study examined the children's imitations of their mother's speech. The researchers found that the children's utterances were not really imitative, and that "grammatical mistakes" the children made revealed their search for regularities in the language.[13]

What children actually do in using the adult language that surrounds them is to try to discover regularities in it, to organize it into patterns or rules. A child who hears *today* and *tonight* and then says *tomorning,* is not imitating adult language, but is instead processing the language heard to discover how it works and then developing a rule to use. When the rule the child has developed is not actually used (as in this example), it becomes very obvious what type of thinking, organizing, and processing is occurring.

Verifying and Revising Rules Developed

Just as children learn to behave in ways deemed acceptable to their parents by a process of being "corrected" when they do not act properly and being "reinforced" or praised when they do, it would seem that parents can and should use this same way to shape their children's language. Think of all the times, though, a parent says, "Say, Thank you" or "Please." Language develops very, very rapidly and "So far no evidence exists to show that either correction or reinforcement of the learning of grammar occurs with sufficient frequency to be a potent force."[14] Cazden cites a conversation between an adult and a four-year-old to show how impervious to correction a child's rule system can be.

Child: My teacher holded the baby rabbits and we patted them.
Adult: Did you say your teacher held the baby rabbits?
Child: Yes.
Adult: What did you say she did?
Child: She holded the baby rabbits and we patted them.
Adult: Did you say she held them tightly?
Child: No, she holded them loosely.[15]

Another such conversation is quoted in McNeill about a parent who is deliberately trying to teach a child a form not within the child's own system.

Child: Nobody don't like me.
Parent: No, say "Nobody likes me."
Child: Nobody don't like me.
Parent: No, nobody likes me.
Child: Nobody don't like me.
(Seven more repetitions of this)
Parent: No! Now listen carefully. Say "Nobody likes me."
Child: Oh! Nobody don't likes me.[16]

An explanation for this resistance to correction is part of the principle of assimilation. In order to be assimilated, there must be a degree of only moderate novelty. Anything that is too new, too novel, is not assimilated because it does not correspond to anything in the child's *schemata* or existing internal organization.

Children receive sufficient information from their environment if they are exposed to mature adult language to use in the process of adaptation without needing specific correction or reinforcement. When they are mature enough linguistically to make these changes, they will restructure their existing linguistic rules and incorporate the new items.

THE SEQUENCE OF ACQUISITION

The preceding section has indicated that the process of language acquisition involves systematic and progressive rule development and then verification or revision of these rules using evidence given by other speakers of the language. This systematic and progressive development is evident in the predictable order of acquisition of linguistic items. Although there may be relatively wide variations in the rate of acquisition or in the age at which particular items are acquired, the order of acquisition of these items is strikingly similar.

Early Language and Motor Development

The following chart of motor and language development is adapted from Lenneberg.[17] The approximate ages corresponding to each section have been omitted in order to focus on the developmental trends involved. The chart covers the period from six months of age to about four years of age.

MOTOR AND LANGUAGE DEVELOPMENT: SELECTED MILESTONES

Motor Development	Language Development
Supports head when in prone position; then plays with a rattle when placed in hand; then sits with props	Makes gurgling sounds usually called cooing; then responds to human sounds; then the vowel-like sounds begin to be interspersed with more consonant sounds
When sitting bends forward and uses hands for support; then stands up holding on and grasps with thumb apposition; then creeps efficiently and pulls to a standing position	Cooing changes to babbling; then vocalizations are mixed with sound play; differentiates between words heard; appears to try imitating sounds, but isn't successful
Walks when held by one hand; walks on feet and hands with knees in air	Identical sound sequences are replicated and words (*mama, dada*) emerge; shows understanding of some words and simple consonants
Grasp, prehension, and release fully developed; gait stiff and propulsive; sits on child's chair with only fair aim	Has a repertoire of 3 to 50 words; still babbling but with several syllables and intricate intonation patterns; may say *thank you* or *come here*, but can't join items into spontaneous two-item phrases

[handwritten marginal notes: "3 months or before", "6–8 months", "around 12 months", "around 18 months"]

Motor Development	Language Development
Runs, buts falls in sudden turns; can quickly alternate between sitting and standing; walks stairs up or down with only one foot forward	Vocabulary of more than 50 items; "telegraphic speech" as tries to join vocabulary into two-word phrases; increase in communicative behavior and more interest in language
Jumps into air with both feet; takes a few steps on tiptoe; good hand and finger coordination	Fast increase in vocabulary; frustrated if not understood; utterances have two to five words; characteristic "child grammar"
Runs smoothly with acceleration and deceleration; makes sharp and fast curves; walks stairs by alternating feet; can operate tricycle	Vocabulary of some 100 words; 80 percent of utterances intelligible even to strangers; grammatical complexity roughly that of adult usage
Jumps rope, catches ball, and walks a line	Language well established; deviations more in style than in grammar

(handwritten margin notes: 24 months, 30 months, 36 months, 48 months)

Acquisition of Syntactic Structures

Numerous studies have been conducted to establish the sequence of acquisition of syntactic structures. Three such studies will be briefly discussed here as they deal with children at different age levels.

In the study of syntactic acquisition of two young children called Adam and Eve, Bellugi and Brown found the identical order of appearance of certain inflections in both children's language although there was a considerable difference—from eight-and-a-half to fifteen months—in the ages of the children when the inflectional forms first appeared.[18] The inflections were items such as -s for plurals and -ed for past tense of verbs. Moreover, the order of appearance of these inflections did not match with the frequency of the forms found in the language of the children's mothers.

Stages of acquisition of syntactic structures were also identified by Menyuk in a study of nursery school and kindergarten children.[19] The language of the children was recorded in family role playing, in answering questions, and in talking about pictures. She found that certain transformations were used by significantly more first-grade children than kindergarten children, showing maturation between nursery school and first grade.

The third study which showed evidence of stages in the acquisition of syntactic structures was Chomsky's study of children between five and ten years of age.[20] She examined four particular constructions—not usually present in the grammar of five-year-olds but normally acquired by age ten—in an effort to determine the order of acquisition and the approximate age of acquisition. Chomsky found that one construction involving understanding of pronoun reference was quite rapidly and uniformly acquired at five-and-a-half. Two of the other constructions appeared to be under control from age nine on, and the fourth construction was not completely controlled by all of the ten-year-olds.

These studies, and others which have examined the acquisition of various syntactic structures, have found that individual structures are acquired in a particular order although the age of acquisition may vary from one individual to another. There is then a sequence of acquisition that is quite regular. It seems independent of experiential factors except in the rate of acquisition.

SEMANTIC ACQUISITION

The acquisition of semantics, or word meaning, is less clear than that of syntax. Early studies dealt mostly with vocabulary frequencies and derivations of words, and linguistic investigations until recently concentrated on phonology and syntax. Although the details of the acquisition of semantics is not clear, there are many similarities between syntactic and semantic acquisition. There seem to be stages in semantic acquisition as children progressively amend their early language until word meanings approximate those of adults.

One view of semantic acquisition is that word meanings are learned by adding "features" or meaning components to the lexical meaning of words. Clark suggests that,

> When a child first begins to use identifiable words, he does not know their full (adult) meaning; he only has partial entries for them in his lexicon. The acquisition of semantic knowledge, then, will consist of adding more features of meaning to the lexical entry of the word until the child's combination of features in the entry for the word corresponds to the adults.[21]

Thus, very young children may call anything on four wheels a car—including trucks and moving vans. As they have more experience with different vehicles, they refine car in various ways until what they call a *car* is just what an adult would. In the process of refining the meaning of words, children both particularize (*car* to *Chevy, Ford, station wagon,* etc.) and generalize (*car* to *pickup, van,* etc.).

With older children an indication of this same process of refining meanings until they approximate the adult meaning may be seen in words that are closely related by having many overlapping features. In word pairs such as boy-brother or girl-sister, one word of each pair may refer to a subset within the other word and yet have additional features. All brothers, for example, are boys, but not all boys are brothers. Brother is a subset of boy with the additional feature of family relationship. Many middle-graders still have difficulty with this distinction, and when asked how many brothers or sisters they have, will include themselves.

The semantic features theory is that there are combinations of the presence or absence of particular features that make up the lexical meaning of the word. The chart below illustrates the features of *before* and *after*.

before	*after*
+time	+time
−simultaneous	−simultaneous
+prior	−prior

This approach to semantics, that of semantic features, is still controversial. Brown and McNeill have explored semantic acquisition using the notion of semantic features and have looked for developmental trends. This theory, if not generally accepted, does represent a major line of thinking in the area of semantics.

Another view of the role of semantics in the language of young children is expressed by Bloom.[22] She examined the telegraphic speech of a number of children and found that grammatical explanations of sentences such as *Mommy sock* neglected to include the connection with cognitive-perceptual development and the inherent semantic relations that underlie the juxtaposition of words in these early sentences. *Mommy sock* meant different things at different times. Once it meant the child was picking up her mother's sock and another time it described the mother putting on the child's sock. In Bloom's view of semantics, language has a surface structure and an underlying semantic (not grammatical) structure.

Another researcher has explored the context within which a particular word or lexical item is used and suggests that until the child is quite mature, somewhat after age ten, lexical items do not have a meaning separate from the sentence context used by the child.[23] Menyuk points out that even when a word is understood and used in one sentence structure, the same word may not be understood in a different sentence structure. This would suggest, as Bloom has, that somehow there are underlying semantic relationships reflected in the particular grammatical context.

In the acquisition of semantics, we may see the two principles of development suggested by Piaget in the development of mental structures: organization and adaptation. The sentence context serves as an organization for semantic properties, and adaptation seems to be the process through which the child acquires increasingly more mature lexical references through experiences with the linguistic community.

Even though we do not have definitive data on the process of semantic acquisition, we do know some of the factors which enable children to increase their vocabulary—increase both the number of words and word meanings they can use and also increase the precision of the meanings of these words. One factor which aids development is contact in a meaningful situation with a wide variety of words, both in speech and in written materials. Another is feedback from adults about word meanings as the words come up in the context of the situation. A discussion of vocabulary development is included in Chapter Five.

DEVELOPMENT OF COMPLEXITY

Complexity in language involves compressing two or more simple structures into a single sentence through compounding, subordinating, and embedding. For example, the following sentences may be combined several ways.

I had a baseball.
It was new.
I took it to school.
I lost it.

They may be made into compound sentences: *I had a baseball, and it was new. I took it to school, and I lost it.* They may be made into complex sentences by subordination: *My ball that was new was a baseball. When I took it to school, I lost it.* Or they may be combined with some embedding into a single sentence: *I lost the new baseball I took to school.* In the latter case, *It was new* becomes embedded as a single adjective.

As children mature there is a developmental increase in the number and kinds of structures they use. This should not imply that young children only use simple sentences, for children at kindergarten age do use compounding, subordination, and embedding. However, there is an increase in the number of transformations used as age and ability with language increase. This is true of both oral and written language. A major study examining the development of children's oral language was conducted by Loban over a period of years. In 1952 a group of over three hundred children was selected and oral language samples were obtained annually throughout their school years. This study found that students showed an increase in complexity of language throughout the years with a noticeable rise about the time of fifth grade. The primary difference in grammatical complexity between the less mature and more mature children was in the dexterity of substitutions within patterns and not in the number of different patterns used.[24]

A key study in examining differences in syntactic maturity in written language used students in grades four, six, eight, ten, and twelve as well as two groups of adults. They were all given a passage containing very short simple sentences and were asked to rewrite it in a better way without omitting any information. Their rewriting was then checked on five syntactic measures. Hunt[25] found that as school children mature, they tend to embed more of their elementary sentences or kernel strings, and that this embedding is done in different ways at different age levels. As with oral language, older students tended to write significantly longer clauses and T-units. A *T-unit* is a minimal terminable unit, an independent clause with its modifiers. It is a more accurate measure of complexity than sentence length since it prevents run-on sentences from increasing length artificially.

These studies, along with others which have examined complexity in children's language, indicate a pattern of increasing complexity in both spoken and written language throughout the elementary grades. Although a variety of means to combine structures is used at all grade levels, it is at first done mostly through coordination and later through subordination and embedding. One may expect a great many "run-on" sentences throughout the early elementary grades, but these decrease as children's language matures.

VARIABILITY IN ACQUISITION

Although the patterns of acquisition are orderly in the sequence of development, both individual differences and social circumstances lead to considerable variation in acquisition at a given age level.

This variation may consist of differences in the structures acquired at a particular time by an individual or in differences in the acquisition of a particular structure by children of the same age.

Individual Variability

A very clear picture of the differences between individuals in the acquisition of particular structures occurs in a study discussed earlier in the chapter. In this study, the researchers were investigating the appearance of various syntactic or morphological inflections in Adam and Eve's language.[26] Of the five inflections reported, the one acquired when the children were closest in age was the -ing on present progressives. Eve used this inflection at nineteen-and-a-half months and Adam used it at twenty-eight months, eight-and-a-half months' difference. On the other hand, the third person ending -s on present tense verbs was reported for Eve at twenty-six months, but not for Adam until forty-one months, a fifteen-month difference. In spite of such tremendous variations in the age at which these children used the inflections, the order or sequence of use was the same.

This kind of individual variability may be found for other syntactic or semantic structures as well as for various elements of motor development. There simply is a great deal of variability in individual children's rates of development. In language acquisition, particularly, the factor that appears to be most important is the individual linguistic environment of the child.

The individual linguistic experiences of children serve as the source from which children process their language. The words they hear, their pronunciations, and the structures which are used by people around them serve as a basis for developing linguistic rules. The particular linguistic environment of the child may also be important in the kinds of interaction opportunities provided—opportunities for the child to test and revise particular linguistic rules.

Social Variability

In addition to the factors mentioned previously which cause individuals to vary in their language, there are also variations used within a particular social context. Within any dialect of English there are varieties or *registers* of that dialect appropriate for use in particular situations. People vary their language depending upon their current situation and what they believe to be correct within their dialect for that situation.

These variations or registers may be signaled by changes in phonology, syntax, lexical items used, and paralinguistics or pause and gesture. An individual speaker of any English dialect usually controls a range of registers varying from informal ones used with peers or family to formal ones which include written registers if the person is literate.

Even children use registers of language. Just ask a seven-year-old to role play an adult and you will observe different inflections, different vocabulary, and different gestures. The use of different language in written modes of discourse is also easily observed in children. By the time they are in the upper elementary grades and have been exposed to a considerable amount of written material, children write quite differently than they talk—showing an understanding of a register of written language.

There is, then, variability in language due to the particular situation in which language is used as well as variability among individual speakers and groups of speakers due to differing linguistic environments. It is this variability within language that the teacher observes so clearly in the classroom and which necessitates varying assignments or experiences for different children.

IMPLICATIONS FOR TEACHING

There appear to be two distinct implications for classroom practice stemming from the theoretical view presented of how children acquire language. If the basic process of acquisition involves using the language environment as a source for language "data," then it is important for the teacher to provide a rich language environment in the classroom. If the rules developed by children about how their language operates are then tested and revised in terms of the feedback they receive as they use language, then there must be many opportunities to use language in various ways.

Need for a Rich Language Environment

Providing a classroom environment full of opportunities to hear rich and varied language would involve selecting and reading literature for children that has a variety of sentence structures and a wealth of words as well as real literary qualities. It also implies that the teacher should not simplify sentence structures or vocabulary unless the children indicate a lack of understanding. Rich language could also be introduced through various media such as films,

Children enjoy hearing and repeating the creative language that appears in so many of today's books for children. (*Photograph by Juanita Skelton*)

audiotapes, and recordings and by inviting guest speakers. This kind of language environment should present language in a meaningful context and offer a variety of experiences from which children can draw language data.

Literature for children Literature is a particularly rich source because so many books and poems for children contain imaginative language and children enjoy hearing it.

Look at the language used in the following selections from literature and poetry written for children of various ages. Examine the complexity of the sentences and the choice of words used. To get a feeling for complexity in mature language, examine sentence length and the use of clauses. Rich vocabulary is apparent in words which are precise and those which create a vivid picture in the mind of the reader.

In *The Way the Tiger Walked*, a picture book for younger children, there is a scene where the tiger tries to get the animals who are imitating him to walk their own way.

> The tiger stalked up to the elephant. Then, suddenly, he spread out his ears until they looked like small golden wings. He walked with

heavy steps, and the ground shook under his feet. Rumble-sway! Rumble-sway!

The elephant's trunk curled up in surprise. "What a powerful way to walk!" he thought.

And then the elephant slowly raised his head. He held his trunk up high. He trampled back to his jungle brush, walking the way an elephant walked, with a rumble and a sway. Rumble-sway![27]

O'Dell has written a book for older children based upon the forced move of the Navahos from Arizona to New Mexico between 1863 and 1865. It is also the story of Bright Morning and her husband, Tall Boy.

I started off, leading the way along the river, to the big rocks that stood at the entrance to the hidden canyon. The rocks and the gnarled sycamores that grew among them formed a low, winding corridor and Tall Boy had to climb down from the horse to get through.

Hidden Canyon was just as I remembered it. The yellow cliffs rose on all sides. The spring flowed from the rock and made a waterfall that the wind caught and spun out over the meadow. On the far side of the meadow was the grove of wild plums, where I had picked many handfuls of fruit. The trees now were covered with white and pink blossoms.

But I had forgotten the cave. Tall Boy saw it at once.[28]

Poetry, too, is a rich source of language. Its sounds appeal to children.

THE PICKETY FENCE[29]

The pickety fence
The pickety fence
Give it a lick it's
The pickety fence
Give it a lick it's
A clickety fence
Give it a lick it's
A lickety fence
Give it a lick
Give it a lick
Give it a lick
With a rickety stick
Pickety
Pickety
Pickety
Pick

David McCord

SKINS[30]

Skins of lemons are waterproof slickers.
Pineapple skins are stuck full of stickers.
Skins of apples are skinny and shiny,
and strawberry skins (if any) are tiny.

Grapes have skins that are juicy and squishy.
Gooseberry skins are vinegar-ishy.
Skins of peaches are fuzzy and hairy.
Oranges' skins are more peely than pare-y.

Skins of plums are squirty and squeezy.
Bananas have skins you can pull-off-easy.
. . . .
I like skins that are thin as sheeting,
so what-is-under is bigger for eating.

Aileen Fisher

Through literature for children the teacher can introduce a variety of language patterns and vocabulary in meaningful ways. There is rich context for understanding, and concrete imagery to delight and capture the child's imagination.

There is research evidence to show that using literature has some effect on children's language ability. Studies such as those by Cohen, Fodor, and Cullinan et al.[31] have found literature to be effective in facilitating some aspect of language acquisition or development. All these studies used an activity program or oral discussion as a follow-up to the stories read to children in the experimental groups.

Language of the teacher   Another source of language input for the classroom is the language of the teacher. Too often teachers working with children in the primary grades attempt to simplify their language so that they will be easily understood. There are, of course, times when this might be necessary for the safety of the children. Other than those few rare times, the teacher can facilitate language development more by speaking in a normal adult way. The context within which language is used helps to clarify much that may not yet be under control of less mature speakers. If the teacher is sensitive to the responses—both verbal and nonverbal—of children, further explanations can make clear any lack of understanding while developing vocabulary at the same time.

Another facet of the teacher's language is the kind of response elicited from children. Teachers must create a need for children to respond in a variety of ways to their experiences. This may occur in individual discussions or as part of a group experience.

Nonprint media   Another source of a rich language environment which may be provided within the classroom setting is the variety of films, audiotapes, and recordings available. These media also provide a context for language that is meaningful. They should be selected for their inherent interest as well as for their language possibilities.

The content of the nonprint media may involve another subject area such as math, science, or social studies. There are also recordings, tapes, films, and film strips of both poetry and prose available. If the teacher can set up a listening area for independent use, children can select what appeals to them and work individually or in small groups with the materials.

The creation in the classroom of a rich and varied language environment is important for all children. It is crucial for children whose home environment does not provide experiences for children to respond to through language. The need to use language to communicate ideas and feelings in an original and creative way is to some extent culturally determined. For teachers working with children who have not been exposed to this need to use language, the richness and response to language in the classroom are vital.

Opportunities to Engage in Language

A major feature of the process of language acquisition and development is the testing and revision of the internalized rules of how language operates. This applies to the acquisition of specific syntactic constructions and also to the acquisition or refinement of semantics or word meanings.

Communicating and explaining   The teacher needs to set up situations that give children opportunities to talk with others. Children need experiences in sharing ideas and explaining things. This may be done with the whole class, with small groups of children, or between individual children. Children should be allowed to talk freely with each other when it will not interrupt classroom activities and as long as that talk is not rowdy or purposeless. In group discussions and in sharing activities, children should be encouraged to describe and explain and interact with each other. The teacher can accomplish this by asking a variety of questions and by encouraging children to ask questions or add their own experiences. Activities

Children need frequent opportunities to engage in meaningful conversations within the classroom. (*Photograph by Thomas England*)

which require joint cooperation, effort, and thinking also prompt meaningful talk among children.

Imagining and creating   Through the various avenues provided in oral composition, the teacher can encourage imaginative and creative uses of language. Dramatic activities and storytelling lend themselves to this kind of language use. Inventing new words and using familiar ones in new ways, rhyming and discovering "found" poetry, and telling real and invented stories all lead to imaginative and creative uses of language.

In classrooms we provide opportunities for children to respond to their experiences creatively in various artistic media. This kind of response should be encouraged in creative language activities also. Children, even at the early age levels, should have an opportunity to tell or write stories and poems. If the task of writing is difficult for them, there should be provision made for dictating to others. Children should share orally as well as in written form the stories and poems they have written.

Playing with words and sounds is natural for children. Rhyming words and making up new words are not unusual at all. It is typical to see this in young children who have not been "disciplined" so much that their creative response has been squelched. If teachers want to foster creative responses by children to their environment, then they must cherish creativity and imagination in children. Students need to be encouraged and given opportunities to work creatively with language in both oral and written forms. They need to hear imaginative language used in both stories and poetry.

SUMMARY

There are some specific classroom practices that may be drawn from the theory of language acquisition presented here. There is a need for the teacher to provide a classroom environment that has rich language experiences for children. There is a need for children to have many varied opportunities to engage in both communicative and creative uses of language. A classroom that permits and encourages these activities not only helps children develop their language potential, but also facilitates growth in all the language arts.

Understanding through Involvement

1. Tape-record several children at different ages telling a story based on the same wordless book (see list of these in Chapter 13). Then examine the stories for differences in complexity of the sentence structures used, the number of words per sentence or per main clause, and the fluency with which the children told the story (no long pauses, fillers like *and-uh*, or completely garbled language).
2. Another interesting activity with different age levels is to see what words children associate with the ones you give. Generally the less mature children will give a word that follows the one you say, somewhat more mature children will give a word that begins with the same letter or sound, and the fully mature children will give a word that will substitute for the one you give because it is the same part of speech or in the same word class.

You might try:

Hat	*Tall*	*Monday*
Walk	*Come*	*Knife*
Red	*Hot*	*Pen*
Mother	*Book*	*Brother*

3. This activity involves asking small groups of first- or second-graders and fifth- or sixth-graders to put two short sentences together into one sentence. They may add words or leave words out or change them around. Look for differences in the ease with which they combine the sentences and the variety of ways they can do it. They should see the sentence pairs, hear you read them, and then give their answers orally. Some sentence pairs you could use are:[32]

   a.) The cat is black.
   The cat likes hot milk.
   b.) Sam watched the clowns.
   The clowns blew up balloons.
   c.) My hat is blue.
   My hat has flowers on it.
   d.) My sister is going to camp this summer.
   She will learn to swim at camp.
   e.) My sister likes to play with her dolls.
   Her dolls all talk.

4. There are differences between what a child understands and what that child can say. This may be seen clearly by asking children between two-and-a-half and three-and-a-half years of age to look at some pictures of various animals. You first point to certain ones asking, "What is this animal called?" After a while, switch and ask the child to point to the wolf (or elephant, giraffe, etc.). There should be a noticeable difference between what the child can name and what that same child can point to when hearing the name.

5. Examine some children's trade books or library books that would be appropriate for primary age or preschool children. In these picture books, look for vocabulary that is interesting and different and also for sentence complexity. Although sentence length is not as accurate a measure as some others in determining complexity, it does work fairly well in professionally written material and is simple to do. Use the first ten or fifteen sentences in five or ten books to get a feel for the kind of linguistic complexity that is used in well-written picture books for children.

REFERENCES

[1] Frank Smith. *Understanding Reading—A Psycholinguistic Analysis of Reading and Learning to Read.* New York: Holt, 1971, p. 50.

[2] E. H. Lenneberg. "A Biological Perspective of Language," IN *Language* (R. C. Oldfield and J. C. Marshall, eds.). Baltimore, Maryland: Penguin, 1968, pp. 32–33.

[3] David McNeill. *The Acquisition of Language.* New York: Harper & Row, 1970, pp. 2–3.

[4] D. McCarthy. "Language Development of the Preschool Child," IN *Child Behavior and Development* (Roger G. Barker, et al., eds.). New York: McGraw-Hill, 1943, pp. 107–128. E. A. Davis. *The Development of Linguistic Skill in Twins, Singletons with Siblings, and Only Children from Age Five to Ten Years.* Minneapolis, Minnesota: The University of Minnesota Press, 1937.

[5] Courtney B. Cazden. *Child Language and Education.* New York: Holt, 1972, pp. 121–125.

[6] Ibid.

[7] H. Ginsburg and S. Opper. *Piaget's Theory of Intellectual Development.* Englewood Cliffs, New Jersey: Prentice-Hall, 1969, p. 17.

[8] Ibid., p. 18.

[9] A. L. Baldwin. *Theories of Child Development.* New York: Wiley, 1967, p. 176.

[10] Dan I. Slobin and Charles A. Welsh. "Elicited Imitation as a Research Tool in Developmental Psycholinguistics," IN *Studies of Child Language Development* (C. A. Ferguson and D. I. Slobin, eds.). New York: Holt, 1973, pp. 485–497.

[11] Ibid., p. 490.

[12] Susan M. Ervin. "Imitation and Structural Change in Children's Language," IN *New Directions in the Study of Language* (E. H. Lenneberg, ed.). Cambridge, Massachusetts: MIT Press, 1964, pp. 163–189.

[13] Roger Brown and Ursula Bellugi. "Three Processes in the Child's Acquisition of Syntax," IN *New Directions in the Study of Language* (E. H. Lenneberg, ed.). Cambridge, Massachusetts: MIT Press, 1964, pp. 131–161.

[14] Courtney B. Cazden. "Suggestions from Studies of Early Language Acquisition," *Childhood Education*, vol. 46, December 1969, p. 129.

[15] Ibid., p. 128.

[16] David McNeill. "Developmental Psycholinguistics," IN *The Genesis of Language* (F. Smith and G. Miller, eds.). Cambridge, Massachusetts: MIT Press, 1966, p. 69.

[17] E. H. Lenneberg. *Biological Functions of Language.* New York: Wiley, 1967.

[18] Ursula B. Bellugi and Roger Brown. "The Acquisition of Language," *Monograph Social Research in Child Development*, vol. XXIX, no. 1, 1964.

[19] Paula Menyuk. "Syntactic Structures in the Language of Children," *Child Development*, vol. xxxiv, June 1963, pp. 407–422.

[20] Carol S. Chomsky. *The Acquisition of Syntax in Children from 5 to 10*. Cambridge, Massachusetts: MIT Press, 1969.

[21] E. V. Clark. "What's in a Word? On the Child's Acquisition of Semantics in His First Language" (unpublished paper). August 1971, p. 12. Further discussion of this theory: E. V. Clark, "On the Acquisition of the Meaning of Before and After." *Journal of Verbal Learning and Verbal Behavior*, vol. 10, 1971, pp. 266–275. H. H. Clark and E. V. Clark. "Semantic Distinctions and Memory for Complex Sentences." *Quarterly Journal of Experimental Psychology*, vol. 20, 1968, pp. 129–138.

[22] Lois Bloom. "Why Not Pivot Grammar?" IN *Studies of Child Language Development* (C. A. Ferguson and D. I. Slobin, eds.). New York: Holt, 1973, pp. 430–440. ALSO SEE L. Bloom. *Language Development: Form and Function in Emerging Grammars*. Cambridge, Massachusetts: MIT Press, 1970.

[23] Paula Menyuk. *The Acquisition and Development of Language*. Englewood Cliffs, New Jersey: Prentice-Hall, 1971, p. 182.

[24] Walter D. Loban. *The Language of Elementary School Children*. Champaign, Illinois: National Council of Teachers of English, 1963.

[25] Kellog W. Hunt. "Syntactic Maturity in School-Children and Adults." *Society for Research in Child Development Monograph*, vol. xxv, no. 1, February 1970.

[26] Ursula Bellugi. "The Emergence of Inflections and Negations Systems in the Speech of Two Children" IN *The Acquisition of Language* (D. McNeill, ed.). New York: Harper & Row, 1970, p. 83.

[27] Doris J. Chaconas. *The Way the Tiger Walked*. New York: Simon & Schuster, 1970.

[28] Scott O'Dell. *Sing Down the Moon*. Boston: Houghton Mifflin, 1970, p. 132.

[29] David McCord. "The Pickety Fence," *Far and Few*. Boston: Little, Brown, 1952.

[30] Aileen Fisher. "Skins," *That's Why*. Camden, New Jersey: Nelson, 1946.

[31] Dorothy Cohen. "The Effect of Literature on Vocabulary and Reading," *Elementary English*, vol. xlv, February 1968, pp. 207–217. Eugene M. Fodor. "The Effect of the Systematic Reading of Stories on the Language Development of Culturally Deprived Children," *Dissertation Abstracts*, vol. xxvii, no. 4, October 1966, p. 952–A. Bernice E. Cullinan, Angela Jaggar, and Dorothy Strickland. "Language Expansion for Black Children in the Primary Grades: A Research Report," *Young Children*, vol. 29, January 1974, pp. 98–112.

[32] Frank Zidonas et al. "Sentence Combining," *Protocol Materials in English Education, Language Development*. Tampa, Florida: University of South Florida, 1975.

RESOURCES FOR PART ONE

FOR FURTHER READING

Almy, Millie. *Young Children's Thinking*. New York: Teacher's College, 1966.

Brearley, Molly, ed. *The Teaching of Young Children: Some Applications of Piaget's Learning Theory*. New York: Schocken Books, 1970.

Brown, Mary, and Norman Precious. *The Integrated Day in the Primary School*. New York: Agathon Press, 1970.

Burling, Robbins. *Man's Many Voices: Language in Its Cultural Context*. New York: Holt, 1970.

Cazden, Courtney B. *Child Language and Education*. New York: Holt, 1972.

Cazden, Courtney B., Vera P. John, and Dell Hymes, eds. *Functions of Language in the Classroom*. New York: Teachers College, 1972.

Dale, Edgar. *Building a Learning Environment*. Bloomington, Indiana: Phi Delta Kappa, 1972.

Davis, A. L., ed. *Culture, Class, and Language Variety*. Urbana, Illinois: National Council of Teachers of English, 1972.

Elkind, David. *A Sympathetic Understanding of the Child Six to Sixteen*. Boston: Allyn and Bacon, 1971.

Francis, W. Nelson. *The History of English*. Urbana, Illinois: National Council of Teachers of English, 1963.

Ginsburg, Herbert, and Sylvia Opper. *Piaget's Theory of Intellectual Development*. Englewood Cliffs, New Jersey: Prentice-Hall, 1969.

Isaacs, Susan. *Childhood and After*. New York: Agathon Press, 1970.

Isaacs, Susan. *The Children We Teach*. New York: Schocken Books, 1971.

Pulaski, Mary Ann Spencer. *Understanding Piaget*. New York: Harper & Row, 1971.

Tough, Joan. *Talking, Thinking, Growing*. New York: Schocken, 1974.

Wadsworth, Barry J. *Piaget's Theory of Cognitive Development*. New York: McKay, 1971.

Wilkinson, Andrew. *The Foundations of Language*. New York: Oxford University Press, 1971.

OTHER INSTRUCTIONAL MATERIALS

Cassette Tapes

Alvina Burrows. *Involving the Child in the Language Arts*. Listener Educational Enterprises, 6777 Hollywood Boulevard, Hollywood, California 90028.

David Elkind. *Piaget in Childhood Education*. Listener Educational Enterprises, 6777 Hollywood Boulevard, Hollywood, California 90028.

Films

The Language of Children (protocol project films). Film Distribution Supervisor, Ohio State University, Dept. of Photography and Cinema, 156 W. 19th Avenue, Columbus, Ohio 43210

Piaget's Developmental Theory: Conservation

Piaget's Developmental Theory: Classification

Piaget's Developmental Theory: Formal Thought

Davidson Films, Inc., 3701 Buchanan Street, San Francisco, California 94123.

Development of the Child: Language

Kagan and Gardner, Harvard University, Harper & Row.

PART TWO

Language Skills: Substance and Strategies

This portion of the text presents strategies for teaching children essential language skills based on developmental learning theory. This theory suggests that content and basic skills are best learned within the context of meaningful and concrete experiences.

Chapter Five is devoted to the teaching of thinking and vocabulary skills. Because experience is necessary for both thinking and vocabulary development, it forms the basis for the instructional program. Through a variety of planned experiences, children can categorize, classify, and label objects. The goal is to extend students' thinking and vocabulary through experiences which include wide reading, discussion, listening, fieldtrips, and neighborhood excursions.

The teaching of language usage and grammar is presented in Chapter Six. Various kinds of grammars found in textbooks are described and discussed for informational purposes. Activities for children are suggested to help them become more flexible and more fluent in using English in oral and written form.

Listening, as a skill, has been ignored in most classrooms. Chapter Seven presents a framework for instruction, suggesting that listening is part of an interchange system. The impact of television on listening behavior is also explored and instructional activities using children's television viewing are included in the discussion.

Four major types of oral composition are discussed in Chapter Eight: sharing, discussing, reporting, and storytelling. Sharing is viewed as a means of facilitating children's language and concept development. The various kinds of discussions are divided into those that are primarily for planning and those used for presentation. Specific ideas for oral reporting and storytelling are included.

Although drama is certainly a form of oral composition, it is discussed in a separate chapter because it is quite different in nature and purpose from the other forms of oral language activities. The kinds of drama expression discussed in Chapter Nine range from dramatic play and movement to pantomime, role playing, and improvisational drama.

A personal letter, report, or invitation can be a creative endeavor just as can the writing of an imaginative story or poem. Therefore, the discussion in Chapter Ten combines instructional approaches for a wide variety of writing experiences.

The final chapter in this section, Chapter Eleven, focuses on teaching the supportive writing skills—punctuation, capitalization, spelling, and handwriting. Instruction is accomplished within a meaningful context and does not interfere with the spontaneous flow of children's thoughts as they write. Transcribing oral material to teach certain punctuation skills, making their own rule books, and individualizing for spelling are a few examples that may be used in the classroom.

CHAPTER FIVE

Extending Thinking and Vocabulary Skills

PREVIEW QUESTIONS

1 What activities would extend children's thinking skills beyond the cognitive memory level?
2 What critical thinking skills and activities are appropriate for elementary school age children?
3 How is vocabulary increased?

A knowledge and understanding of Piaget's theories of intellectual development provide a basis for planning an environment that will stimulate and extend children's thinking. Piaget suggests that children, until about age eleven, think best with something in their hands; therefore, students' learning should be tied to concrete materials and experiences throughout most of their elementary school years. For instance, it is possible for a student to read about rocks and then write a report concerning the hardness of certain ones versus the softness of others. However, wouldn't the learning be more lasting and meaningful if the student had the actual rocks to touch, observe, and use in conducting experiments? Instead of a report taken solely from a reference book or encyclopedia, the student could present firsthand findings and observations. A written record of the experiments might be kept, shared with others, and the results confirmed using several published sources. Children who are encouraged to become actively involved in finding out, discovering, problem solving, model constructing, project sharing, and touching, seeing, and describing their world around them develop language and thinking skills that will serve them for the rest of their lives. Such experiences also facilitate an understanding of concepts and the vocabulary associated with them.

DIRECT EXPERIENCES AND THE DEVELOPMENT OF THINKING SKILLS

What kind of thinking is required of most students? Are they usually given low-level cognitive memory tasks that require them to recall facts and predetermined answers? Or do teachers provide activities that will develop a wide range of thinking skills, including the ability to evaluate and make judgments about oral and written material? Are young children given enough opportunities to sort and group objects? Are older students encouraged to make close observations and then write about their findings? These tasks, and others similar to them, extend children's thinking abilities by challenging them to use skills that demand flexibility of thought. These experiences also can be a natural part of the daily classroom curriculum as shown through the following discussion of several different types of thinking experiences.

Sorting

Children can participate in a variety of sorting activities as part of their everyday learning. For instance, a group of students went on a neighborhood walk and collected a number of interesting items.

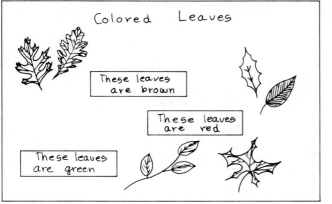

Figure 6

An autumn display

These were sorted, labeled, and attractively displayed. One group of four children sorted their collections of leaves by placing the green leaves in one pile, the brown leaves in another, and the reddish colored leaves in still another. They then selected representative leaves from each of the three piles, attached them to a large piece of posterboard, and wrote brief descriptions to identify each of the categories, as in Figure 6.

Another class decided they could help the appearance of the school by cleaning up the area around it. They spent part of a morning picking up litter—bottles, cans, gum and candy wrappers, and old pieces of newspapers. When the students returned to the room, they sorted and counted the different items to find out what seemed to be littered most often around the school. They discovered that they had collected more gum and candy wrappers than any other item. This finding led to a discussion about why there were so many gum and candy wrappers and what might be done to correct the litter problem.

Besides offering children a variety of sorting experiences such as these, items for sorting may be available on a special table in the classroom or sorting boxes can be made with very little effort. Counters, balls, blocks, toothpicks, small toys, straws, pencils, paper clips, and rubber bands are only a few of the items that might be placed in sorting boxes. If you cover the boxes with wrapping paper or contact paper, they will be much more attractive.

Very young children usually will sort objects according to color. For example, given a collection of green, yellow, and red buttons, a child will place all the red ones together, all the green ones together, and so on. Asked if there is another way to sort them, the child may say *no,* even though some buttons are square and others are round. A child whose thinking is more advanced may quickly sort the but-

EXTENDING THINKING AND VOCABULARY SKILLS

Sorting activities can be a natural part of the everyday learning environment.
(*Photograph by Thomas England*)

tons according to color, size, and shape. The student who is in the concrete operational stage of cognitive development may be able to sort objects according to a wide variety of attributes, including texture and weight. By asking a few thought-provoking questions, a teacher may also help a child see new ways of sorting objects and thus extend the child's thinking.

Observing

Opportunities to observe closely are helpful in developing and extending children's thinking. What does it mean to observe closely? We have all admired a beautiful piece of furniture or lovely garment. Without close observation, however, it is difficult to evaluate the quality of the furniture or the garment. What about the workmanship? the design? the quality of the wood or fabric? These are questions that we answer by using and applying critical observations.

We need to help children become better observers. Having students observe details and describe them in writing is one way of doing this. For example, some children were interested in caring for a budding plant that their teacher had brought to school. To extend the learning experience, the teacher suggested that they record their observations of the plant each morning when they checked on it. Over a period of several weeks the students wrote their precise observations of the plant. They described the different stages of blooming and recorded observations about its size, shape, color, number of leaves, quantities of buds and when each opened, and the amount of water that the plant required. One student wrote her observations in the form of a diary and another student shared a poem that he had written about the plant. Their final project was to compare their writings and compose a group experience story about their observations.

These students were becoming close observers. A variety of experiences that will develop children's observational skills are close at hand in most elementary school classrooms—observing the birds that come to the window each morning, the weather as it changes from day to day, the goldfish, hamster, or guinea pig, the trees as their leaves change to the autumn colors, or indoor plants that the students have planted.

Comparing

As adults we are required to make comparisons; for instance, when we buy a car, we compare the qualities of one automobile over another based on our individual needs. After comparing and contrasting several makes of cars, we make some type of decision. Children, too, make comparisons when they shop for such things as toys, candy, or gifts.

Experiences that involve comparing one thing with another can be included very easily in the school day. Students can increase their skills at recognizing likenesses and differences as well as making certain kinds of judgments. A teacher's questions can create situations where children are asked to make comparisons: *How are these two shapes different? How is this story like the one we read yesterday? How are these two shells alike? What can you say about their size? Who is taller, Jimmy or Kay?* Questions such as these can be asked during any part of the day.

Students may also enjoy comparing and contrasting books. A number of children's stories have similar themes, plots, characters, or illustrations. Book comparisons can inspire conversations between the teacher and young children; and for older children, they provide opportunities for in-depth discussions. Are the characters Dandelion and Dazzle, in the books titled with their names, alike in some way? How is the book *The Very Hungry Caterpillar* similar to the book *Inch by Inch*? What similarities do you find between the two stories *Island of the Blue Dolphins* and *Julie of the Wolves*? In planning the questions that you ask about books, you will need to consider the children's level of cognitive development. However, there are many picture books that may be used with older children.

The following presents a partial listing of books that may be compared.

Picture books to compare

Lionni, Leo. *Fish Is Fish*. New York: Pantheon, 1970.
Massie, Diane Redfield. *Walter Was a Frog*. New York: Simon & Shuster, 1970.

Carle, Eric. *The Very Hungry Caterpillar*. Cleveland: World Publishing, 1969.
Lionni, Leo. *Inch by Inch*. New York: Pantheon, 1960.

Keats, Ezra Jack. *The Snowy Day*. New York: Viking, 1962.
Bourne, Miriam. *Emilio's Summer Day*. Illustrated by Ben Shecter. New York: Harper & Row, 1966.

Wildsmith, Brian. *The Lion and the Rat*. A fable by La Fontaine. New York: Watts, 1963.
Steig, William. *Amos and Boris*. New York: Farrar, Straus, & Giroux, 1970.

Freeman, Don. *Dandelion*. New York: Viking, 1964.
Massie, Diane Redfield. *Dazzle*. New York: Parents Magazine, 1969.

Lionni, Leo. *Swimmy*. New York: Pantheon, 1963.
Valens, Evans G. *Wingfin and Topple*. Illustrated by Clement Hurd. Cleveland: World Publishing, 1962.

Shecter, Ben. *Conrad's Castle*. New York: Harper & Row, 1967.
Shulevitz, Uri. *One Monday Morning*. New York: Scribner, 1967.

Raskin, Ellen. *Nothing Ever Happens on My Block*. New York: Atheneum, 1966.
Seuss, Dr., pseud. (Theodore S. Geisel). *And To Think That I Saw It on Mulberry Street*. New York: Vanguard, 1937.

Asbjornsen, P. C., and J. E. Moe. *The Three Billy Goats Gruff*. Illustrated by Susan Blair. New York: Holt, 1963.
Asbjornsen, P. C., and J. E. Moe. *The Three Billy Goats Gruff*. Illustrated by Marcia Brown. New York: Harcourt, Brace, 1957.

Middle-grade books to compare

O'Dell, Scott. *Island of the Blue Dolphins*. Boston: Houghton Mifflin, 1960.

George, Jean. *Julie of the Wolves*. New York: Harper & Row, 1973.

George, Jean. *My Side of the Mountain*. New York: Dutton, 1959.

Little, Jean. *Home from Far*. Boston: Little, Brown, 1965.

L'Engle, Madeleine. *Meet the Austins*. New York: Vanguard, 1961.

Kerr, Judith. *When Hitler Stole Pink Rabbit*. New York: Coward-McCann, 1972.

Reiss, Johanna. *The Upstairs Room*. New York: Thomas Y. Crowell, 1972.

Fitzhugh, Louise. *Harriet the Spy*. New York: Harper & Row, 1964.

Sachs, Marilyn. *Veronica Ganz*. New York: Doubleday, 1968.

Rodgers, Mary. *Freaky Friday*. New York: Harper & Row, 1972.

Burch, Robert. *Queenie Peavy*. New York: Viking, 1966.

Gold, Sharlya. *Amelia Quackenbush*. New York: Seabury, 1973.

Classifying

Sorting and classifying are somewhat related activities. Both require a person to group items according to identifiable characteristics and both involve the same type of thinking. However, classifying is usually a more complex and abstract task than sorting. Whereas sorting involves the manipulation of objects, classifying usually does not. For example, classify or group the following words: *Mustang, Love Bug, Pinto, Maverick, Rabbit, Super Beetle*. One way of classifying the words might be to group them in a class called *automobiles;* or, they may be placed in a class called *small cars*. When we classify, we may also have subclasses. For example, some of the cars are Fords and others are Volkswagens. Fords are American automobiles and Volkswagens are German automobiles. When we classify objects, places, people, animals, and so on, it is possible to categorize them in a variety of ways.

Classification experiences can occur in the classroom as students set up science displays, label collected objects, or design bulletin boards. Observational experiences can also provide opportunities for children to use classification skills. The automobile classification activity might begin with observing and recording the types of vehicles that pass in front of the school within a two- or three-minute period. Using those data, students can develop a classification scheme, perhaps something similar to Figure 7.

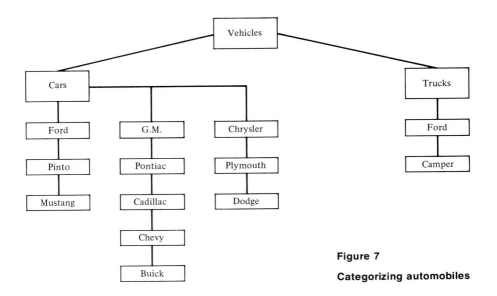

Figure 7

Categorizing automobiles

There are an infinite number of possibilities for children to develop classification skills. As students have more experiences with classifying, they will be able to identify things around them that may be grouped into classes and subclasses. A popular activity, which is certainly not new, is called "animal, vegetable, or mineral." Using these three classes, group the following: horses, paper, tire, gasoline, lettuce, broccoli, milk, bread, people, mink, pencil, and emerald. This type of classification activity is difficult for young children. It requires not only abstract thought, but also background knowledge and experience. This is true of most classification activities.

Summarizing

Telling or writing a summary requires a different type of thinking than that used in sorting, observing, comparing, and classifying. We must take a body of content and briefly capture the essence of it. The main points of what we have read or heard need to be summarized in the appropriate and logical sequence. If we summarize a story, we have to decide what content, events, and characters are most important to include. If we summarize a speech that we have heard, we must be able to distinguish between relevant and irrelevant points.

It is very important that children have a purpose for telling or writing a summary. So frequently the word *summary* is associated with the formal written book report, a traditional assignment that has made more children nonreaders than readers. The skill of summarizing can be developed through a variety of purposeful and meaningful activities.

Outside speakers can be valuable resources for the elementary school classroom. When a speaker is invited to speak about a subject of interest, prepare the students to listen for main points or ideas. Later, conduct a discussion that requires students to summarize what has been said. If they have difficulty, ask them to think of the main points. These may be listed on a chart or the chalkboard and then written in the form of a summary.

Children can tape-record summaries of books which they have enjoyed reading. The cassette tape may be placed in the library area or listening center for others to hear. Book summaries may also be tape-recorded to accompany a bulletin board that displays scenes from favorite books.

DEVELOPING CRITICAL THINKING SKILLS

Critical thinking is related to critical reading and listening. There are activities in listening that you will want to refer to in Chapter 7 that relate to critical thinking. In this section we will limit the discussion to what is meant by the term *critical thinking* and ways one might critically analyze oral and written statements.

What is critical thinking? Ennis defines critical thinking as the correct assessment of statements based on certain judgments.[1] How are these judgments made and applied to the material that is being evaluated? Appropriate questions need to be answered depending on the type of statements that you are assessing. The following represents a range of questions from which to choose:

Is there ambiguity in a line of reasoning?
Do certain statements contradict one another?
Does a conclusion follow necessarily?
Is the statement specific enough?
Is the statement actually the application of a certain principle?
Is an observation statement reliable?
Is an inductive conclusion warranted?
Has the problem been identified?
Is something merely an assumption?
Is a definition adequate?
Is a statement made by an alleged authority acceptable?[2]

Students in the upper elementary grades can critically evaluate newspaper and magazine articles, statements made on television or radio, and reading material available in the classroom. Certain questions may be asked regarding statements in textbooks, basal readers, or library books.

If we are to develop good thinkers—individuals who can make wise decisions and objective judgments—then we need to be concerned about teaching a variety of thinking skills beginning in the elementary school. Teachers need to evaluate the activities and experiences that are provided for their students. If they are primarily pencil and paper tasks requiring rote recall or a limited response, then children are involved in low-level thinking tasks. However, if they are developing classifications, writing detailed observations, comparing and talking about books, making critical judgments concerning written and oral statements, then they are participating in stimulating and higher-order thinking activities.

DEVELOPING AND EXTENDING VOCABULARY SKILLS

Vocabulary growth occurs very rapidly during the preschool years. When children enter school, they possess an extensive vocabulary on which to build. How do children learn their first several thousand words? According to Dale, O'Rourke, and Bamman, ". . . they heard them from parents, older children, playmates, on television and radio, on the playground and at the store. Second, they experienced them—they said things, they touched things, they smelled things, they drank things."[3] Through experiences and available models, children develop a basic and workable vocabulary. The extent of a child's vocabulary, however, depends largely upon both genetic and environmental factors.

Kinds of Vocabularies

Vocabulary is frequently divided into four types: listening, reading, writing, and speaking. Why is this? It is possible for people to understand words they hear, and yet not use the words themselves in speaking and writing. It is also possible that a word can be read and understood, and yet not handled easily when heard in a listening situation. Listening, reading, writing, and speaking vocabularies all overlap to some extent and, at the same time, contain different words that are understood or used frequently by individuals. There is also a fifth vocabulary that we might consider—our "understanding" vocabulary. We know certain words well enough that we can respond to them. We may, however, need to see or hear them in context, or need someone to say something that helps us recall the word meanings.

Gray[4] coined the term "permanent vocabulary," referring to words that we know and understand well enough to use effectively in both speaking and writing. Unfortunately, however, we do not all possess large permanent vocabularies. There are actually several levels of comprehension when we consider a person's knowledge of words: (1) *I never saw it before;* (2) *I've heard of it, but I don't know what it means;* (3) *I recognize it in context—it has something to do with . . . ;* and (4) *I know it.*[5] When we refer to these four stages of word knowledge, we must also keep in mind that only a single meaning of a word may be known. In teaching vocabulary, we need to determine if children understand and can use all the meanings of a particular word.

VOCABULARY AND CONCEPT DEVELOPMENT

We cannot divorce vocabulary development from conceptual development. Every word is essentially a concept. By understanding the concept associated with a word, we understand the meaning of the word. For example, the word *water* is meaningful to us because we understand the concept of water. We have had experiences with water—we swim in water, we drink water, we wash dishes in water.

Certain concepts are more concrete than others, and the words associated with them are easier to learn. For instance, if you want children to understand the concept of squareness and the word associated with it (*square*), you show them pictures of squares, have them cut out squares, and perhaps even draw squares. The concept is very teachable because it can be demonstrated in very concrete and tangible ways. But how do you teach children the concept of honesty? How do they learn the meaning of the word *honest?* Intangible and emotive concepts such as this are learned through experience—either direct experience, vicarious experience, or a combination of both. When children have had plenty of experiences related to the concept of honesty, they will understand the concept and the word *honest.*

Vocabulary develops through experiences and the association of these experiences with words. Intelligence and environmental factors cannot be overlooked when we are assessing the depth and breadth of children's vocabularies, but a learning environment that offers a wide variety of experiences can only promote and extend children's vocabulary development.

METHODS OF TEACHING VOCABULARY

"Vocabulary development in school must be a planned program. . . . Incidental teaching, alone, tends to become accidental teaching."[6] There is no doubt that a teacher needs to provide learning experiences that will incorporate the development and expansion of children's vocabularies. Opportune moments for developing concepts and associated vocabulary are often overlooked in the classroom. As an example, a small group of children came to the word *jostled* in their reading. None of the children knew the meaning of the word, but one child attempted to give a definition using the context of the story. The teacher interrupted the child, gave the definition of the word *jostled*, and then announced it was time for the next reading group. What might this teacher have done instead? The students could have been encouraged to predict the meaning of the word by using contextual clues. They might have demonstrated the meaning of the word by participating in a role play situation, such as being jostled on a crowded bus. Other situations in which one might be jostled could have been discussed, and the word itself could have been found in the dictionary to determine if there were other meanings.

All types of learning and communication experiences offer opportunities to develop a child's vocabulary. "All education is vocabulary development, hence conceptual development; we are studying words and symbols all the time."[7] We do know that planned experiences can be used effectively to extend and broaden children's vocabularies and they can be incorporated easily into the ongoing learning environment.

Direct and Concrete Experiences

Involvement in direct and concrete experiences helps to develop all types of vocabularies. Children need a variety of sensory experiences—touching, listening, tasting, and smelling. Along with direct experiences go conversations and discussions. By talking with children, a teacher can help them understand concepts and word meanings. For example, a child walked into class one morning carrying a lizard. Instead of placing the lizard aside in a nearby box, the teacher gathered the children around to look and talk about the lizard. They discussed the shape and size of the lizard, his color, the texture of his skin, and what he ate. They composed a class story about the lizard and each child copied the story from the chalkboard. The students added the story, *Jim's Lizard,* to a growing collection of experience stories that they were keeping. Needless to say, these students had developed not one but several concepts through this experience and the words associated with it.

Using Context Clues

Children may need help in using context clues as a means of discovering word meanings. Some children intuitively use context clues to unlock the meaning of unknown words, and others do not. Children simply need to be made aware of how context clues can be helpful to them (see Chapter Thirteen for ways of doing this).

Motivating an Interest in Words

Motivation is an important part of word study. The direct teaching of words using lists can be a boring as well as an ineffective method. A traditional approach to teaching new words and their meanings has been to assign students a list of words and have them look up the definitions in the dictionary. They copy the definitions directly from the dictionary and write a sentence using each word in the list. Unfortunately, many teachers still feel that students learn words in this manner.

Teachers who are successful in extending children's vocabularies know the significance of motivation. Fieldtrips can provide opportunities to introduce new words, discuss them, and do something with them after the experience. One teacher did this using special class activities, such as trips to the symphony, and reported that students were anxious to learn new words related to the experience.[8] Another teacher took advantage of commercial television programs to promote word study and found it to be a successful teaching technique. Students discussed new words that they had heard while watching their favorite television programs.[9] These are only two of the many possibilities for motivating children's interest in words—children can study the origins of words, identify words in their reading that they would like to learn, or make their own dictionaries to use when they are writing.

Books and Reading

According to research, it is possible to develop and increase a child's vocabulary by reading books aloud frequently.[10] The following story was retold and tape-recorded by a student after a well-known Aesop's fable had been read aloud and discussed. Notice the words and phrases in the child's retelling that have been taken from the original fable—*King of the forest, roars, nibble, paw, trap,* and others.

> Once there was a mouse. He forgot where he was going and he ran over a poor lion and the lion said, "What do you mean by this?" And he put his paw over the mouse. He was fixing to eat the mouse. And the mouse said, "Oh, King of the forest, please do not do this to me, for one day I may be able to help you." And then he set the mouse free. And a short while later the lion got caught in a trap and he roars and all the animals heard him. And then, the mouse heard him. And the mouse said, "That was the lion that set me free." And then the mouse woke up and came running and never stopped till he came to the lion and the trap was made of rope and the mouse began to nibble the rope. He made a big hole so the lion could get out. And then the lion said, "I'll always remember this: Little friends can be great friends."

Vocabulary is also increased the more a child reads independently. Therefore, more needs to be done in a classroom than simply providing a few books for children to read. Make a concerted effort to select a wide variety of books rich in vocabulary that will stretch and extend students' language. Provide time each day to read a book aloud and then place it in the classroom library area. Encourage students to reread it if they are interested, and call attention to other books in the area they may wish to explore and read. Your enthusiasm for and about particular books can have considerable influence on children's reading.

Discussion of particular words after reading a story aloud can extend children's knowledge of words. For example, when reading aloud Leo Lionni's book *Alexander and the Wind-up Mouse,* we find such words as *sneaked* and *ordinary.*

> One day, when there was no one in the house, Alexander heard a squeak in Annie's room. He sneaked in and what did he see? Another mouse. But not an ordinary mouse like himself. Instead of legs it had two little wheels, and on its back there was a key.[11]

Because books such as *Alexander and the Wind-up Mouse* present words in context, children have little difficulty understanding

A child's vocabulary may be extended through frequent experiences reading a variety of children's books. Paperback collections can provide students with many choices within the classroom setting.

their meaning if they are unfamiliar. Calling attention to certain words and briefly discussing them can ensure they are noticed. After reading the story, talking about the words *sneaked* and *ordinary* and using them in other contexts helps children incorporate them into their own vocabularies. "How did Alexander move when he *sneaked* into the room and saw the wind-up mouse?" "If you *sneaked* into a room, how would you move?" "What did Alexander mean when he called himself an *ordinary* mouse?" "What can you see around you that we might call *ordinary*?"

It is just as important to read books aloud to older children as it is to younger children. After reading aloud a chapter of a middle-grade book, spend some time talking about a few of the special words in the story and how the author used them. Look at the following passage from Engdahl's *Enchantress from the Stars,* a science-fiction book with many interesting possibilities because of its rich language.

So Georyn and Terwyn again went forth from the Enchantress, and though it was hard to turn their backs on the lighted hut and pass beyond even the reach of starlight, they did not hesitate. And after a time, a faint point of light appeared in the depths of the forest far ahead of them, and they followed it; but it moved before them so that they could not approach. Then finally as dawn was spreading up out of the east, they came upon it, where it had been set upon a rock in the midst of a small glade; and as they reached out to take it, the first ray of sunlight pierced the trees. And although the globe still contained a piece of the Sun, it was no longer of fiery brilliance, for its parent Sun now outshone it; so Georyn extinguished it once more as the Lady had bid them. But a light now waxed within him at the knowledge that such wonders as he had been shown could exist.[12]

Word Study

Many children can have an enjoyable time studying the history of words. The study of word origins is intriguing and can entice some children into a lifetime fascination with words. If word-history study is to be successful with elementary school age children, two key points are necessary for consideration:

> (1) The children must be personally involved, suggesting, contributing, experimenting in terms of history or etymology (at their level), and thereby seeing the relationship of word history to their everyday lives. This goal can be reached by encouraging the children to use key words studied in discussion and conversation (for example, making adjectives such as *jovial* from *Jove*, *solar* from *Sol*, *lunar* from *Luna*, etc.). (2) The teacher must become as expert as he can in words and word origin as they relate to general language development. He must, in effect, become 'word-conscious,' bringing to the classroom a knowledge of the 'new' words to be discussed.[13]

Teaching Affixes

A knowledge of affixes can increase an individual's word power. Prefixes and suffixes are meaning-bearing units (morphemes), and an understanding of them can enlarge a child's vocabulary.

In teaching affixes, the inductive approach is the best method. You might ask the children to name all of the words they know that begin with the prefix *un* and write them on the chalkboard or a large piece of chart paper. For example: *untidy, unlucky, unable, undone, unhappy, uncovered, unknown, uneasy, unpaid, unattractive, unpopular, unwrap, unloved, unpack,* and *unsewn.* Discuss the collection of words, letting the children form their own generalization about the prefix *un-* and how it alters the meaning of base words.

Word study can be a challenging and enjoyable experience for both teachers and children. The prerequisite for an effective program is a teacher who is interested and enthusiastic about teaching and learning new words. If that same teacher looks for ways to motivate an interest in word study and provides experiences that lead to concept and vocabulary development, the program should be very successful.

PRELIMINARY LEARNING ACTIVITIES

1. Plan and make several sorting boxes that may be used with children of different ages. For additional information regarding the preparation and use of sorting boxes, refer to the section on sorting in this chapter.
2. Plan and prepare several classification activities that may be used with students in the upper elementary grades.
3. A study of word origins can be interesting to some students. Plan a study that you think a small group of older students might enjoy. Include the books that may be used as references, and develop a number of motivating experiences that will be an integral part of the study, such as having the students prepare a booklet of their findings to be put in the school library.
4. Plan and develop several direct experiences (such as fieldtrips, neighborhood walks) that may be conducted for the purpose of developing concepts and vocabulary words associated with them.

PARTICIPATION ACTIVITIES

1. Plan a fieldtrip or excursion (perhaps to the neighborhood shopping center) for the purpose of presenting new concepts and words to children. While on the trip, the children should collect words that they want to discuss when they return to the classroom. Students may form small groups, pool their words collected on the trip, and write them on large sheets of paper. These may be discussed and used in a number of ways. The students may want to classify their words and identify words that have more than a single meaning.

2. Read two books aloud that may be compared. Prepare several questions that will stimulate a discussion of their likenesses and differences. After the discussion, encourage the children to make a chart or construct a bulletin board to illustrate the similarities between the two books.

3. Collect a variety of items to be sorted. Have kindergarten children sort the items. Next, have fourth-grade children sort the same items. Compare how the young children sorted the items with how the older students sorted them.

4. Select a book to read aloud based on its vocabulary and language value, as well as its general appeal to children. Read the book aloud to a small group of students. Afterward, discuss some of the special or unfamiliar words in the story.

5. Plan a classifying experience. Try it with both young and older elementary-age students. Compare their responses.

REFERENCES

[1] Robert H. Ennis. "A Concept of Critical Thinking," *Educational Leadership,* vol. 21, October 1963, pp. 17–20, 39.

[2] Ibid.

[3] Edgar Dale, Joseph O'Rourke, and Henry A. Bamman. *Techniques of Teaching Vocabulary.* Palo Alto, California: Field, 1971, p. 8.

[4] William S. Gray. "Reading and Understanding," *Elementary English,* vol. 28, February 1951, pp. 148–159.

[5] Edgar Dale, Joseph O'Rourke, and Henry A. Bamman. *Techniques of Teaching Vocabulary,* p. 3.

[6] Ibid., p. 5.

[7] Ibid.

[8] Mabel Lindner. "Vitalizing Vocabulary Study," *English Journal,* vol. XL, April 1951, pp. 225–226.

[9] George Mason. "Children Learn Words from Commercial TV," *The Elementary School Journal,* vol. LXV, March 1965, pp. 318–320.

[10] Dorothy H. Cohen. "The Effect of Literature on Vocabulary and Reading Achievement," *Elementary English,* vol. XLV, February 1968, pp. 209–213, 217.

[11] Leo Lionni. *Alexander and the Wind-Up Mouse.* New York: Pantheon, 1969.

[12] Sylvia L. Engdahl. *Enchantress from the Stars.* New York: Atheneum, 1970, p. 96.

[13] Edgar Dale, Joseph O'Rourke, and Henry A. Bamman. *Techniques of Teaching Vocabulary,* p. 247.

CHAPTER SIX

Considering Grammar and Usage

PREVIEW QUESTIONS

1 What is the difference between grammar and usage?
2 What kinds of grammar appear in language arts textbooks for children?
3 In what ways does usage vary?
4 What grammar should be taught to elementary school children?
5 How can a teacher help children become more adept in making appropriate usage choices?

The very word *grammar* produces a variety of responses. Historically grammar became associated and almost synonymous with the teaching of English in our public and private schools. Even today some teachers and some parents feel the school should teach more grammar while others are vehemently opposed to any grammar instruction. Part of this wide range of opinion is due to the fact that the term *grammar* is used in several different ways to mean many different things.

Traditional grammars or "school grammars" are *prescriptive* in nature. They prescribe or decree what is correct to say or write based on written material by well-known classic authors; and this material, of course, followed the traditional rules of Latin. They include such typical practices as underlining the subjects and predicates of sentences or even diagramming them. They also include making choices between such pairs as *who* and *whom, sit* and *set,* or *shall* and *will.* Studying grammar is supposed to make one a better writer and a more "correct" speaker. Thus, in one sense of the word, grammar is a set of rules which tells how language should be used.

Newer grammars which have appeared in recent textbooks are built upon a completely different basis. Grammar is used to mean a theory of language or a description of how English operates. Instead of prescribing what should or should not be, these more recent grammars have attempted to describe how native speakers of the language actually use that language. The two major kinds of descriptive grammars are structural and transformational generative. Both have attempted to look at language in a scientific, analytical way and describe how language is actually used, rather than decreeing how it should be used.

There are still choices of language forms which the speaker or writer must make since English has a number of options. The choice that an individual makes within a particular situation will be called *usage.* We recognize, for instance, that *The cat gray here isn't* is not a sentence a native English speaker would say. It is not grammatical, even though we can probably understand what the speaker is trying to communicate. It is a matter of usage, however, when deciding to say, *The gray cat isn't here* or *The gray cat ain't here.* In discussing grammar and usage, we will use the term *grammar* to describe how language works and the term *usage* to describe the choices or options within the language that one makes. Pooley compares this distinction between grammar and usage to the difference between behavior and etiquette.[1] Grammar, like behavior, is what happens without any judgments being made; usage is like etiquette, and varies because of social and situational forces.

We feel that the abstract and rather theoretical study of grammar is not appropriate subject matter for children of elementary school age. The focus on language in the elementary school years should be on helping children become more able to use language to express their ideas and to communicate with others. We should be able to help children put their ideas into words and sentences in a variety of ways. We also need to help children become more adept at making usage choices. It should be understood that certain usage items may bring about strong social exclusion or penalty when used in particular situations or with particular groups, but may be completely acceptable in other situations. *I ain't got none* instead of *I don't have any* is probably the kind of usage choice that would get strong reactions in many social situations. Other usage choices do not bring about such strong reactions. An example of such a choice might be *May I go?* versus *Can I go?* or *Whom did you see?* versus *Who did you see?* We are suggesting then that there are no absolute right or wrong usage choices. There are only "more acceptable in this situation" and "less acceptable in that situation" choices. It is the teacher's job to be sensitive to each child's usage patterns and then help each child become increasingly more flexible in making more appropriate usage choices.

KINDS OF GRAMMARS

Although we consider the abstract and theoretical study of grammar inappropriate for elementary school children, we think it is necessary for teachers to become familiar with and understand different grammars. There are at least three major kinds of grammar to be found in school textbooks today: traditional grammar, structural grammar, and transformational generative grammar. The most recent work in linguistics has centered on the relationship between meaning and structure. Newer grammars such as case grammar[2] or generative semantics[3] have delved into semantics rather than syntax as a prime component of our system of language. This chapter, however, will examine the grammars used with children.

Traditional Grammar

Traditional grammar, mainly based on Latin, classifies words into various parts of speech such as nouns, verbs, adjectives, prepositions, and conjunctions. These parts of speech are defined primarily in terms of meaning or content, as in "A noun is the name of a person, place, or thing." This can present problems to students when using such words as *blue* and *walk*. What parts of speech are they? Blue describes so it must be an adjective, as in *My blue shirt is dirty.* But what part of speech is *blue* in the next sentence? *Blue is the best color.* The word *blue* is now a noun. Let's use one other example. *Walk* is quite obviously a verb in *I walk to school,* but it becomes a noun in the sentence *The walk is icy.*

Traditionally, sentences are classified as simple, compound, complex, or in some cases as compound-complex. Sentences can also be described as declarative, interrogative, exclamatory, or imperative. One of the practices most closely associated with traditional grammar is the diagramming of sentences developed by Reed and Kellogg.[4] The most important sentence elements are put on a horizontal line and separated by shorter vertical or diagonal lines. Minor elements of the sentence are placed below the main line in a way that shows their relationship to the other elements of the sentence. An example of this is:

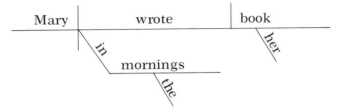

The above diagram indicates that *Mary* is the subject, *wrote* the verb, *book* is a direct object modified by *her*, and that *in the mornings* is a prepositional phrase modifying *wrote*.

The most important elements of this grammar are the word and the sentence. Little attention is paid to paragraphs or other larger units of writing. Also, there is little emphasis on word order although English, an analytic language, is based on this. The sentence diagrammed above might have been *In the mornings, Mary wrote her book* or *Mary wrote her book in the mornings.* There is no way to determine from the diagram how to reconstruct the original sentence.

Recognizing that usage varies, authors of traditional grammars only accept the practices of the best speakers and writers of English as a standard. This implies a prescriptive "best" and therefore traditional grammar in the classroom usually operates in a highly structured fashion. *Do this* and *Don't do that,* or *This is right* and *This is wrong* become the daily instructional routine for the English teacher.

Structural Grammar

Structural grammar is descriptive; it attempts to describe how people use language rather than prescribing how language should be used. An early and exhaustive explication of structural linguistics was made by Charles Carpenter Fries with the publication in 1952 of *The Structure of English*. One of the most important principles of structural grammar is that grammatical function is independent of word meaning. In order to make this point, many structuralists used sentences made up of nonsense words. In *Sligy bobbles wugged ziches, bobbles* is a noun modified by *sligy, wugged* is a verb, and *ziches* is another noun. The fact that we don't know what action *wugging* represents or what a *zich* looks like does not interfere with our identification of what parts of speech they are. Fries stated that the grammatical function or structural meaning is signaled by particular devices (such as word endings, articles, and so on).

Fries rejected the traditional parts of speech and defined or categorized words into four major form classes and fifteen groups of function words. Since these do not all correspond to the traditional parts of speech, he gave each of them different names such as *Class 1* and *Class 2* or *Group A*. He also uses the terms *determiner* for words such as *the, a, an* and *intensifier* for words such as *very* or *much*. Sometimes structural grammar is called "slot and filler" grammar because of the pattern substitution concept used to establish the parts of speech in these new categories without referring to the meaning of the words. Class 1, for example, includes all the words that fit in the following blank:

The _____ *is/are good.*

Similar "test frames" help describe the nature of the other classes of words.

Structural grammarians also use the Stimulus-Response (S-R) model in psychology to explain not only how language functions as a means of communication, but also how children acquire language. This theory emphasizes the view that behavior is learned through reinforcement. Fries felt that children learn language by associating certain language forms with the situations that called them forth. In dealing with novel sentences, he contended people use analogy to sentences already known. They are able to do this, Fries thought, by using structural signals and sentence patterns.[5]

The emphasis in Fries's *Structure of English* is on sentence structure and it was a radical departure from traditional grammar.

It became known as the "new" grammar or "linguistics" although it represented only part of the linguistic community at that time and today represents an even smaller part.

Transformational Generative Grammar

Transformational generative grammar also represents a descriptive approach. It attempts to describe not only how language is used, but also how related sentences are changed from one form to another (transformed) and how new sentences can be formulated (generated) from our unconscious or conscious knowledge of how our language operates. The person most closely associated with transformational generative grammar is Noam Chomsky who first published this theory in 1957 in *Syntactic Structures* and further delineated it in his 1965 *Aspects of the Theory of Syntax*.

One of the characteristics of transformational generative grammar is the distinction made between the surface structure and the deep structure of language. Linguists have noticed that many sentences which appear to be parallel are actually very different. Malmstrom and Weaver give the following example of three sentences which appear on the surface to be formed identically:[6]

> *Jon wanted the guest to eat.*
> *Jon wanted the baby to eat.*
> *Jon wanted the hamburger to eat.*

In the first two, both the surface structures and deep structures (or underlying structures) are similar; the noun preceding *to eat* is to do the eating. The third, although it resembles the other two in its surface structure, is very different. The noun preceding *to eat*, the *hamburger*, is not to do the eating, Jon is. Therefore, the underlying structure of the latter is different from the other two.

Another type of problem sentence that interested transformationalists was the ambiguous sentence that might have more than one underlying structure. An example of this is:[7] *Visiting relatives can be a nuisance.* This might mean that it is a nuisance to visit relatives or that having relatives visit you is a nuisance.

The final problem leading to the concept of deep and surface structures is shown by pairs of sentences which do not look similar on the surface, but are closely related at the deep structure level since they are nearly synonymous:[8]

> *A new student painted the picture.*
> *The picture was painted by a new student.*

These parallel sentences occur because of the different transformations that have been made in the deep structures before they appear in the surface structures.

Transformational generative grammar has rejected the Stimulus-Response model as an inadequate explanation of how children acquire their native language. Transformational generative linguists do not believe that children understand a sentence simply by recalling a prior experience with the sentence. Instead they propose that children attempt to organize a system of language rules subject to their cognitive capabilities and language environment. Transformational generative grammar, therefore, attempts to duplicate the rule system that adult speakers of the language employ.

Transformational generative grammar describes two sets of rules. The first set is called *phrase structure rules* and represents the grammatical relationships indicating meaning between the words in the deep structure of the sentence. The second set of rules, *transformational rules,* accounts for changing the deep structure form into the surface structure form of the sentence.

The phrase structure rules are written like an algebraic formula and are often represented by tree diagrams.

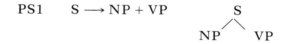

PS1   S ⟶ NP + VP

This phrase structure rule and its matching diagram indicate that a sentence (S) may be rewritten as a noun phrase (NP) and a verb phrase (VP). A second phrase structure rule is:

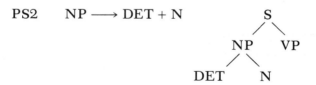

PS2   NP ⟶ DET + N

This states that the noun phrase may be rewritten as a determiner (DET) plus a noun (N). As you might imagine, when the sentences become more complex, the rewrite rules and tree diagrams also become more complex.

Transformational rules are also written like a formula, but are labeled T instead of PS and use the double arrow instead of the single arrow to indicate what may be transformed into what. The transformational rules are applied in order, although some may not be used if they aren't relevant to a given sentence.

T1 accounts for changing subject pronouns into object pronouns after a transitive verb. It is written as:

$$T1 \quad V_t + \begin{bmatrix} I \\ we \\ he \\ she \\ they \end{bmatrix} \Rightarrow V_t + \begin{bmatrix} me \\ us \\ him \\ her \\ them \end{bmatrix}$$

Rule T2 applies when the pronoun *I* is used with a form of *be* in the present tense. Following this transformational rule we would say *I am watching* instead of *I are watching*.

$$T2 \quad I + PRES + BE \Rightarrow I = PRES_1 + BE$$

These rules appear quite complex and are certainly inappropriate for elementary school students; they do, however, illustrate the kind of thought process that native English speakers unconsciously use in producing sentences. This is the process that children have under basic control by the time they enter school.

Studying grammar brings to a conscious level what we do subconsciously with language. However, there is little need for elementary school age children to study formal grammar. Research indicates such instruction rarely improves a student's facility with oral and written language. However, grammar-related activities such as combining or expanding sentences may improve both oral and written communication. This will be discussed later in the chapter.

GRAMMATICAL KNOWLEDGE

Although most adults have some instruction in grammar by the time they finish school, most of the rules which they apply in their everyday language have not been learned. Some of these relate to phonemics or pronunciation. For example, the *-ed* suffix on past tense verbs may be pronounced /d/ or /t/ or /əd/. Teachers do not teach children the rules for this, and yet both children and adults can pronounce *-ed* properly whether it appears in real or nonsense words. Try the following:

walked	*prepared*	*waited*
backed	*ignored*	*adopted*
priced	*hurried*	*disconcerted*
chopped	*behaved*	*headed*
zitched	*wugged*	*regicated*

The words in the first column, including the final nonsense word, all end with the /t/; those in the middle column all have the /d/ ending; those in the third column all end with the /əd/ phoneme.

Adults unconsciously adhere to rules of syntax or word order. We were not taught the rules for the proper order of multiple adjectives preceding a noun. Even so, if given some examples of possible combinations of these adjectives, we will all come up with the same order or orders. Try the following and see if you agree with others:

1.	*small*	*green*	*two*	(Martians)
2.	*enormous*	*red*	*one*	(geranium)
3.	*purple*	*big*	*four*	(monsters)

The regular order of these adjectives of size, color, and number is (1st) number, (2nd) size, and (3rd) color. For emphasis, however, the second and third may be reversed. Other "rules" for other combinations of adjectives exist, and all native speakers use them without any formal instruction. Young children operate with these same rules—usually by the time they are four or five years old. Some of the rules are used in all of the dialects of English, and others may vary with particular dialects. Examples of phonemic and syntactic differences in dialects are illustrated in Chapter Three.

The kinds of rules which have traditionally been the job of the English teacher are those for formal or proper usage. "Don't end a sentence with a preposition" or "Don't use a double negative." These maxims actually deal with options or choices which a speaker may make depending on dialect, social situation, and mode of communication (whether oral or written). Teachers need to recognize the extensive amount of knowledge about language that children possess and use by the time they enter school, instead of focusing on the knowledge they may lack.

LANGUAGE USAGE

In the past we have frequently discussed language usage in terms of being formal or informal. This is an oversimplification since the ways in which we use language vary. It also perpetuates the traditional idea that usage is either "right" or "wrong." This dichotomy may make usage easy for a teacher to deal with, but it is neither accurate nor productive information for language users.

Gleason[9] has done some revision of Joos's examination of styles in speech and writing that may illustrate some of the variation in language that we make because of the degree of formality in a given situation. These "keys" or styles of language are somewhat general, but they do reflect different situations that affect our pronunciation, word choice, and language structures. One set of terms is used in oral language situations and another in written language. Learning theory, as well as experience, suggests that children begin with the informal keys and progress towards the more formal ones.

LANGUAGE KEYS

Informal ⟵————————————————————⟶ Formal

(spoken) Intimate—Casual—Consultative—Deliberative—Oratorical

(written)   Informal—Semiformal—Formal

The general language situations used in the language key indicate some of the major situations which affect language usage choices, although particular language choices made within each of the language keys depend on what is considered appropriate usage within a dialect.

Spoken Language Keys

Oral language keys are usually more informal than their counterparts in written language. This becomes obvious when speech is recorded and then transcribed. The speaker, more often than the writer, responds to the nonverbal or verbal cues given by listeners and modifies the language accordingly. The speaker is able to use a variety of oral devices to clarify meaning, while written language must depend on other devices to lead the reader along.

Oratorical key   The oratorical key is used primarily by professional speakers such as lawyers, clergymen, and politicians. It is very carefully planned, and parts of the speech may be written out beforehand. Oratorical key language often uses rhetorical devices to clarify a particular point. One such device is repetition of a particular word or group of words; another is the use of parallel structures in adjacent sentences.

Deviations from what is expected help to make the point. President John F. Kennedy used parallel structures in such a way in his well-known "Ask not what your country can do for you. Ask what you can do for your country." Ralph Bunche used repetition effectively in the following: "I have a number of very strong biases. I have a deep-seated bias against hate and intolerance. I have a bias against racial and religious bigotry. I have a bias against war, a bias for peace."[10] How carefully the repetition of *bias* is handled! It is repeated five times, but with variations such as *a deep-seated bias, a bias against, a bias for.*

Deliberative key The deliberative key is used particularly when speaking to large groups. Although the basic ideas and sequence of topics may be planned in advance, there is not the degree of planning involved in the oratorical key. The speaker is not able to adjust to all nonverbal cues and proceed freely along. Instead each sentence is "thought out" just before it is spoken. This is the quality that gives the deliberative key its name.

Gleason in his discussion of this key suggests that children's early experiences in speaking before the entire class are difficult for them because these are their first attempts to use the deliberative key. He suggests that previously they depended on verbal and nonverbal feedback from the listener, and it is the lack of this feedback rather than being frightened or a lack of fluency that causes their problems.

Consultative key The consultative key is the common key used in everyday interaction with another person or a small group of people who are not close friends or family. It is basically unplanned and depends to a great extent on cues from the other person. Even though one person may take a major role in the discussion for a period of time, the listener(s) responds with sounds or short phrases such as, "Yea, Um-hmm, That's right." This may be a new experience for many younger children. When they first attend school, they are more accustomed to speaking with close friends or their own family. This key is used with the teacher and with many other children in the school.

Casual key The casual key is used among people who have a well-established relationship with each other in informal situations. It is characterized by the use of slang and an almost total lack of preplanning. Gleason suggests that a characteristic feature of casual speech is the omission of unstressed words—especially those at the beginnings of sentences: "Anyone home?", "You wanna go?", "Won't tell anyone about it." These are typical of what many speakers in many dialects actually say in casual situations, but speakers of other dialects may make other variations of their language in any given language key. At this point, we simply don't have enough information about language variation in all dialects in each key to be very definitive about those variations. Classroom teachers who are sensitive to the situational language keys and who listen carefully to their own students can pick up cues about the kinds of language changes a particular child makes in a given situation.

Intimate key   The intimate key is a very private language used with very close friends or within the family. Because it is so private, there is not as much information available about it as with some of the other keys. Teachers of young children often get glimpses of language in the intimate key as children interact with each other before they have become very sophisticated about what variations in their own home language are appropriate to make in a classroom.

The spoken keys most frequently used within classrooms that teachers may observe are the central three: deliberative, consultative, and casual.

Written Language Keys

Written language is not as varied as oral language and Gleason suggests that nearly all edited English may be described in terms of the three central literary keys: formal, semiformal, and informal.[11] There are certain features of written English which require uniformity. For example, the pronunciation of a word may vary, but the conventional spelling of the word is always the same in written language. There are also certain conventions of punctuation which are quite uniform across most edited English. Therefore, the differences among the main literary keys are not as great as those among the various oral keys.

Formal key   The formal key in writing has the same function as the deliberative key does in speech. It involves thoughtful planning of ideas in sequence, sentence construction, and choice of words. It is used for professional writing purposes rather than for social correspondence. This written key would not ordinarily be used by children of elementary school age, although it might be used by high school students in essays or term paper writing.

Semiformal key   This key corresponds to the consultative key in oral language. It follows most conventional mechanical writing devices and does involve planning of ideas and vocabulary. This key is used when writing to distant acquaintances or to unknown persons. This type of writing requires more careful language choices and will, at first, be difficult for many elementary school age children.

Informal key   Informal writing is almost parallel to the casual key used in speech. Thus the informal written key is used when writing to friends or close acquaintances. There is much less adherence to the conventions of writing and dashes may replace periods and colons, reflecting genuine informality. Informal key writing reflects the speech patterns of the writer more closely than any of the other keys of written language.

These keys of oral and written language take into account the *mode of discourse*—whether the language is spoken or written. They also deal with the major *styles of discourse;* that is, whether the style is casual, intimate, formal or informal. Another factor present in adult language that Gleason does not deal with within the framework of the keys is the *field of discourse*. This involves considerations about whether the language is used in medicine, in shopping, or in games. Each field has its own effect on the language used. The preceding discussion of the language keys will give you, we hope, some idea of the changes in mode and style of language that speakers and writers make all the time in the process of communication.

Registers of Language

There are two dimensions of variations in language which occur: first is the dialect or the general variety of language which each person employs, second is the range of distinctions everyone has to choose from at various times. The latter is sometimes called *register*.[12] Registers are similar to keys of language although they are more inclusive because they deal with a wider range of variations. As mentioned earlier in presenting the language keys, it is difficult to give specific examples of what language choices might be made within each of the keys or registers—what is appropriate in one register in one dialect may not be appropriate in that register in another dialect.

Reflected in the concept of register is the fact that speaking a particular dialect will affect the span of choices available within a particular situational context. This is especially important for teachers to recognize because it explains many of the language differences among children who speak different dialects in the classroom. It accounts for some of the observations that researchers not familiar with register variations have made about particular dialect groups. For example, many of the comparative studies of the language of white and black children did not take into account the situation in which the black children were speaking and what kind of language would be appropriate for them to use in this particular register in their dialect. The same physical situation is no guarantee of equality in both groups because what is appropriate language behavior for one dialect-speaking group in a given situation is not necessarily appropriate behavior for speakers of another dialect.

Children are aware of the need to make differences in their language depending on particular situations. Even very young children take on different vocabulary, intonations, and sentence structures when playing adult roles. Listen to some preschoolers playing house or some primary school children playing school. Their language reflects their knowledge about how adults act in those roles. Older children are more adept at making changes in their language. In talking with each other they may say, *bugs and stuff* and then change that wording to *insects and other things* when reporting their group's discussion to the teacher and the rest of the class. Adults, too, make similar changes in their language depending on the situation. A teacher may report to the principal or parent that a child *has very little self-control.* This same teacher may say to peers or friends that the child *is driving me crazy with all the pushing and hitting.*

Many teachers are startled at some of the language used by children in their class who speak a dialect significantly different from their own. This is especially true of younger children who are less aware of appropriate changes to make from the intimate family and friends situation to the more formal classroom situation. Their intent is not to shock or to be unruly; they simply have selected language inappropriate for use in the classroom because of their immaturity and lack of experience. If the teacher can remain calm and suggest that the language they have used is fine in certain situations, but is not appropriate in this situation, the incident becomes useful instruction instead of rejection.

Register, then, includes the idea of keys of language as the distinction in mode of discourse (oral or written) and styles of discourse (oratorical to intimate and formal to informal). It also takes into account the field of discourse (politics to shopping) and the interaction of an individual's dialect with the mode, style, and field of discourse.

GRAMMAR IN THE CLASSROOM

The primary aim of the language arts program is to help children become more able to use language to express their ideas both orally and in writing. The formal study of grammar does not help them meet this goal. However, there are activities based on grammar that can be productive in helping children become more fluent and more flexible in their use of language.

Expanding Basic Patterns

One of the activities that can help children be more effective in their use of language is expanding simple sentence patterns in various ways. This activity should be done within the language and the experiences of the child. A format that is particularly useful with this kind of expansion work is the group experience story. Suppose that the children had visited a nearby doughnut shop and were now writing about this trip. The teacher could first ask for ideas about what to write. One child might say, *We saw a man cut out the doughnuts.* Another might mention, *I like doughnuts.* The teacher would then write these ideas on the chalkboard or a large sheet of chart paper. The children would then find various ways to add ideas to the original sentence.

    For: *We saw a man cut out the doughnuts.*

        What could we add about the man?

           a man in a white jacket

           a man in the back room

           a man with a chef's hat

           a young man

        What did he do besides cut them out?

           roll and cut out

           cut out and twist

           cut out and fill

        How did he cut them out?

           carefully

           real fast

           with a knife

           with a special cutter

    For: *I like doughnuts.*

        Why do you like them?

           because they're sweet

           because they're good

        Which doughnuts do you like best?

           chocolate ones with frosting

           twisted ones with cinnamon

    The children might talk about ways to add to the original sentence before writing it on a chart.

We saw a man in a white jacket cut out and twist the doughnuts.
I like twisted doughnuts with cinnamon because they're sweet.

Or, after children have had experience in expanding sentences, they may work individually adding ideas to original sentences.

Combining Ideas

Children become more effective in their use of language if they have meaningful practice with various ways of combining ideas. This may be done individually with their own writing or with a group. The use of group experience story charts or an overheard projector works well for this activity. For example, a group of children that have experimented with water erosion would have the following from their notes or memory:

We poured water down a hill.
Part of the hill was grassy.
Another part was just dirt.

The teacher would then ask how these could be combined to make one sentence. The ideas must be kept, but words can be added, dropped, or the order changed.

We poured water down a hill that was partially grassy and partially plain dirt.

In working with combining sentences, there is the danger that children will assume that long sentences are better than short ones. In some cases this is true. In other cases, the short sentences are very effective and can create a mood of excitement or suspense. One short sentence in the midst of longer ones can serve as a point of emphasis. The aim for older children is that a whole series of short sentences becomes somewhat boring, and there is a great deal of unnecessary repetition in such a series of short sentences. The purpose of doing work in combining sentences is to give children alternatives to use in their own writing and to make them aware of additional ways to use language more effectively to express their own ideas.

Finding Movables and Selecting Words

Certain words or phrases may be placed in different parts of a sentence. For example, the sentence, *I knew he had to be my pet when I saw him* can be changed to read *When I saw him, I knew he had to be my pet.* Changes such as this sometimes subtly alter the emphasis or effect of a sentence.

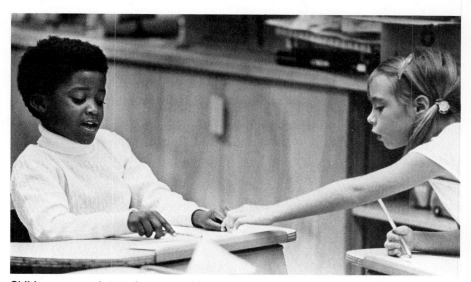

Children can work together to combine and expand their sentences. (*Photograph by Thomas England*)

There are several ways to use sentences from a reading text, a weekly children's news magazine, or a collection of sentences reproduced on a transparency or ditto sheet. Children may want to use their own writing—moving words, phrases, or clauses around and then comparing the new version with the original piece of writing.

Some of the words or phrases that may be used as movables within a sentence are:

adverbs (*eventually he moved/ he moved eventually*);
adjectives (*gigantic orange balloon/ orange gigantic balloon*);
prepositional phrases (*he walked in the house/ in the house he walked*);
clauses (*Since he came early, we . . ./ we . . . since he came early*).

The selection of specific words to convey a particular meaning— or words that are appropriate for a particular kind of writing—is very helpful for the older child. This is the area of field of discourse (discussed in the section on register) that determines some of the vocabulary or lexical items that one chooses to use in a particular piece of writing. Scientists, for example, make a distinction between *soil* and *dirt*. In the earlier discussion of combining sentences about erosion, *soil* would be preferable to *dirt*.

Other words are chosen for the particular shade of meaning they convey. Children in the upper elementary grades may examine a thesaurus which lists synonyms and antonyms. In *Roget's College Thesaurus* the listing for *walk* as a verb is: *ramble, stroll, promenade, saunter, travel (on foot), march, parade, tramp, hike, tread, pace, step.* Although these are synonyms for *walk,* there is a great deal of difference between *strolling* and *tramping* or between *sauntering* and *pacing.* If you do not want to use a thesaurus, you can have the children list words that have almost the same meaning and conduct a follow-up discussion on the connotations. What are a few synonyms for the word *thin? Slender, skinny, underweight, bony.* If you are not talking about a person, but about material, what words might describe it? *Sheer, fine, delicate, filmy.*

Developing an awareness of what effect a particular word has or what moving a word, phrase, or clause to a different part of a sentence does is important in developing writing skills. The function of language in a particular and meaningful situation is the most appropriate way of working with grammar in the elementary school. In contrast to teaching a formal grammatical description of English through traditional, structural, or transformational theory, working with language in this way offers potential for improving the quality of children's writing.

USAGE IN THE CLASSROOM

Usage was compared earlier in this chapter to etiquette. It involves the choice of word selection among the various alternatives that are available. Traditional school grammar attempted to say what was "correct" by tying usage choices to grammatical constructions. Thus, usage became more prescriptive than the language used by well-educated and politically, socially, or economically powerful individuals when the choices were determined by the traditional grammarian. "This is *she.*" "With *whom* did he go?" "*May* I go with you?" Because there was little oral communication except between immediate settlements, the early development of the prescriptive choices was related to written language. Written language is considerably different from oral language in a number of ways. Since it is often written for an unknown audience, it is usually more formal than oral communication. The prescriptive usage-grammar choices often did not reflect what people actually said or wrote. To further increase the difference between what was used and what was prescribed, the English language has changed considerably over the years. Prescriptive usage-grammar no longer reflects what even the most traditionally oriented people use.

To clarify the term *usage* further, the following is a list of some alternatives available to speakers or writers of English.

May I go versus *Can I go*
I shall be there versus *I will be there*
I ain't got versus *I don't have*
tastes good like _____ versus *tastes good as* _____
he don't want versus *he doesn't want*
me and Tom can go versus *Tom and I can go*
they dove into the pool versus *they dived into the pool*
to feel bad versus *to feel badly*
it's a elephant versus *it's an elephant*

Many things determine the choice of options that exist in our language. For most children, usage choices are a reflection of the language used in their home and immediate environment. There are also regional differences in preferred usage, as well as socio-economic differences. The amount of formal education of the adults in a child's environment helps to determine the choices that an individual child makes. If a family is bilingual, there will be an influence of the other language on the English usage patterns of the child. The child's dialect and the registers of that dialect, as they relate to particular situations in which language is used, will cause certain patterns of usage choices.

It no longer seems reasonable to treat usage as a "right" versus "wrong" situation. The purpose of instruction should be to help children make usage choices which are appropriate for a particular register or situation.

Opportunities for Usage Experiences in Oral Language

There are several ways that children can become familiar with varying choices in usage. Very young children can be given the chance to become involved in dramatic play. As they play the father, mother, or police officer, they assume the language that is appropriate to that person's situation. Teachers may raise the quality of the dramatic play by adding props such as hats or costumes to the play area or by intervening with questions which will extend children's thinking about the role or situation. At this stage the children are involved in exploring situations, and it is not a time for the teacher to give instruction about what they should say or how it should be said.

Older children can work with role playing. As they are active in taking on various roles, the teacher can discuss what kinds of talk a doctor uses, what a teenager would say, or how a musician or judge would express an idea. Role playing can also put the same person in a variety of situations that would call for changes in language. What would a parent say about their child's misbehavior to their best friend, to the school principal, to the child? How would a child tell about a bad test grade to parents, to friends, or to the teacher? How would you report an accident you had seen to the police officer, how would it be reported on the evening television news, how would you tell it to friends? Using role playing situations and language changes and various usage patterns to help create believability in a particular character is both an interesting and an effective way to deal with various usage patterns.

There are also opportunities for working with usage patterns within the framework of classroom discussions and presentations. This is particularly true for those children who have been exposed to very little formal usage. In informal classroom discussions or conversation, the usage choices reflect this informality. As you move into presentational discussions such as round table or panel discussions, there is a call for a somewhat more formal language. By helping children make distinctions between the formality of the situation and the kind of group involved in the discussion and the appropriateness of particular usage items, you are helping children grow in their ability to select appropriate usage for particular situations. Making distinctions between home talk and school talk or between talk with friends and talk with others can help children become more flexible in their choices.

Usage Opportunities in Written Language

There are several kinds of work in written language that provide children with opportunities to select among options in usage. These activities are more appropriate for older children for several reasons. Younger children are more involved in simply getting their ideas into written language, and making fine distinctions in written usage becomes too much of a task. Working with the teacher on group stories or recordings of events does help younger children make distinctions between the oral and written modes of expression. Written language is not merely talk written down; there are conventions in writing that do not exist in oral expression, and there are ways of expressing ideas orally that have no parallel in writing.

The teacher can help older children take into account whether the audience is known or unknown, and what the purpose of the writing is, and then determine suitable usage selections. A teacher can structure opportunities for writing that call for various registers of language to be used. Instead of isolated practice that has little meaning for children, there are real writing situations that call for realistic choices.

Children can assume roles in writing much as they might take roles in oral dramatizing. An event from a story or from real life may be described from several viewpoints. Children who have read *A Taste of Blackberries*[13] might describe Jamie's accident as it would have been reported in the newspaper, as a diary entry by one of his friends, or as Mrs. Houser would have written about it to her daughter. The dedication or improvement of a nature trail or of some new playground equipment for the school might be described by children in a thank you letter to the parent's group who had developed it, in an article for the school system's monthly newsletter, or in letters to their pen pals in another part of the country.

Letter writing offers an opportunity for variations in language usage. A few examples are letters to various business concerns ordering free or inexpensive materials for their classroom, writing letters to their favorite author or to pen pals. Some may want to write former classmates who have moved away. Although teachers would not necessarily proofread or correct *personal* letters, they can give guidance before the writing period about the kinds of language that might be appropriate. In writing business letters the teacher may want to go over the draft of the letter before it is recopied and sent. Guidance in the prewriting period can be extremely helpful to children when doing this type of letter writing.

Children in the upper grades would be doing some written reporting. At times this may involve describing some firsthand observations or the results of a survey or experiment. They might also collect recipes or directions for making something as part of a unit of study. All of these reporting situations call for variations in usage.

As children participate in grammar-based activities or work within the usage area in either oral or written formats, there are several important principles to remember. Children's language reflects their strong emotional and linguistic ties to family and close friends. There is rarely a way to change language patterns without saying or implying that the teacher is right and family and friends are wrong. The initial goal of the teacher is to develop security in expressing ideas. It is the content of the talk or writing that is important. If children want to change their language at a later time, for whatever reason, they may. In the elementary school, though, the objective is more *fluent* and *flexible* use of language to express ideas. Viewing usage as a range of choices dependent upon the situation leads children to accept their familiar language and that of other children and adults as variations instead of levels of correctness. We are building in choices based on knowledge of how people use language in various situations.

PRELIMINARY LEARNING ACTIVITIES

1. Try some role playing experiences with others and with some observers to record differences in register or usage from situation to situation. The observers should look for differences in pronunciation, lexical items or vocabulary, and in syntax. Some possible situations are:
   (a) You receive a D in a course in which you were expecting at least a B. What do you say to (1) friends, (2) your teacher, and (3) an appeals board headed by the dean of your college?
   (b) You are involved in an automobile accident because the person ahead of you turns right from the center lane of a four lane road just in front of you. What do you say to (1) the police officer, (2) your parents or spouse, and (3) your close friends?
   (c) You order something from a mail-order catalog and when it arrives it is not the color, or size, or brand you paid for. What do you write to (1) your friend about it and (2) what do you write to the company? Be your own observer in this one.
   Now try to think of some situations that would relate to children's experiences that they could role play to discover differences in their own language in different situations.

2. Examine the following four samples of exercises like those in textbooks for children. Then label them traditional or "school" grammar, structural, or transformational generative.

   Sample 1
      Write the following sentences putting in the correct word for each dash:
   (a) One girl _____ (is, are) absent today.
   (b) Many books _____ (is, are) in our room.

Sample 2

    Combine each of the following pairs of sentences by joining the noun phrases with either "and" or "both . . . and."

(a) An orange is on the counter. An apple is on the counter.

(b) The girls were on the bus. The boys were on the bus.

Sample 3

    Write four sentences using two of the words below in each sentence. Use "a," "an," "the," or a number as a determiner before each:

    park, ball, lake, boats, birds, trees

Sample 4

    Transform the affirmative sentences below to negative ones by adding a form of "do" and "not" and changing verb forms when needed.

(a) Jane caught the ball bunted toward first base.

(b) The jockey carried a good luck charm.

(c) The buses stop in front of the grocery.

PARTICIPATION ACTIVITIES

1. Take a trip with a group of children—to a nearby store, florist or nursery, to an area of the playground or neighborhood—or have someone bring something interesting to school (a motorcycle, electric car, show dog, antique, and so on). Then work on an experience story with the group doing some expansion of basic sentences or sentence combining.

2. Try out one of the role playing situations discussed in the preliminary learning experiences with children and see what they can observe about how they change their language.

3. If you have older students, try having them write in at least two different ways some item pertaining to current events. See the suggestions given on pages 120–121.

4. Test whether children can accurately describe the order of adjectives preceding a noun. Give them sets of cards on which the adjectives and the noun have been written and ask them to arrange the cards in order. Another alternative is to see if children will pronounce accurately the -ed suffix on verbs that they may not know. You can do this by using words from the lists in the section on Grammatical Knowledge or other words that you make up. The words should be printed or written on separate cards.

5. Develop a game that would involve sentence expansion or sentence combining and try it with a group of children.

REFERENCES

[1] Robert C. Pooley. *Teaching English Grammar*. New York: Appleton-Century-Crofts, 1957, p. 106.

[2] Jean Malmstrom and Constance Weaver. *Transgrammar*. Glenview, Illinois: Scott, Foresman and Co., 1973, p. 259.

[3] Ibid., p. 273.

[4] Alonzo Reed and Brainerd Kellogg. *Work on English Grammar and Composition*, 1877, in H. A. Gleason, Jr., *Linguistics and English Grammar*. New York: Holt, 1965.

[5] Mark Lester. *Introductory Transformational Grammar of English*. New York: Holt, 1971, pp. 16–20.

[6] Malmstrom and Weaver. *Transgrammar,* p. 61.

[7] Ibid., p. 62.

[8] Ibid., p. 63.

[9] H. A. Gleason, Jr. *Linguistics and English Grammar*. New York: Holt, 1965, pp. 357–361, 367–375.

[10] William S. Chisholm and Louis T. Milic. *The English Language Form and Use*. New York: McKay, 1974, p. 391.

[11] Gleason. *Linguistics and English Grammar*, pp. 369–373.

[12] This concept is discussed in M. A. K. Halliday, A. McIntosh, and P. Strevens. *The Linguistic Sciences and Language Teaching*. Bloomington, Indiana: Indiana University, 1964, pp. 77–110.

[13] Doris Buchanan Smith. *A Taste of Blackberries*. New York: Thomas Y. Crowell, 1973.

CHAPTER SEVEN

Listening and Language

PREVIEW QUESTIONS

1 Why is listening an important language skill?
2 How can listening be taught?
3 What are the possibilities of using television to develop listening skills?
4 What critical listening activities are appropriate for elementary school children?

Of all the language arts, listening continues to be the most neglected area. It is frequently ignored by educational researchers as well as classroom teachers. Why? One obvious reason is that most people do not differentiate between hearing and listening. Because the two abilities are equated, there is seldom an apparent concern for teaching listening in the elementary school. This has to be viewed as a faulty generalization, however, since the two abilities—hearing and listening—are quite different, yet related. For example, there are individuals who turn on the radio or television immediately when they come home with no intention of really listening or watching; they are mostly interested in hearing the sound. Listening demands much more from us. To listen, we must comprehend what we are hearing; listening requires us to think about what we are hearing.

TIME SPENT IN LISTENING

How much time do you spend in listening? If you are like most people, your answer is "a lot!" We listen to the radio, records, 8 track and cassette tapes, and of course, television is a prime consumer of listening time. Statistics show that television owners watch television an average of 45 hours a week.[1] Certainly we are more engaged in listening than in any of the other language arts areas (reading, speaking, or writing). An early study by Rankin[2] reported 68 percent of an average person's waking hours are spent in some form of communication, with listening being the most frequently used mode. This research has been confirmed by later investigators.

Children, like adults, spend a great deal of time listening. Outside of the school environment, the preschool child watches and listens to television an average of 28½ hours a week. And the elementary age child who spends about 25 hours a week in school views television approximately 24 hours each week.[3] A classic study conducted by Wilt[4] suggests that children spend more than half of their time inside the conventional classroom listening. When asked to estimate, teachers said students learned by listening an average of 74.3 minutes per day. Classroom observations showed that students were actually listening 158 minutes per day, and the majority of this time was spent in listening to the teacher. The findings of the Wilt investigation indicate that teachers were unaware of how much time they required children to listen. It is no wonder that many students eventually become passive listeners if they are in this type of learning setting. A classroom environment where active children are expected to listen to the teacher most of the school day will only produce children who learn to ignore the speaker. You have seen both children and adults do this. Even now, in your college courses, you sometimes "tune out" the instructor. Adults, as well as some children, develop the ability to look as though they are listening, but the behavior of most children will show the teacher that their thoughts are elsewhere. They will talk to their neighbors, read a book that is carefully hidden under the desk, or stare out the window at something that interests them.

SOUNDS, NOISE, AND A VERBAL BARRAGE: OUR WORLD TODAY

The world we live in today is filled with sounds, noises, and verbalizations. We become so accustomed to sound in our environment that we are sometimes bothered when it is too quiet.

The problem with our sound-filled world is that we tend to become passive listeners. We hear birds singing but we do not think to listen for the song of the cardinal or mockingbird. Listening is an *active* process and listening is an *alert* process.

Today's schools are also bombarded with sound. Marjorie Hart's description of a preschool is certainly not atypical.[5]

> Our nursery school stands near a frantically busy boulevard, one of the heaviest traffic lanes in the San Fernando Valley. From our playground, we can observe every possible type of vehicle, moving along in an unrelenting roar. In addition to this, we have had heavy machinery out there lately, digging up the street to lay down new storm drains. They are jack-hammering, bulldozing, digging, hauling; our yard and classrooms vibrate with the racket. Furthermore, one of the world's busiest airports keeps the sky over our heads dotted with a variety of aircraft and flooded with noise.

Hart began a special program in her preschool classroom after realizing a need to teach listening skills. She set a goal to eliminate "language immunity" in her preschool children. Through a variety of planned experiences, the group of four-year-olds became more discriminating and discerning listeners. A comment made by one little girl to Ms. Hart illustrates the success of the classroom instructional program: "To hear everything you have to squint your ears."[6] This young student was learning to *listen*.

TEACHING LISTENING

We need to view listening as a valuable and legitimate component of the elementary school curriculum as well as an area that can be taught. To support this, there are findings from a number of research studies that indicate instruction can improve children's listening skills. Pratt[7] concluded, after conducting an experimental program designed to develop specific listening skills, that listening instruction can be effective. Working with fifth-grade students, Hollow[8] found that a planned instructional program improved students' listening abilities. She reported that pupils at varying levels of intelligence benefited from the program.

We have talked in earlier chapters about providing a rich language environment for children. In such an environment children are encouraged to converse about topics of interest, share and discuss favorite books, read aloud to book partners, and freely talk with their teacher and peers. This rich language environment is also the rich listening environment. Children are not required to listen to the teacher two-thirds of the time; instead, purposeful listening is continuous throughout the school day. Skills in speaking and listening develop more naturally in this type of learning setting —and rightfully so. *Oracy*, a term originally coined at the Birmingham University School of Education, refers to the skills of listening and speaking, just as *literacy* refers to the skills of reading and writing. The reciprocity between listening and speaking is natural and can occur within classrooms where teachers value language. In such classrooms teachers make opportunities for both speaking and listening because it is through them that language develops. However, we need to differentiate between a qualitative and quantitative language environment. If the classroom is organized and managed in a *laissez faire* fashion where children merely "chat" with one another and there is no direction given to their conversations and discussions, little learning of any kind can take place. Rather, it is the carefully planned and organized environment that facilitates skills in oracy. It is a setting where learning experiences are continuous and not chopped up in little time segments. Andrew Wilkinson, a British educator, describes an effective classroom learning climate in this way:

> The English teacher has special opportunities for providing a rich variety of speech situations, amongst which discussion is prime. The traditional English time-table assigned different aspects of the subject

to different periods. Now we think of the time-table in terms of a central continuing theme or experience out of which emerge opportunities for various aspects of production (writing and speaking) and reception (listening and reading). We start, not with the skill to be taught, but with the central experience upon which the skills may operate. Within this framework many opportunities for speaking and listening occur naturally.[9]

In such a skillfully organized environment children are actively involved in interesting and meaningful experiences. Skills in both oracy and literacy develop naturally within the framework of the experiences themselves. To cite an example, a group of children were particularly interested in making fudge after visiting a candy factory. The teacher brought several fudge recipes to school and told the children they could choose the one they liked the best. The students gathered on the large area rug and began sorting through the recipes. Two children suggested that the recipes be read aloud and then compared. The group thought this was a good idea so they began to read and talk about each recipe. Throughout their discussion, a number of questions were raised: "How many ingredients will we need for this recipe? Does this fudge have to be cooked? Will this recipe make enough fudge for everyone in the class?" Finally, narrowing their choice to two, they decided to write the recipes on large sheets of chart paper and tack them on a nearby bulletin board. Having done this, the students continued the discussion until they reached a consensus. The recipe they chose, "Mother's Old-Fashioned Fudge," did not have to be cooked and was the least expensive to make.

These children were speaking and actively listening to one another. No one withdrew from the discussion; they were all involved listeners because they were engaged in an activity that interested them. The children in this rather brief follow-up experience were deeply involved in using their listening skills to make an important choice. The activity also included meaningful practice in reading and handwriting as well as considerable skill in a planning discussion. Comparing the recipes involved some rather complex math, and the original trip was related to a study of their community.

When teaching listening, the most important factor to remember is *integration*. Listening is not taught as an isolated subject in the elementary school curriculum; it permeates all the language arts and the entire school day.

RAISING THE QUALITY OF CHILDREN'S LISTENING

Within the context of ongoing classroom learning experiences, the teacher can raise the quality of children's listening. The teaching of specific listening skills or good listening habits can occur within this framework, without formally saying, "Today children, we are having a lesson in listening," or continually repeating, "Children, you are not listening! Let's pay attention!"

What skills should you be concerned with teaching? If you help children improve their listening comprehension, you will subsequently help them in all learning areas. Pratt[10] suggests the following skills are involved in the comprehension of ideas:

Noting details
Following directions
Organizing into main and subordinate ideas
Selecting information pertinent to a specific topic
Detecting clues that show the speaker's trend of thought

Within the organization of daily classroom learning experiences, children can be taught to note details, determine main ideas, select the most useful and pertinent information about a topic and follow directions. They can detect clues that point out the speaker's trend of thought or draw inferences from what has been said. If a group of students is listening to a cassette recording of a children's book, the teacher can guide a discussion of the story. A planned series of questions can involve children in identifying significant details. A discussion may center on the main ideas of the story or the author's purpose in writing the story. Reading books aloud provides the teacher with many opportunities to develop skills in listening comprehension.

An excellent example to mention is the Listen-Read Project.[11] This study put listening and books together to improve children's reading, and the findings showed many valuable side benefits to the program. Each day children used a listening center and heard cassette recordings of books. While listening, they each had a paperback book of the story being read. There was a choice of activities that followed the listening sessions: paired reading, writing of group experience stories, role playing of the stories, and discussions in which children were asked inferential and evaluative questions. The outcome is described as follows:

Descriptive data collected from the teacher indicated that the children became more adept at handling books, displayed increased

A listening center can offer many valuable learning experiences. These students are listening while following the printed text of a story that has been recorded on cassette tape.

attention spans in reading and far greater facility in oral language. The high level of concentration, made possible through the use of headsets, was still further evidence of the efficacy of the program in developing listening skills. Because of smaller groupings with part of the class administering its own Listen-Read activity, the teachers were less controlling and encouraged more open discussion. As a result, children who had been quiet and shy began to offer their ideas about the books they had enjoyed.[12]

The use of books is not the only means of teaching listening comprehension skills. For instance, children are continually asked to follow directions in order to complete learning tasks. Teachers can correlate the teaching of this listening skill with daily learning activities, keeping in mind the age and cognitive stage of the children. For example, children listen and follow directions when they make books (Chapter Thirteen), prepare certain types of art

Listening carefully to what children say is an important aspect of teaching.
(*Photograph by Thomas England*)

projects, participate in movement experiences, or role play scenes from a favorite story.

The evaluation of children's listening skills is an immediate and continuous process if you teach listening within the context of daily classroom learning experiences. You have instant feedback that suggests that John can or can not follow directions. A group discussion focusing on the significant points made by a visiting speaker will enable you to assess quickly children's listening comprehension abilities.

Teacher intervention can raise the quality of listening and thus affect learning. Intervention usually takes the form of asking students questions. The questioning focuses on suggestions, ideas, or information that will extend and further develop the child's learning experience. To illustrate, a small group of children went on a listening walk with the teacher. When he asked them to describe various sounds as they walked through a park, the teacher discovered the children were listening on a very superficial level. They had not heard the chirping of a cricket, the sound of the wind as it rustled through the trees, or the sound of an annoyed and irritated blue jay. They had only heard the predominant or "big" sounds—the buses and cars as they passed by, a man yelling at his dog, and a baby crying. The teacher's questions encouraged the children to listen and describe all kinds of sounds that they heard around them. Do you hear the birds? What kind of birds are they? Can you imitate the call of the cardinal? How is the cardinal's call different from the blue jay's?

The teacher who listens to what children say and encourages them to talk and ask questions has an accurate guide to children's thinking abilities. You can only intervene in children's conversations and discussions to raise the level or quality of the learning if *you* listen. Evaluating children's listening skills depends upon listening to all that they say. The teacher of listening needs to be a model listener.

TELEVISION: ITS POSSIBILITIES FOR TEACHING LISTENING

Television is a source of pleasure for both children and adults. As mentioned earlier in the chapter, television is a prime consumer of much of the American population's time. Witty[13] reported that first-graders viewed television 15 hours per week; fifth-grade students watched television 25 hours per week; and the viewing time for high school students was 12 to 14 hours per week.

If primary age children are watching television approximately 15 hours per week and upper elementary age students about 25, one wonders about its effect. Are children learning and becoming more knowledgeable because they view television to this extent? The research is inconclusive at this time, but present findings tend to lean toward the negative side. Himmelweit[14] compared a group of children who were television viewers with a group who were not and found the nonviewers were more knowledgeable. In fact, the more intelligent television watchers tended to do less well in school if they were avid viewers of television. Slater,[15] working with third-graders, found that school achievement, reading, arithmetic, and intelligence had a negative correlation with television viewing. Another study reported by La Blonde[16] suggests there is no significant relationship between fifth-grade students' television habits and school achievement. However, the findings did indicate a positive relationship between television viewing and students' performance on Word-Study Skills of the Iowa Tests of Basic Skills. This finding is not too surprising since a number of other studies have conclusively shown that television contributes to vocabulary development. Both Himmelweit[17] and Schramm[18] indicate that television helps to build the vocabulary of the beginning school age child. Children who watch and listen to television are from six months to a year ahead of nonviewers in vocabulary development.

Bringing Television and the Language Program Together

Why not capitalize on the amount of time children spend watching television? Studies show that students enjoy and learn from instructional television, and the same results can be obtained using commercial television. Savage,[19] in promoting the idea of using children's out-of-school television experiences to build a language program, says, "A common criticism is that television is creating an unthinking generation. The trick for teachers is to get their pupils reacting to what they see and hear on TV." The potential that exists for increasing children's language and listening skills through commercial television is certainly great. If students receive guidance and direction, they will surely become more knowledgeable about the world around them. Television is also an excellent source for teaching students to become critical listeners. When educators talk about beginning where children are, they need to consider commercial television as a potential learning device.

Here are some ideas for using children's television viewing to increase their language and listening abilities. Once you begin using children's television experiences as a viable part of the language arts program, you will probably think of many more useful ideas.

1. Dramatization and television may be used together. After viewing the same TV show, children can dramatize a favorite scene or episode.
2. Have the children view a daytime serial. Ask them to predict what will happen tomorrow and then watch it to see how accurate their predictions were.
3. Discuss different endings that could have been written for an episode of a popular series show they watched the night before.
4. Ask children to view an informative show that has been well reviewed and use it as a basis for discussion.
5. Children can compare and contrast television news coverage with newspaper coverage of significant events.
6. Children might produce a news show of their own after interviewing school faculty and students.
7. When a new program premieres on television, ask your students

to watch. Discuss and evaluate the program the next day with the children. Some students may enjoy writing a review of the new show.

Critical Listening and Television

We live in a society where we are constantly being sold something. Have you watched any commercials recently and said to yourself, "Such ridiculous ads! Who would rush out and buy any of those products after seeing the commercials?" The answer—a lot of American people buy these products! Television executives contend viewers often complain bitterly about a commercial being irritating and then go right out and buy the product advertised.[20] The evidence indicates a certain amount of gullibility on the part of adults, but what about children? Working with students ages eight to ten, Cook[21] found they were willing to accept the propaganda presented in television commercials, regardless of their level of intelligence. One can conclude from the available research that skills in critical listening should be taught in the elementary school and not left until students are in high school or college.

It is difficult to divorce critical listening from critical reading, and critical thinking is basic to both. Research investigations by Devine[22] and Lundsteen[23] show a positive relationship between critical reading and critical listening. Evidence from both studies reveals that the ability to listen critically can be taught. For this reason, Devine recommends that skills in critical reading and critical listening be taught together. The skills are so interrelated that teaching them concurrently will provide reinforcement.

How do you go about teaching critical listening and critical reading? You might begin with teaching children certain propaganda techniques that are widely used by advertisers. Older students can identify the use of these techniques in newspapers, magazines, billboards, radio, and television.

Widely Used Propaganda Techniques[24]

Bandwagon: Everybody is doing it. All members of a group are doing it.

Card Stacking: Falsehoods that distract. Illogical statements to give the best or worst possible case for an idea.

Glittering Generalities: Virtue words like *truth* and *honor.* Empty, yet colorful words.

Name Calling: Giving an idea or product a bad label.

Plain Folks: Attempts to delude an audience into thinking the speaker is just like them.

Testimonial: A respected or hated person can say that a given idea is good or bad.

Transfer: The authority and prestige of something respected is carried over to something else.

Students can also learn to distinguish fact from opinion. Young children might look at a selection of pictures and discuss statements about them. For Figure 8 those statements might be: The girl is happy. The girl is wearing a sweater and skirt. The dog likes the girl. The dog is small. The dog belongs to the girl.

Students can choose their own pictures from newspapers or magazines and write their own statements about them. These may be exchanged with a partner or displayed somewhere in the classroom. Small and large group discussions can focus on why certain statements are factual and why others are opinion.

Older students can listen to radio or television news reports and analyze what is fact and what is opinion. The same activity can be done with newspaper editorials. After having a number of experiences, some students may want to write and record their own editorials about current topics or events. Reading aloud a biography of a famous person or a book that is historical fiction offers opportunities to determine fact from fiction, too. Questions such as — *Did this really happen? Was the person like the author describes? Is this a true event?*—can lead to some interesting and enjoyable research for upper-elementary age children. Authenticity may also be questioned—*What qualifies this author to write about this subject? How much research was necessary in order to write this book? Is the factual information accurate?*

All good fantasy is grounded in reality, and children can learn to distinguish between the two. A picture book such as *Where the Wild Things Are*[25] can be read aloud and discussed, focusing on what parts of the story are reality and what parts are fantasy. Because the illustrations in this book depict both fantastic and realistic situations, they too can be included in the discussion.

In an age when listening is rapidly becoming a primary means of obtaining information as well as a source of enjoyment through radio and television, it seems that it deserves much more attention than it is presently getting in our schools. Given an interesting and meaningful learning environment along with appropriate instruction, students' listening skills can be improved; and children can become critical listeners and thinkers.

Figure 8

Critical interpretation of pictures

PRELIMINARY LEARNING ACTIVITIES

1. Plan a listening library to use later with children. Your library may include:
   (a) stories recorded on cassette tape—if possible, have paperback copies of the stories for children to look at while listening;
   (b) records that children will enjoy listening to more than once;
   (c) poems recorded on cassette tape that will interest most children;
   (d) tape-recorded instructions that provoke a listening situation ("Listen to the sounds around you for the next five minutes and write about as many as you can");
   (e) open-ended stories read on cassette tape—after listening to an open-ended story, children write or tape-record their own original endings;
   (f) recordings on cassette tape of a series of television or radio commercials that represent all seven propaganda devices— children can identify each propaganda device as they listen;
   (g) a recording of two contrasting reports—children can compare the two by listening for similarities and differences.
   Now it is your turn. How many other listening experiences can you add to your library?

2. The idea of using a sharing basket is discussed in Chapter Eight. Sometime each day, children who wish to share (perhaps an imaginative story, poem, painting, and so on) place a note or the project itself in the basket. Make a sharing basket and plan the listening and speaking rules that will guide its use.
3. Children enjoy listening walks and a number can be planned in and around the school. The purpose for listening is established prior to taking the walk. For example, children or a teacher may plan a walk around the school grounds to listen for unusual sounds. Or, after reading the book *The Tiniest Sound*,[26] the walk may focus on listening for "tiny" or "soft" sounds. Plan a variety of listening walks that may be taken in and around most schools.
4. Prepare a sample letter to be sent to parents informing them about upcoming television shows that their children might watch. You may wish to include possible follow-up activities, related books, questions, etc., to promote parental participation.

PARTICIPATION ACTIVITIES

1. Have children write open-ended stories that can be read aloud and then completed by other children. The ending to the stories may be written or verbalized. If you are working with a small group of children, you may ask each child to add a sentence to the story until they reach a logical ending—or the last child in the group may end the story.
2. Develop and use a listening-reading transfer lesson. You will plan two similar lessons: the first lesson will require children to *listen* and demonstrate certain skills; the second lesson will require children to *read* and demonstrate the same skills.

    For more information read: Patricia M. Cunningham's "Transferring Comprehension from Listening to Reading," in *The Reading Teacher*, vol. 29, no. 2 (November 1975), pp. 169–172.
3. Ask your children to view and listen to their favorite television show and write an experience story about it. Children may do their writing at home or even the next day at school. If some children have watched the same television show, you might encourage them to write a group experience story.
4. There are innumerable activities related to critical listening that children will enjoy. Here are a few:

(a) Have several children tape-record a number of Saturday morning television commercials. As a class, analyze the commercials according to the seven propaganda devices mentioned in this chapter.

(b) Tape-record several television cereal commercials. Using the cereal boxes that correspond with the commercials, make a comparison. Ask children to contrast the television advertising with the advertising shown on the cereal boxes.

(c) Older students can role play television commercials. Working in small groups, they can choose a commercial to dramatize for other class members. Some students may prefer to write and role play their own commercials.

5. Take a listening walk. After reading *The Listening Walk*[27] aloud, take your children on a similar walk.

REFERENCES

[1] Figures are based on 1970 statistics of the A. S. Neilsen Media Research Division.

[2] Paul T. Rankin. "The Measurement of the Ability to Understand Spoken Language." Doctoral dissertation, University of Michigan, Ann Arbor, Michigan, 1926.

[3] 1970 A. S. Neilsen Media Research Division.

[4] Miriam E. Wilt. "A Study of Teacher Awareness of Listening as a Factor in Elementary Education." *Journal of Educational Research*, vol. 43, April 1950, pp. 626–636.

[5] Marjorie Hart. "Language Immunity: A Preschool View." *Elementary English*, vol. 50, no. 4, April 1973, pp. 625–627; 646.

[6] Ibid., p. 625.

[7] Edward Pratt. "Experimental Evaluation of a Program for the Improvement of Listening." *Elementary School Journal*, vol. 56, March 1956, pp. 315–320.

[8] Sister Mary Kevin Hollow. "Listening Comprehension at the Intermediate Grade Level." *Elementary School Journal*, vol. 56, December 1955, pp. 158–161.

[9] Andrew Wilkinson. "Oracy in English Teaching." *Elementary English*, vol. 45, no. 6, October 1968, p. 743.

[10] L. E. Pratt. "The Experimental Evaluation of a Program for the Improvement of Listening in the Elementary School." Doctoral dissertation, State University of Iowa, Iowa City, 1953.

[11] Helen E. Schneeberg and Marciene S. Mattleman. "The Listen-Read Project: Motivating Students through Dual Modalities." *Elementary English*, vol. 50, no. 6, September 1973, pp. 900–904.

[12] Ibid., p. 902.

[13] Paul Witty. "Studies of the Mass Media." *Science Education*, vol. 50, March 1966, p. 120 (pp. 119–126).

[14] Hilde T. Himmelweit, A. N. Oppenheim, and Pamela Vance. *Television and the Child.* London: Oxford University Press, 1958, p. 21.

[15] Betty Rech Slater. "An Analysis and Appraisal of the Amount of Televiewing, General School Achievement, and Socio-economic Status of Third Grade Students in Selected Public Schools of Erie County, New York. *Dissertation Abstracts*, vol. 25, April 1965, p. 5651A.

[16] J. A. LaBlonde. "A Study of the Relationship between Television Viewing Habits and the Scholastic Achievement of Fifth Grade Children," *Dissertation Abstracts*, vol. 27, February 1967, p. 2284A.

[17] Himmelweit et al., *Television and the Child.*

[18] Wilbur Schramm, Jack Lyle, and Edwin B. Parker. *Television in the Lives of Our Children.* Stanford: Stanford University Press, 1961, p. 16.

[19] John F. Savage. "Jack, Janet, or Simon Barsinister?" *Elementary English*, vol. 50, no. 1, January 1973, pp. 133–136.

[20] Clark M. Agnew and Neil O'Brien. *Television Advertising.* New York: McGraw-Hill, 1958, p. 22.

[21] Jimmie E. Cook. "A Study in Critical Listening Using Eight to Ten Year Olds in an Analysis of Commercial Propaganda Emanating from Television." Doctoral dissertation, West Virginia University, 1972.

[22] Thomas G. Devine. "The Development and Evaluation of a Series of Recordings for Teaching Certain Critical Listening Abilities." Doctoral dissertation, Boston University, 1961.

[23] Sara Lundsteen. "Teaching Abilities in Critical Listening in the Fifth and Sixth Grades." Doctoral dissertation, University of California, Berkeley, 1963.

[24] Alfred M. Lee and Elizabeth B. Lee, eds. *The Fine Arts of Propaganda.* New York: Harcourt, Brace and Company, 1939, p. 105.

[25] Maurice Sendak. *Where the Wild Things Are.* New York: Harper & Row, 1963.

[26] Mel Evans. *The Tiniest Sound.* New York: Doubleday, 1969.

[27] Paul Showers. *The Listening Walk.* New York: Crowell, 1961.

CHAPTER EIGHT

Oral Discourse— Discussing and Presenting

PREVIEW QUESTIONS

1 How can a teacher improve the quality of oral communication?

2 What kinds of questions and what strategies of questioning produce responses from children?

3 What kinds of discussion groups are there and for what purposes is each best?

4 How do you select materials and prepare for storytelling and choral reading?

5 How should teachers evaluate oral presentations?

A group of Ms. Clark's children took a walk around their school and looked for signs of various kinds. During the excursion, the teacher carefully wrote down what the students noticed. When they returned from their walk, Ms. Clark brought out some replicas of a few signs they had seen. After a brief discussion, the children decided to make copies of some other signs that the teacher had not constructed. When all the signs were completed, Ms. Clark brought out a pocket chart—a large poster-type sheet with narrow strips of paper stapled across it to make slots in which the sign replicas would fit. One row was for traffic signs, one for advertising or ads, and the third was for information. The children selected a sign from the ones they had seen and went up to the chart to put it in the right place. The Burger King sign went into the "ads" pocket, the stop sign went into "traffic," the street sign went into "information," and then one of the children put *Buses Only* into "information." Some of the children protested that it should be in "traffic." A somewhat heated discussion followed. In the process of that discussion, the group learned a great deal about the purposes for having traffic signs and they came to narrow their meanings of all three labels— ads, traffic, and information.

As a follow-up Ms. Clark had the group select one sign (*Railroad Crossing*) and write an experience story about the railroad crossing sign. They read and reread their story as they were in the process of composing it. When the story was just as they wanted it, she copied it on a large sheet of lined chart paper and they decorated it with cutouts done in poster paint of trains and tracks, of children and cars waiting at a crossing, and of the railroad crossing sign itself.

The next day they used an assortment of small boxes, clay, toothpicks, colored paper, and paint to make a table display map of their walk. Three of the children who had wanted to do the experience story on the Burger King sign dictated their own story to a fifth-grader who comes to their room three days a week for thirty minutes. Two others decided that there should be a sign for children from their school telling them where to wait for the crossing guard at a busy street nearby. They talked to their teacher about their idea for a few minutes and then went off to get poster paper and paint to make a sign for this. The teacher came back to help them decide what the sign should say and how to spell the words for it, but then they were on their own. The rest of the group wrote up their own ads for various products, getting help in spelling the words they needed from another fifth-grader.

The children shared all their projects when they were finished.

They read the stories, told about their walk, and showed all the signs they had seen along the way. The group who made their own advertisements displayed these on a bulletin board and told about them. The children also told about their new school sign and decided to write about the idea and send it to the city council to see if it could be adopted for their city.

What were they studying? Reading? Language Arts? Social Studies? Actually, they were working on all of these. Most important of all, they were actively involved in their learning. They were using language to communicate, to clarify ideas, to compare and contrast. They were also using language creatively as they chose words for their stories and for their ads. There was an honest need to use language in a variety of ways and all the activities were rooted in personal firsthand experience. Another significant point is that they went into a subject in enough depth to learn something instead of skimming the surface. There were a variety of activities related to the same topic. Although they worked together on one story about the railroad crossing sign, there was the opportunity for children who wanted to do something else to have choices. They worked with concrete materials instead of working entirely with ditto work sheets and a textbook story. If the children had been interested in the new international road signs—one of which was on their walk— the teacher might have asked questions which would have led to an interesting research task. With a slightly older or more experienced group, the teacher might also have suggested the construction of a conventional but more abstract paper map rather than the table display map.

The teacher capitalized on several areas of oral discourse. Informal conversation was involved on the original walk and during the work on the table display map. Informal planning discussions took place while they were deciding what to say in their group experience story, during the classification of the signs, and while they were planning the table display map. Oral presentations occurred when they shared their own ads, stories, and the new proposed pedestrian sign. All of these are part of the language arts skills that are considered here as oral discourse. Other activities in this area are oral reporting, book discussions, choral reading or speaking, making announcements or relaying oral messages, giving directions, making introductions, using the telephone, reviewing orally, conducting meetings or group discussions, and asking questions or giving explanations orally. Drama, also a part of oral discourse, is discussed in the next chapter.

THE ENVIRONMENT THAT PROMOTES ORAL LANGUAGE SKILLS

The best plans of the teacher and the most stimulating topics for oral language activities will be of little value if the classroom environment does not encourage children's free and active participation. What kind of environment is necessary?

A key component is the removal of criticism and pressure to conform to some predetermined standards. Although the teacher may want to remind children before the activity to talk loudly enough for others to hear or to keep to the topic, the main emphasis is on what the child says rather than how it is said. It is not the time to correct word usage, criticize children's ideas, or suggest that they did not prepare adequately. Although you may feel that you can listen to children and at the same time do some clerical task, don't. You would be communicating nonverbally that what the child is saying isn't important or worth hearing. Sometimes it is tempting to suppress a child who is dominating group talk. However, the verbal student may not be subdued for very long, and you may inhibit another child who is on the verge of adding something to the discussion. Too many standards and too much adherence to them can hinder discussion instead of improving it.

A second component of a classroom environment that encourages participation is the establishment of *talk* as a significant vehicle for learning. Often, owing to evaluative measures and grading policies, teachers tend to place a higher value on written work than on oral work. Because of this, both student and parents begin to think written work is the most important. By seeking new ways to apply information that is acquired orally, teachers can provide experiences that can be evaluated according to children's contributions in oral language situations.

Another reason that oral activities do not receive the same emphasis as written ones is because words, once spoken, are quickly gone. There does not seem to be time to reexamine them or evaluate them. It is possible, however, to tape-record or take notes during discussions. Summarizing orally as the discussion proceeds may help children realize that their ideas do make a difference, and that as a group they have accomplished something in the process of oral work. Finding a system such as a chart to record those who participate, distract, and so on, will also help in your evaluation.

The establishment of meaningful conversation as a general classroom pattern is another facet of an environment conducive to oral skill development. This does not mean that children should be allowed to detract from other learning activities. It does mean that

Purposeful conversation is an integral part of a rich oral language environment. (*Photograph by Thomas England*)

children should be allowed to converse with those nearby as long as the conversation does not interrupt others who are working on something else. There are times when you will need to have all their attention focused on you. There are other times—while building a model, writing a composition, planning a puppet play, doing art work—when encouraging conversation is developmentally sound.

Children can learn from each other, and they can learn from working together. When you are evaluating your students, you need to know what they can do independently; however, a large portion of time, children can work together on assignments, projects, or papers.

The final component of a classroom rich in oral language activities and language expansion is the development of a real need for children to discuss, describe, compare, and categorize things orally. Discussions should be an integral part of the daily classroom routine because there is always a need for something to be shared, discussed, or decided. The teacher must be perceptive and recognize moments when talk needs to be encouraged. A teacher can structure the classroom, the presentation, or a situation so that it calls for some phase of oral discourse.

For children who are in the preoperational stage of development—approximately two to seven years old—oral discussion experiences are especially important. The egocentrism of children at this stage of development leads them to assume that others know and think the way they do. And when others show that they do not, young children are often exasperated by this lack of understanding. An important way for children to realize that words do not carry all the information they suppose is to allow them many chances to talk with others, to explain their ideas, and to describe their experiences.

At the next stage of development—the concrete operational period from about seven to about eleven—egocentrism becomes much less apparent and the child develops a social awareness and the understanding of another's point of view. Discussion and conversation are still very important, because at this stage of development they serve to help children communicate their thoughts and refine their concepts. Children at this stage of development cannot work from abstract ideas; their thought processes are still grounded in concrete, firsthand experiences. Their thinking is facilitated by using real objects and events. Through communicating with others, children's concepts and views are accommodated into the internalized organizational patterns.

What we are suggesting is not just that talk of various kinds is a nice thing to do in elementary classrooms; rather, talk is a critical part of the school experiences of elementary-age children. Oral language activities cannot be dismissed as a nuisance or unimportant. They need to be considered a major part of the school curriculum for every child—and they are especially important for children whose background of experience does not include conversations or discussions of various kinds with linguistically mature adults.

SHARING

This section is entitled *sharing* instead of *show-and-tell* for several reasons. First, show-and-tell is confined almost exclusively to the primary grades, and upper elementary-age children would feel that having show-and-tell was childish although they might like to share hobbies or collections if it seemed like a grown-up thing to do. Another reason for using the term *sharing* is that it is more descriptive of the activity at any age or grade level. Show-and-tell implies one person at a time showing something and telling about it without any interaction from those listening. And that is exactly what it usually turns out to be—except that those who are supposed to be listening usually are not. Young children are too egocentric to be totally interested in what others say and are really more interested in what they have to say. Too often it is the same few children who get up to show-and-tell, and they may not be the ones who need the experience the most.

Sharing, on the other hand, is a very adultlike activity. Its name directly implies give-and-take, response from the listeners, a mutual participating in the topic. Sharing, however, cannot take place with an entire classroom very successfully. Twenty to thirty people of any age cannot participate in a discussion. When show-and-tell shifts from a speaker/audience situation to a sharing activity, it becomes an interactive situation where the listeners' responses, questions, and experiences are also of value. This means that the teacher needs to provide a small group situation for sharing.

Teachers play an important role in sharing. It is their responsibility to encourage personal involvement in the sharing discussion. Through the questions they ask and the strategies of questioning they use, teachers can explore the topics dealt with in greater depth and can extend children's contributions. The interaction between children is also part of the teacher's role in sharing discussions.

Encouraging Personal Involvement

Getting children really involved in a discussion means selecting topics that interest them and grouping children together who have some common experiences. In the early primary grades many teachers have found that sharing is better placed at the end of the school day than at the beginning. During the day children either do things such as paint, write stories, and so on, that they would like to share with others, or they are reminded of ideas or experiences they wish to tell about. One successful teacher uses a "Sharing Basket" to encourage discussion. Children may put a note in the basket during the day about what they would like to share. This has a dual purpose: It reminds them of their ideas and it points out a purpose for writing. Older children may enjoy and profit from sharing a book they have read or a movie or television program they have seen. Teachers have used this kind of sharing as a substitute for the formal oral or written book report with great success. For this, you could group children according to those who have read books by the same author, books dealing with the same time period, or perhaps books dealing with the same theme.

Using Effective Questions and Questioning Strategies

One very important factor in developing sharing discussions is the use of appropriate questions and questioning strategies. Research suggests that the level of teachers' questions determines the level of children's thinking. Cunningham[1] has developed a model of questioning, shown in Figure 9, that seems helpful in considering the various kinds that may be asked.

Narrow questions are divided into two subcategories, cognitive-memory questions and convergent questions. Cognitive-memory questions are those which require that the person responding recall or recognize information which has previously been made available. It involves only remembering the answer. On a topic such as seashells, the following are examples of cognitive-memory questions.

Recall—*Where did you find this shell?*
Identify-Observe—*What colors are there in these shells?*
Yes-No—*Is this the biggest shell?*
Defining—*What do you mean by spiral shell?*
Naming—*What is this shell called?*
Designating—*Which is the smallest shell here?*

The other type of narrow questions are called convergent. These are questions which may involve more than simply remembering, but they lead to one specific answer. The aim of the question is to reach a predetermined right answer. The following are sample convergent questions on the topic of shells.

Explain—*Why are these shells called bivalves?*
State Relationships—*How are clams and oysters related?*
Compare-Contrast—*In what ways are these shells similar or different?*

Broad questions are also divided into two main subcategories: divergent questions and evaluative questions. Divergent questions are open-ended questions that call for a variety of responses rather than a single answer. The following illustrate kinds of divergent questions.

Predict—*What would make some shells more valuable than others?*
Hypothesize—*If you continued collecting shells, how many would you have in five more years?*

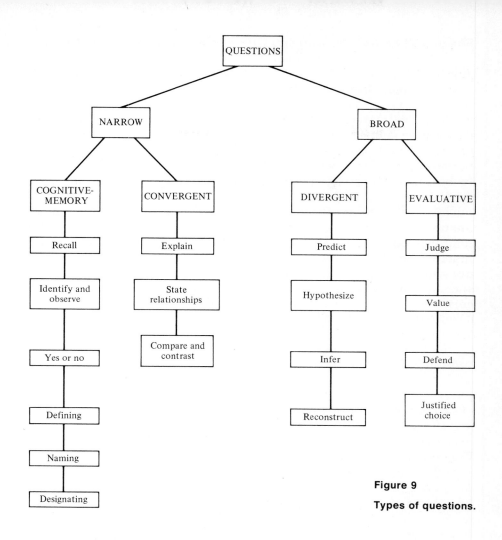

Figure 9

Types of questions.

Infer—*What problems would you have collecting shells along the Alaskan coastline?*

Reconstruct—*Can you tell us how you first became interested in shell collecting?*

The other kind of broad questions are evaluative questions. These questions ask the student to make or support some kind of judgment. Sample questions of these evaluative subcategories are as follows:

Judge—*Describe the most unusual shell you have.*

Value—*What makes shell collecting an enjoyable hobby?*

Defend—*Why did you say that other classes in our school should know about your shell collection?*

Justified Choice—*If you could only keep three shells, which ones would you keep and why would you choose those three?*

The illustrations of the various kinds of questions within each of the four subcategories are given primarily to illustrate the types of questions that would be classified as cognitive-memory, convergent, divergent, or evaluative. It is not important for the teacher to be able to classify questions; what is important is that each teacher be able to predict what amount of response a particular question will generate and what kind of thinking is involved in answering the question. Too often teachers, in attempting to check reading comprehension or oral listening comprehension, ask primarily cognitive-memory questions. Generally speaking, the broad questions, both divergent and evaluative, provoke the greatest response from several different children. Use cognitive-memory or convergent questions to clarify facts and gain information; then use divergent and evaluative questions to extend thinking beyond that level.

Questions that begin in the following ways tend to increase the number of possible responses from students: *What could you tell someone about . . . ? How can you tell that . . . ? What are the differences between . . . ? What things does this picture tell you about . . . ? Under what circumstances . . . ? What reasons for . . . ? What are the possible values of . . . ? What might happen if . . . ? How could you summarize . . . ? What evidence can you find that . . . ? What could have caused . . . ? What are the effects of . . . ?*

The teacher's role in questioning, then, is to ask questions that are penetrating and provocative. These are the questions that make one think at a more complex level and that elicit several answers or reasons. Of course you cannot predict ahead of time which way a discussion may lead, but as a teacher you should prepare ahead of time a few key questions to ask. During the discussion itself, you can supplement the key questions you planned with others that seem necessary because of the direction the discussion takes.

In addition to the particular questions that are used during a discussion, there are four strategies that are used to improve discussion.

Ask fewer questions and balance the ones you do ask between broad and narrow questions. Use narrow questions to establish a common area of information; ask broad questions to extend the thinking of your group.

Balance participation in the discussion by calling on children who do not volunteer as well as those who do. Do not let a few children who always raise their hands to answer close out others who could also contribute to the discussion. Many children who are less able students because of problems with reading and writing are perfectly capable of responding orally within the discussion. They may be rather shy about answering a question, but they will gladly do it if called upon. You can even refocus a child who is not really involved in the discussion by saying his name and then asking him a question. However, do not do this to trap someone. Ask a question you think the child can answer.

Use questions that not only allow but encourage several children to answer. Children are the world's greatest experts at determining what teachers actually want. If you can convince them that there is not a preset, predetermined answer for every question and that it is the child's job to find out what that answer is, children will reward you with some highly original ideas or solutions.

Improve children's responses to questions by giving them time to think, and ask additional questions to make them correct, clarify, or extend their first answers. Silence is an uncomfortable element in a discussion. Too often the teacher who feels responsible for the discussion will give an answer or just go on to another question. If, however, the teacher will make an effort to be quiet, one of the children will break the silence. Children often need some time to think, to figure things out, to make connections between the question and their experiences. Give them time. There will be moments when a teacher may want to extend an answer. A puzzled look and perhaps saying, "Ohhh?" or "Explain a little more" will elicit additional information.

Questioning plays a very large part in teacher-led discussions. The questions themselves and the strategies of questioning that the teacher uses are significant. Through the questions posed, teachers raise the level of children's thinking and further their language development.

Promoting Child-to-Child Interactions

The questioning strategies above will help develop a pattern of discussion in which children do more talking than the teacher. Asking questions that do not focus on a single short answer will also promote child talk. After all, the teacher does not really need the experience of explaining, describing, categorizing, and speculating; the necessity to use language in a variety of ways is a part of language development and therefore what children need. Teachers can deliberately promote interaction among children by asking them to verify or add to what someone has said without implying that their first response is incorrect. Another way of facilitating interaction in the classroom is to make children responsible and comfortable in asking questions as well as in giving answers. With young children you can prompt their questions by suggesting what they might ask, "Who would like to ask George what other ways people use to display their collection?" With children of any age, teachers can praise the questions that students ask. If you can make your class feel that asking questions as well as answering them is important to you, they will try to do it.

A critical feature of good discussion as well as good conversation is a small group in which each participant feels comfortable. With the large group—and perhaps with a small group in the primary grades—children may need to raise their hands and be called on in order to limit constant interruptions. As children have more experience, this should gradually become unnecessary.

Some teachers have found other ways to control interruptions. A "speaker selector" is highly effective if not used excessively. This is an object, something intrinsically interesting such as a marble egg, feather, or large button that is passed around the group. Only the person having the speaker selector should be speaking. As the object passes around the circle or group, the person having it may talk and then hand it on when finished. If the child who has it does not want to contribute an idea or comment, it is simply passed on. This eliminates all the raising of hands and being called on, and it also guarantees that each person will have their turn. Even with young children it is a workable idea—perhaps because of its visibility and its guarantee of a turn. It is difficult to get young children to take their turn and not interrupt because of their strong egocentric drive and because of the amount of competition for attention present in the classroom which is not present at home.

Because sharing is an important part of the emotional development of children and offers such potential for developing thinking skills and language skills, it should be more than the conventional show-and-tell. Try to make the sharing time a vital part of the curriculum by arranging it in a way that affective, cognitive, and linguistic skills are developed.

DISCUSSING

In addition to conversation and sharing there are two other kinds of classroom discussion: planning discussions and presentational discussions. These should be used in your classroom when there is a real need to plan or to present something meaningful to the children.

Planning Discussions

There are two kinds of discussions that are appropriate for planning or generating ideas. These are brainstorming groups and buzz groups. *Brainstorming* has been successfully used by adults as well as by children and is effective in generating ideas, especially innovative or creative approaches to a problem. In brainstorming there is no need to come to a decision or agreement. Every idea is accepted as stated, although others may combine ideas or add to an idea which has been suggested. It is a free-wheeling approach which may include a wide range of suggestions from the very practical to the improbable. Most teachers will use it with caution, clearly stating ahead of time that the object is to get a lot of ideas without coming to a decision. *Buzz groups* are also used to get ideas or to plan. In contrast to brainstorming, buzz groups focus on a particular conclusion or decision. A small group or several small groups of children are given a specific problem and a certain amount of time to reach their objective. The discussion may require children to consider a number of pros and cons, but the group eventually reaches closure on an idea or suggestion.

Planning discussions can be used for a wide range of topics in the classroom. Their content may be related specifically to the language arts as children plan, for example, the cover for an invitation to their parents to visit their room. These discussions may also be related to another content area, such as how to care for and record their observations of the gerbils as a part of a science experiment or how to set up a softball tournament between the fifth and sixth grade.

If you allow children to participate in planning activities, you should be willing to agree to any reasonable plan which they decide upon. If you feel there are constraints on what they might decide, then note these ahead of time. You may wish to say what theme should be followed in the invitation, what supplies are available, what the cost or time limits are, and so on. If you have already made some planning decisions, then announce them or state the alternatives from which the children may choose.

Presentational Discussions

These discussions are intended as a way for individuals or a group to present to others something they have learned or information they have gathered. The two main kinds of presentational discussions are round table discussions and panel discussions. The more informal and less audience-oriented of the two is the round table discussion. *Round table discussions* involve a small group of students and a moderator. They are relatively informal with the group members sharing ideas or findings with each other or an audience. The moderator's main responsibility is to keep the group moving along and on the topic. You may want to have the moderator summarize the discussion in some way, but keep in mind that summarizing an oral discussion is a rather high-level thinking skill and is fairly difficult even for adults. *Panel discussions* are clearly intended for presenting ideas to an audience. Each member of the panel takes responsibility for some aspect of the topic. The members tend to take turns in presenting their part, although panel members may add to one another's information as the presentation continues. After the panel has made its presentation, members of the audience may ask questions of the panel as a whole or of one individual panel member. The panel discussion, in contrast to the round table discussion, is more formalized and requires more preplanning.

The topics for presentational discussions tend to be primarily in content areas such as science or social studies, although some topics in literature are appropriate. One classroom had been doing a combination study of the stars and constellations: astronomy, astrology, and mythology. Each of the subgroups presented their information in panel discussions. This was the fact-finding part of their work reported orally; later, they extended the activity in many directions. Some went into writing fictitious horoscopes and various kinds of poetry. One group improvised a play about the Pleiades (the seven daughters of Atlas who were transformed into a cluster of stars according to Greek mythology). Another group improvised brief scenes in the lives of famous astronomers as they made their discoveries. One trio actually built a telescope and recorded changes in the positions of the stars. In spite of all the different activities that followed, all the children gained a basic knowledge of astronomy, astrology, and mythology from the original panel discussions.

Discussion Procedures

The purpose for the discussion, whatever kind it is, should be clear to you and to your students. If children have not had much experience with discussion groups, you should move them into these oral discussions slowly and with a considerable amount of structure. Give clear directions, have some sort of signal to use to stop the discussion if it becomes necessary, and put someone in charge of each group. If the discussion will involve children getting up and moving around to get materials, perhaps at first you will want to

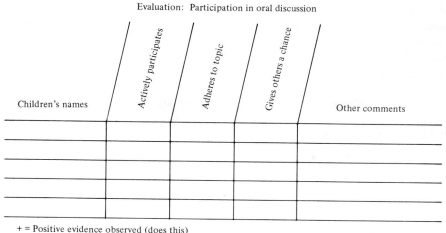

Evaluation: Participation in oral discussion

Children's names	Actively participates	Adheres to topic	Gives others a chance	Other comments

+ = Positive evidence observed (does this)
− = Negative evidence (does the opposite)

Figure 10   Evaluation of discussion.

assign one person from each group to be the messenger. Keep the early experiences with discussion rather simple with a clear-cut purpose and some guidelines which are discussed ahead of time. As children become more used to working in groups, less structuring is necessary and they can work on more complex or involved projects. Age is not as important a factor as being familiar with working in groups this way.

You may want to start with only one small group working on something jointly while the other children are involved in independent projects. This will leave you free to work with the discussion group and get things started. Then you can add a second group, and finally a third, fourth, or fifth—whatever seems appropriate for their interests and needs. It is important, though, that children's early experiences with discussion work well and that they feel good about the group work.

Students may want to set up their own evaluation of their group work, or you may want to set guidelines ahead of time and then comment on those that were followed and those that the children need to work on more the next time. These might include such things as: keeping on the topic, listening to others, giving everyone a chance to talk, and doing one's share to reach the group's goal. You might also decide not to evaluate a particular discussion session with your students. Usually, though, it is a good idea for the teacher to keep some record of the discussion session and how children participated in it. This might be done on a checklist basis with each child's name and labeled columns for their performance as in Figure 10. As you move about the room working with the discussion groups, you can make mental notes of children's contributions or responses. These can then be recorded on the checklist. You will not get a chance to check on each child each time, but over a period of time you can record several sessions for everyone.

REPORTING

Two typical forms of oral reporting are discussed here: informational reports and book reports. These very words seem to summon visions of children coming, one at a time, to the front of the room and reading a written report (some of which is probably copied directly from another source). Surely, there must be a better way. The description itself suggests three things to be avoided: standing up in front of the room, reading a written report, and putting down on paper another writer's words. Avoiding the possibility of children presenting reports orally in this way can make the reporting situation more appropriate and pleasant for children of elementary school age.

Informational Reports

Reporting may be done through a group presentation if children have worked on related informational reports. A panel discussion is less formidable to children than individual reports. If the report topics are not closely related and a group presentation seems unsuitable, there are other ways of helping children present interesting oral reports without reading a prewritten text.

One way to improve oral reporting is to show children how to take notes from the encyclopedia or from other reference materials using their own words. This is not a skill that develops independently without instruction. Note-taking skills can be taught by showing children short paragraphs of material on chart paper or an opaque projector. After they have had a chance to read the paragraph, remove it from their view and have them tell or write down one or two important ideas from the paragraph in their own words. These can be telegraphic in nature rather than written in full sentence form. Your students will need quite a few experiences like this with note-taking before they are ready to work with their own research materials. When they make that step, they will still need some help and supervision before they can work completely on their own. Children need to develop confidence in their own ability to take notes in their own words instead of relying on copying sentences or even whole paragraphs from other sources.

By changing the format of oral reports, the teacher can do a lot to improve the reporting situation. One effective way is to split the focus of attention from being entirely on the individual giving the oral report. One possibility is to have children prepare chart paper strips with each idea they are going to talk about on a single strip. These can then be pinned up one at a time as they give the report. This same idea can be accomplished by writing the main ideas on a transparency and using an overhead projector. It is reassuring for many children to think the audience is looking at the main ideas instead of at them. The information for the report can also be given in an interview-show technique. You can have your own class version of "The Today Show." To do this, children who are reporting will prepare three to six questions about the topic for someone else to ask them. They can rehearse their answers with the master of ceremonies who will interview the guests for the day's show. The element of role playing involved in this makes most children more comfortable. A third possibility for some topics is to have the children prepare slides, gather printed pictures to use with an opaque projector, or make their own illustrations to accompany their report. Children can talk about the pictures as they present information about their topic. Thus, the attention of the class is focused on the pictures—particularly when using a projector—instead of on the person giving the report. These are a few of the ways you can make children more at ease with oral reporting.

In evaluating children's oral reports, it is extremely important that the emphasis be on what the child says and not how it is said. The whole purpose of oral reporting is the giving or sharing of information; it is not oral language usage, projection of voice, and so on. Many teachers like to list (on the board or on a chart) reporting guidelines for children to consider while preparing their reports. If you choose to do this, keep the guidelines very simple and few in number. Too long a list will make anyone feel that there is no way to live up to such expectations. After the report you will no doubt want to make some evaluative comments. Keep in mind that every child needs to feel successful and good about the experience, and that your comments may serve as instruction for others. You can comment on one or two things that the child did well, and save any further suggestions for an individual conference. Think of evaluation as searching for value in what children do; after all, the word *value* is an inherent part of the word *evaluation*.

Sharing Books

This section is intentionally entitled "sharing books" instead of "book reports." Why? Because the term *book report* usually carries negative connotations. Did you ever have to write and turn in weekly book reports? And what was the purpose of all those book reports? To check to see if you had really read the book? Our intention here is to present ways that children can share their experiences with books and, at the same time, be motivated to continue their reading. Not every book the child reads has to be shared in some way. Just as adults sometimes read a book they don't find particularly meaningful or a book that is too close to them to want to share, so children should be able to choose what books they want to share.

There are a number of alternatives to formal oral book reports. Books may be shared orally in interesting ways, they may be dramatized, or they may be shared through art. Books may also be shared through enjoyable writing experiences, and you will find a discussion of these in Chapter Ten. Consider the following suggestions as examples of alternatives that you might use.

Through talking

1. Children who have read the same book or who have read books by the same author might discuss the books with each other and with you. This encourages both description and comparing or contrasting which are important cognitive skills.
2. Once in a while children might enjoy giving sales talks for their books. A sales talk should be finalized with some kind of decision which can be a simple vote, or it can be done by listing others in the class who want to read the book after the sales talk.
3. Children might like to tell the story or a part of it to some musical accompaniment of their choosing. This can involve using cut-out illustrations, drawings, or a flannel board.
4. Children can read orally a short scene from their book. They should practice this first so that the oral reading is prepared and smooth.
5. Older children might like to hold an interview with one of the characters in the book. The reader prepares the questions for someone else to ask and then impersonates the character in the book, answering the questions as the character would.
6. Children might enjoy preparing a talking bulletin board that will motivate others to read their book. Suppose four children have read *Harriet the Spy* and enjoyed it. They might work together

in making a display to show the main characters, a favorite scene or episode from the book, and so on. A brief dramatization following the content of the bulletin board would then be recorded on cassette tape.

Through drama Dramatic activities based on a book are an interesting and enjoyable way for children to share a book they have liked with others. Some possibilities for dramatizing are:

1. Make stick puppets to dramatize one scene from a favorite book. Children who have read the same book may share this, or one child can ask a friend to help with the presentation.
2. Children may pantomime characters from familiar stories they have read. This might include some simple costumes.
3. They might enjoy doing a television commercial for their book. This suggests less content of the book will be shared, but also that greater selection of ideas is required.
4. If the children have been reading books that are suitable for improvisation, a group who has read the same book might like to do some improvised scenes from the story. They would not

These students are preparing to dramatize a scene from one of their favorite books. (Photograph by Thomas England)

memorize any lines, but use their own words in the dramatization.

5. Children who have read two different books can work in pairs and do puppet dramas showing the two main characters meeting and talking. This is particularly effective if the two characters have something in common, that is, having lived in the same area at different times, having been president, or having fought in different wars.

Through art Art, as a creative medium, is appropriate for sharing responses to another creative medium. In working with art and literature, try to vary the media used. Crayons and manila paper get pretty tiring after a while and limit potential creativity. Think of painting, crayon engraving, color washes over crayon, chalk, modeling in clay and *papier maché*, collages, sculpture in soap or paraffin, dioramas, and printing using vegetables or corrugated cardboard. Some art work done on 9 × 12 inch paper is fine, but other times children need to work with very large sheets of paper. Let the children choose the materials they would like to use, or work with them to suggest various possibilities.

1. Children could make original illustrations for their story. This might be one illustration or a series of them.
2. They might make an original book jacket for their book.
3. They can create a cartoon strip of one special incident in their story.
4. Making a map or time line of events in historical fiction or biography can be an appropriate activity.
5. Children can make models or sculptures of characters or objects in the book. This idea can also be extended and children can create mobiles.

Whatever means you select to have children share their reading, keep in mind two important suggestions: the focus of the reporting activity should be on sharing and stimulating reading, and children should have a choice of how they want to share their book.

STORYTELLING

There is a very special quality in storytelling that is not present in other kinds of oral experiences. Reading aloud to children is important to language development and to increasing children's interest in literature and ways of using language in writing. Storytelling provides these same possibilities for development and offers a personal contact not present in reading aloud. The teacher as storyteller can focus attention on the children and immediately respond to their reactions. When reading a story, the teacher's attention is at least partially on the printed page. Storytelling is highly personal and intimate.

A teacher who has a number of stories tucked away and ready to tell is prepared for the kind of situations that seem to come up all too frequently. These are the times when a scheduled speaker is late or calls to cancel out at the last minute, when the bus is twenty minutes late picking your group up from a fieldtrip, or when you have two classes settled in your room to watch a special film and the projector breaks. Teachers who have several stories ready to tell do not need a book or any other equipment. They can entertain, instruct, and enchant a group of children on the spot.

Selecting material for storytelling depends mainly on two factors: a story should have a relatively simple plot and sequence of events and clear characterization, and the overall style or effect of the story should suit the personality of the teller. Because of the need for exciting but simple plot development and characterization, folktales are particularly suited for storytelling. Folktales were originally part of the oral tradition and served a number of functions, some of which are still appropriate. Some of the functions met by various kinds of folklore are those of education, social protest, escape from reality, and converting work into play. American folklore—as well as the folklore of other lands—offers a tremendous variety of materials to the teacher. There are myths, legends, fairy tales or märchen, and tall tales. A teacher with a soft voice and a quiet way of moving about might be more comfortable with one of the fairy tales or wonder tales rather than the swaggering tall tales. What you choose to tell should seem comfortable for you.

Because folklore was originally part of the oral tradition and was passed from storyteller to storyteller, there are numerous versions of many folktales. How a particular tale with the same basic features can occur in places apparently removed from each other is one of the unsolved mysteries of folklorists. For example, versions of *Puss in Boots* can be found in Sweden, Spain, Poland, the Dominican Republic, Greece, Turkey, India, the West Indies, Africa, and Indonesia. While the basic features of a folktale are similar, the details will vary quite widely. In an Italian version of 1502,[2] the *Puss in Boots* tale begins with the death of a very poor lady named Soriana who leaves her three sons only a kneading-trough, a rolling-board, and a cat. In a Greek version[3] it is a King who dies after losing all his wealth. He offers his three sons a choice of a golden strap and his curse or the cat and his blessing. The two elder sons, of course, take the strap and the curse, but the youngest son takes the cat and the blessing. In the French version,[4] which is more familiar to most Americans, it is a miller who dies and leaves only the mill, his ass, and his cat. The eldest takes the mill, the second the ass, and the youngest son is left with the cat. Although your introduction to the folktale may be in written form, you should feel perfectly comfortable changing any of the details of the tale to something more meaningful to the group you are telling the story to. You do not have to memorize the story, only the basic events and their order. Occasionally a story has a particular phrase that is "just right" for it that you will want to memorize. This is the case for most of us with, "Mirror, mirror on the wall, who's the fairest one of all?" from *Snow White and the Seven Dwarfs*.

Some advice from an expert storyteller is to strip away any pretenses of being good or exciting, and simply be yourself. If you try to recall the experience or story you are going to tell and get a vivid impression of it, you will find it much easier to tell. You don't have to tell every detail, but select one or two and let the audience fill in the rest.

Children in the upper elementary grades may also enjoy telling a favorite story. They may want to use a flannel board or shadow figures arranged and moved on an overhead projector to supplement their telling of the story. You can encourage them and help them be successful, but insisting on their doing it is probably counterproductive.

Some of the values in storytelling are so important that teachers should make the effort to become able to tell stories as well as to read them aloud. Perhaps the main value in storytelling is in developing children's desire to learn to read for themselves because through storytelling the teacher introduces them to many kinds of literature. Storytelling is one of the few kinds of talk done by the teacher that offers experiences with rich, complex, vivid language. This is especially important in developing complexity of language and acquiring a wide vocabulary. For children who speak a lower prestige dialect than the teacher, storytelling is an opportunity to expose these children to another more socially accepted dialect without interfering with communication between the teacher and the students and without suggesting that the children's own dialect and that of their home environment is unacceptable in any way. It is a way of exposing children to stories that are still too difficult for them to read on their own. This is particularly true in the upper elementary grades when the distance between what interests many children and their ability to read independently is very wide. Storytelling occupies a very special place in the realm of oral discourse and should be important in the elementary school classroom.

SUPPLEMENTAL ORAL LANGUAGE SKILLS

There are a number of other oral language activities that should be included in any elementary language arts program at some time, but which are not as basic as sharing, discussing, reporting, or storytelling. They include a wide range of proficiencies, such as oral directions, messages, interviews, and choral reading or speaking. Some may be such an integral part of other activities or of classroom management that they are not obvious to the teacher. This is perfectly all right, even desirable, as long as the children are given adequate help in developing the oral skills.

Making Announcements, Introductions, and Giving Messages

Children of all ages can participate in making announcements orally. In the early primary grades or with children who have had little experience, the announcements should be very brief. With more age and experience, teachers can expect competence with more complex and lengthy announcements. These can be worked into other content areas or into the regular classroom procedures. Children might report on the temperature or weather or something special about the day or week in the morning "opening exercises." Teachers who use a calendar might incorporate these facts with the month, date, and day of the week. This could be a rotating duty all during the year. Other teachers ask someone at each table or group to announce how many are buying lunch, how many are bringing lunch or ordering milk, and who is absent from their group. In an informal classroom where children help plan some of the activities, various children might announce special activities that they are planning and that others could share in. Teachers often make many announcements during the day that children in their classes could make, and children need the experience of making them.

Introductions are also part of classroom procedures. Appointing one child per week or per month to welcome visitors to the classroom and to introduce them to others is excellent practice. It also makes visitors feel welcome. Often children do not get any training at home about how to make an introduction, so you will need to teach or at least remind children how to do this graciously. Instead of instructing the whole class at once in an artificial situation, why not take the three or four children who are the first to be hosts and hostesses and work with them? Role playing is especially effective here. Perhaps you will want to provide signs on strings. In that way, the child who is playing the role of a parent can quickly slip on a sign saying *parent* and enter the room to be introduced to others. Other signs for principal, room mother, guest speaker, university observer, intern or student teacher, and so on, can be used. Role playing a situation before it actually happens makes it much easier for children; and using children who will actually need to do the introductions establishes a meaningful learning setting. Sometime during the year every child should have an opportunity to assume introduction responsibilities.

Giving accurate messages orally is an extremely important skill for every child. It requires careful listening and remembering, as well as the skill of relaying the information accurately. Pick up on any opportunities that occur to have children practice this skill. As with announcements, the first experiences with this that children have should be simple informational messages. If the information to be relayed is critical, you may want to send a written message along with a child who has had little practice. Every child needs the experience at some time, so be careful not to limit the privilege to only the more mature children in the group.

Giving Directions or Explanations

Anyone who has asked for directions at a service station or from someone walking by has at sometime thought the informant was deliberately making things difficult or even giving directions to another place. Giving directions is a highly skilled task which requires that persons giving the directions or explanations put themselves in the place of the person asking for help. This makes the task difficult for young children in the preoperational stage of development since their egocentric view of the world makes taking another point of view virtually impossible. They naturally assume that everyone understands by a word or statement just what they do. "Go this way until you get to Julia's house, and then turn." Experiences with young children at this stage of development should involve having them explain things by giving concrete demonstrations as they talk. Older children who are in the concrete operational stage of development have less difficulty taking another's point of view, but they still need practice in using a step-by-step explanation.

Some teachers have found it very helpful, when involving the whole class in a project that requires following directions carefully, to work with five or six children first so that they can execute the steps correctly. Then these children can assist others in their group or at their table by supplementing the teacher's directions or explanations. It certainly precludes the teacher being called on for help from every direction at once. Children should also be encouraged to take a leadership role in explaining things to other children. Older children may also work with directions when developing map reading skills. This kind of map work often starts by making a map of some familiar area. The children might then do some role playing in giving directions from one place to another on their map.

Using the Telephone

The telephone is such a vital part of our communications that even very young children should be taught to use it to obtain emergency assistance; and older children should be able to answer courteously, get the person asked for, take a message, or handle a wrong number. Many telephone companies provide a kit with working telephones that may be used in the classroom. If this is not available in your area, you can probably borrow a toy telephone from a student or a friend who has young children. Telephone courtesy can be handled in a learning center with a set of situation cards for older children or a tape-recorded problem for younger ones. Every child of school age should know how to call the fire and police departments and be able to give whatever information is necessary (name, address, telephone number, and the problem). If they cannot memorize the police number, they should know how to dial for the operator and explain what they want. In metropolitan areas, this means being able to ask for the correct city department that handles their area. Children need to learn not to tell strangers information about where their parents are or that they are alone in the house. Courtesy is certainly desirable, but safety is an absolute necessity. Using the telephone is not necessarily something that needs a full instructional unit each year, but teachers should verify that the children in their class can use the telephone for emergencies.

Choral Reading and Choral Speaking

Choral reading and speaking are very special oral language activities which are enjoyed by many children. Early experiences should involve very brief passages of material. If possible, the children involved should participate in choosing the selection they are to read or learn. You can easily identify a well-liked poem because the children will start to repeat part of it with you as you read or say it, and it will be the one they ask for over and over again. These early experiences should probably be done in unison to develop the idea of speaking in perfect time and rhythm. The important thing here is that children have some opportunity to respond to the poem and suggest ways of interpreting it. One poem that allows for a lot of unison work and illustrates the concept of choral reading or speaking is the old nursery rhyme, "One, Two." Have one half of the children say the first line of each verse or couplet, and the other half say the second line. Even nonreaders in kindergarten or first grade can say the first of the pair of lines.

NUMERICAL NURSERY RHYME[5]

One, two,
Buckle my shoe;
Three, four,
Shut the door;
Five, six,
Pick up sticks;
Seven, eight,
Lay them straight;
Nine, ten,
A good fat hen;
Eleven, twelve,
Let us delve;
Thirteen, fourteen,
Maids a-courting;
Fifteen, sixteen,
Maids in the kitchen;
Seventeen, eighteen,
Maids a-waiting;
Nineteen, twenty,
My stomach's empty.
Please, Mother,
Give me something to eat.

Another poem that is suitable for reading and which does not involve a lot of difficult words is "There Was an Old Woman."[6]

THERE WAS AN OLD WOMAN

There was an old woman who swallowed a fly;
I wonder why
She swallowed a fly.
Poor old woman, she's sure to die.

There was an old woman who swallowed a spider;
That wriggled and jiggled and wriggled inside her;
She swallowed the spider to catch the fly,
I wonder why
She swallowed a fly.
Poor old woman, she's sure to die.

There was an old woman who swallowed a bird;
How absurd
To swallow a bird.
She swallowed the bird to catch the spider,
That wriggled and jiggled and wriggled inside her.
She swallowed the spider to catch the fly,
I wonder why
She swallowed a fly.
Poor old woman, she's sure to die.

There was an old woman who swallowed a cat;
Fancy that!
She swallowed a cat;
She swallowed the cat to catch the bird,
She swallowed the bird to catch the spider,
That wriggled and jiggled and wriggled inside her.
She swallowed the spider to catch the fly,
I wonder why
She swallowed a fly.
Poor old woman, she's sure to die.

There was an old woman who swallowed a dog;
She went the whole hog
And swallowed a dog;
She swallowed the dog to catch the cat,
She swallowed the cat to catch the bird,
She swallowed the bird to catch the spider,
That wriggled and jiggled and wriggled inside her.
She swallowed the spider to catch the fly,
I wonder why
She swallowed a fly.
Poor old woman, she's sure to die.

There was an old woman who swallowed a cow;
I wonder how
She swallowed a cow;
She swallowed the cow to catch the dog,
She swallowed the dog to catch the cat,
She swallowed the cat to catch the bird,
She swallowed the bird to catch the spider,
That wriggled and jiggled and wriggled inside her.
She swallowed the spider to catch the fly,
I wonder why
She swallowed a fly.
Poor old woman, she's sure to die.

There was an old woman who swallowed a horse;
She died of course!

Traditional American and English

Two poems that work well with a chorus and a single voice for inexperienced children in any of the elementary grades are "Speaking of Cows" by Kaye Starbird and "June" by Aileen Fisher. In the first, the solo voice can read the second line—the one in parentheses, while the other lines are read in unison.

SPEAKING OF COWS

Speaking of cows
(Which no one was doing)
Why are they always
Staring and chewing?
Staring at people,
Chewing at clover,
Doing the same things
Over and over?

Kaye Starbird[7]

In "June" the solo voice or solo voices can say the lines indicated while a larger group says the unison parts.

JUNE

	The day is warm
	and a breeze is blowing,
Unison	*the sky is blue*
	and its eye is glowing,
	and everything's new
	and green and growing . . . .
Solo	*My shoes are off*
	and my socks are showing . . . .
Solo	*My socks are off . . . .*
Solo	*Do you know how I'm going?*
Unison	*BAREFOOT!*

Aileen Fisher[8]

John Ciardi has written a poem that simply cries out for some large group participation. It is a perfect example of a poem that can be used for choral reading in front of an audience of other children. It allows the audience to participate in the reading by filling in the missing words.

SUMMER SONG

By the sand between my toes,
By the waves behind my ears,
By the sunburn on my nose,
By the little salty tears
That make rainbows in the sun
When I squeeze my eyes and run,
By the way the seagulls screech,
Guess where I am? At the . . . . . !
By the way the children shout
Guess what happened? School is . . . . !
By the way I sing this song
Guess if summer lasts too long:
You must answer Right or . . . . . !

John Ciardi[9]

With older children, the poetry you read to them and the poetry they select to read chorally may be considerably more complex. You might use one of the following poems as an introduction and then let them choose and arrange the readings themselves. The process of doing choral reading or speaking is important; the end result is really not important as long as it pleases the children. The last two lines of each stanza of "This Old Hammer" make it especially appealing for choral reading.

THIS OLD HAMMER

This old hammer
Shine like silver,
Shine like gold, boys,
Shine like gold.

Well don't you hear that
Hammer ringing?
Drivin' in steel, boys,
Drivin' in steel.

Can't find a hammer
On this old mountain.
Rings like mine, boys,
Rings like mine.

I've been working
On this old mountain
Seven long years, boys,
Seven long years.

I'm going back to
Swannanoa Town-o,
That's my home, boys,
That's my home.

Take this hammer,
Give it to the captain,
Tell him I'm gone, boys,
Tell him I'm gone.

Traditional American

Another poem with sound appeal is "The Ballad of Red Fox."[11]

THE BALLAD OF RED FOX

Yellow sun yellow
Sun yellow sun,
When, oh, when
Will red fox run?

When the hollow horn shall sound,
When the hunter lifts his gun
And liberates the wicked hound,
Then, oh, then shall red fox run.

Yellow sun yellow
Sun yellow sun,
Where, oh, where
Will red fox run?

Through meadows hot as sulphur,
Through forests cool as clay,
Through hedges crisp as morning
And grasses limp as day.

Yellow sky yellow
Sky yellow sky,
How, oh, how
Will red fox die?

With a bullet in his belly,
A dagger in his eye,
And blood upon his red red brush
Shall red fox die.

Melvin Walker La Follette

Choral reading or speaking is one way of enhancing children's responses to poetry and this should be the prime concern of the teacher. A rich exposure to poetry of all kinds serves as a basis for enjoyment. However, today's children seem particularly fond of some of the newer poetry that uses modern language and content. The real learning and enjoyment in choral activities depends upon the children being involved in interpreting the poem through using low and high voices, soft and loud passages, and unison speaking contrasted with solo voices. The whole effect may not be as polished as one arranged by the teacher, but the learning involved will be considerably greater.

Other Oral Language Skills

Some of the other oral skills that may become part of the classroom activities are particularly appropriate for upper elementary age children. These skills include conducting meetings or group discussions, using simple parliamentary procedures, making oral reviews of movies or television programs, and interviewing others. Many of them can be easily integrated with other content areas, but some-time during the upper elementary school years the children should have experiences with each.

PRELIMINARY LEARNING ACTIVITIES

1. Suggest three questions for each of the following situations that you believe would generate responses from children in a sharing discussion.
   (a) Tommy has brought his collection of eight to ten arrow-heads to share.
   (b) Susan has her collection of postcards from around the United States to share.
   (c) Kim has examples of several kinds of homemade candles.
   Some possible questions that might be asked are included at the end of this section. Check your questions to see what the answer might be. If they can be answered in a few words, try again.
2. Read three to five children's trade books and suggest a different way to share each through writing, talking, drama, or art. (You may refer to the section on "Sharing Books.")
3. Find a group of people and try doing some choral reading your-self. Use one of the poems from this text that has suggestions for ways to read it, and then select another of your own choosing.
4. Collect ten to fifteen poems that would be suitable for choral reading for the grade and age level with which you want to work. Print or type these on cards.

PARTICIPATION ACTIVITIES

1. Record several children participating in a discussion using the chart on page 155 in the section on "Discussion Procedures."
2. Prepare and tell a story to a small group of children. You might select a folktale or another story you particularly like.
3. Conduct a discussion with a group of children on some experi-ence they have had. Get someone else to record or check off your use of strategies to encourage interaction and participation. If

you prefer, you could tape-record the discussion and do your own analysis later. Look at the questions you ask, the time intervals left before going on to something new, and so on.

Answers to Preliminary Learning Experience, Activity 1

Tommy's arrowhead collection:
How can you tell a real arrowhead from a piece of rock that is accidentally shaped with sharp edges?
Where are the best places for finding arrowheads?
If prehistoric hunters had lived in an area where there were no rocks, what might they have used for spear or arrow tips?

Susan's collection of postcards from the United States:
Which place shown on your postcards would you most like to visit?
Which postcard picture do you think would be most interesting or even surprising to a visitor from another planet?
What reasons can you give for collecting postcards as a hobby?

Kim's group of homemade candles:
What do you do to make candles?
How do you make the candles look so different?
What safety rules do you need to follow in making them?

REFERENCES

[1] Roger Cunningham. "Developing Question-Asking Skills" IN *Developing Teacher Competencies* (James Weigand, ed.). Englewood Cliffs, New Jersey: Prentice-Hall, 1971.

[2] Thomas F. Crane, *Italian Popular Tales*. Boston: Houghton Mifflin, 1885, p. 348.

[3] Laurits Bodker, Christina Hale, G. D'Aronco (eds.). *European Folk Tales*. Hatboro, Pennsylvania: Folklore Associates, 1963, p. 197.

[4] Jacques Barchilon and Henry Pettit. *The Authentic Mother Goose Fairy Tales and Nursery Rhymes*. Denver: Alan Swallow, 1960, p. 59.

[5] Josephine Bouton (comp.). "One, Two," *Poems for the Children's Hour*. Garden City, New York: Garden City, 1927, p. 3.

[6] Traditional American. "There Was an Old Woman" IN *Junior Voices, The First Book* (Geoffrey Summerfield, ed.). London: Penguin, 1970, p. 24.

[7] Kaye Starbird. "Speaking of Cows," *Speaking of Cows*. Philadelphia: Lippincott, 1960.

[8] Aileen Fisher. "June," *Going Barefoot*. New York: Thomas Y. Crowell, 1960.

[9] John Ciardi. "Summer Song," *The Man Who Sang the Sillies*. Philadelphia: Lippincott, 1961.

[10] Traditional. "This Old Hammer" IN *Junior Voices, The First Book* (Geoffrey Summerfield, ed.). London: Penguin, 1970, p. 42.

[11] Melvin Walker La Follette. "The Ballad of Red Fox" IN *Junior Voices, The Second Book* (Geoffrey Summerfield, ed.). London: Penguin, 1970, p. 55.

CHAPTER NINE

Dramatic Expression

PREVIEW QUESTIONS

1 Why is dramatic expression preferable to doing a play?

2 How can a teacher get children involved in dramatic activities?

3 How do you select or plan motivational activities as well as major dramatic activities to extend children's understanding of concepts or of literary works?

4 In what ways can dramatic expression be evaluated?

After hearing their teacher read *Mr. Miacca,* Evaline Ness's version of an old English folktale, a group of children decided to dramatize the story—improvising the lines and scenes as they went along. In their first scene, Mrs. Grimes warns her son Tommy.

MG: "Now, Tommy Grimes, I've told you before and this is the last time I'm going to tell you. Don't go away from home. Mr. Miacca catches bad boys, and he'll get you and eat you!"

T: "Sure, Mom. I'll stay right here."

Unfortunately Tommy doesn't remember his mother's warning and he "goes round the corner" and is caught by Mr. Miacca. When they get back to the Miacca's house, Mr. Miacca finds he doesn't have any herbs to cook along with Tommy so he entrusts Tommy to his wife while he goes out shopping. The scene with Tommy and Mrs. Miacca:

T: "Mrs. Miacca, don't you ever eat anything but boys? Don't you have *anything* else?"

MM: "No. Most of the time it's just boys. But I do like pudding, and I don't get that very often."

T: "Say! My mom's making a pudding this morning. She'd let me give you some. Why don't I go and get some for you?"

MM: "Well . . . . O.K., but be sure to be back for dinner, or Mr. Miacca'll be real mad at me."

The lines in these improvised scenes are not memorized or rehearsed. There were not any costumes or props except for a dowel rod the children used for the leg of the sofa that Tommy stuck out to be chopped off instead of his own leg. There wasn't an audience either, except for some of the other children in the room who took these parts in another scene or in recreating the same scenes. The children never performed the "play" for others; they simply enjoyed doing their own dramatized version of the story.

The authors of the stories that the children choose to dramatize might well flinch at what has happened to their carefully chosen words, but they can not help but react favorably to the children's enthusiastic responses to their books. This form of dramatic expression permits children to respond to a book that they love in a most meaningful way. In the enactment of the story they are developing language skills—listening and speaking—as well as cognitive, affective, and psychomotor skills.

This is dramatic expression, not theater. Drama in the elementary school is a way of exploring the world and oneself. It may be based on a story or simply on a situation. Each "performer" will do the same part differently—as he or she sees it, as experience suggests. The *doing* of the play or the scene is the important part. It does not need an audience; in fact, an audience usually inhibits children. It does not require practicing to "get it right" because there is no right way. Sometimes a suggestion of a costume or a prop will help children feel the character, but an old terrycloth towel will do for the wolf's furry back, a paper crown will do for Max as he sails to "Where the Wild Things Are," or a yardstick will do for the fishing pole Tom Sawyer uses while rafting downriver. The learning and fun come from participating and not from the applause of an audience. "Theater concerns performances before an audience, whose point of view is included and for whose benefit effects are calculated. Theater is a secondary effect of drama, an outgrowth appropriate only much later, after elementary school."[1]

FORCES ENCOURAGING DRAMATIC EXPRESSION

It is difficult to single out one factor that has changed the educational scene. Although an individual or a group may initiate a new program or a new emphasis, the "climate" must be ready to receive it. The climate was receptive in 1966 (after a period of emphasis on the scientific and the technological) for a more individualistic and humanistic influence. That was the year of the Anglo-American Conference on English Teaching at Dartmouth College, New Hampshire. The British participants had already become deeply involved with drama in the classroom in the process of academic desegregation. This same emphasis on drama existed at a second international conference at York, England in 1971 where participants from Great Britain, Canada, and the United States met to continue the dialog on English teaching. Reports from these conferences suggest a number of bases for renewed interest in dramatic expression.

Emphasis on Creativity

As we begin to accept diversity in lifestyle and values, it becomes more important for children to explore a variety of responses to their environment. In society today there is a wide range of attitudes, opinions, and values; some of these contradict one another. Children must learn to cope with these contradictions and even recognize and communicate their own diversity. They must find what is uniquely personal, what their potential is, and where they stand. Language arts teachers are becoming more interested in imaginative writing—in all areas of written composition—where there is an opportunity for original thought and expression. Dramatic activities in the classroom offer a comparable avenue for original and individual oral expression. Dramatizing offers the possibility of trying out attitudes, roles, and emotions and creating new possibilities for ourselves without real risk.

Emphasis on Oral Modes

School used to be a place for developing reading and writing skills (along with arithmetic) rather than oral skills. Information from the cognitive psychologists clearly suggests that children need to be active in the learning process, that children of elementary school age who are in the preoperational or concrete operational stages do not learn by merely reading about things, but from doing them and from talking about them. We also know from the language learning process that children need to use language in a variety of ways. Research on the amount of time most adults are involved in oral speaking and listening suggests that writing is not the prime communication channel in terms of functional use. Dramatics offers meaningful practice in both listening and speaking. One must listen to what the other person says in order to respond appropriately. What one says must be clear and meaningful so that someone else can reply. In addition, dramatic expression offers the "intellectual challenge of finding language true to one's subjective experience."[2] The need for developing children's ability to use language orally in an effective way leads directly to increased use of dramatic activities in elementary classrooms.

Interdependence of Language-Based Arts

Language, and especially oral language, is an inseparable part of the entire language arts program. It is the basis for literature, for writing, and for vocabulary and thought development. Literature provides a special way of helping children interact with their surroundings and with others. Through literature children can discover that books offer special satisfaction. "Part of the satisfaction comes from the knowledge, the information, available through literature. This knowledge is not the same as that on the reference shelf; literature is not factual as an encyclopedia article is factual. . . . Literature is concerned with why things happen, on the motivations of man."[3]

One of the ways of helping children respond more deeply to a piece of literature is through dramatizing it. In that process, the child moves one step closer to experiencing life in another time, another place, another situation. In the active oral response to the book children come closer to its view of reality. They are in on the "doing" and are no longer passive receivers. They use the language of the book and make it their own.

Dramatizing stories or situations is an important factor in developing skill in using written language. Dixon asserts that "the neglect of talk and drama has had disastrous effects on writing."[4] Children write best from their own experience just as adults do. Their direct firsthand experience is limited, and they need additional input. Experiences with drama which place children in new situations are a rich source of material for writing. In writing stories of their own, characterization is richer for having experienced other people's ideas and personalities; setting or environment is more vivid from insight into other situations; plot is better developed from observing the patterns of events.

Language and thought are advanced through dramatizing. Moffett notes that "dramatic interaction [is] . . . the primary vehicle for developing thought and language."[5] Complex cognitive skills are involved in the process of selecting, interpreting, and arranging the material from which the dramatization evolves. Whether the children are working from a piece of literature or from a particular situation, they must choose the relevant and meaningful parts and arrange them so they are significant. They must select words that carry this significance—words from the book or those directly related to the situation. The more familiar one is with a word and the more importance it assumes, the deeper and richer is its meaning.

These three forces—emphasis on creativity, emphasis on oral modes, and interdependence of the language-based arts—point to the necessity for developing dramatic interaction and expression in elementary classrooms. As we come to know more about how children learn, we find more need for active involvement and experience. Participating in dramatizing events, problems, situations, and stories is a uniquely appropriate way of providing this active involvement and experience.

LEVELS OF DRAMATIC EXPRESSION

There are two major levels of drama, the exploratory level and the performance level. In the exploratory level children can examine a variety of roles and possible situations. They can put on high heels or a racing helmet, jump into their car or plane, and zoom off alone or with some friends. At a later stage they can test their courage as they face a hostile band of Martians or join in the gold rush in California as they pan for gold at Sutter's Creek. At this level there is constant interplay between investigating and representing, finding out and trying on. It doesn't matter if someone else is there; there is not any real attempt to communicate to anyone outside those participating. There is no sense of audience, no need to communicate with the audience. Exploring ideas and feelings and situations is all-important.

At the performance level in drama the players have gone through the exploring and are now trying to communicate with and to others their sense of the experience. Exact words become more important as they must express ideas and findings; certainly other information must be communicated to the audience so they can know what is happening. The "play" is formalized and structured—rehearsed for effects. The values in it shift from the players to the audience. Only the skilled performers participate. It becomes theater. The discovery and the exploration are over as the play is set. It is no longer a learning process, but has become a demonstration of specific sophisticated communicative skills.

FORMS OF DRAMATIC ACTIVITIES

Although there is no set sequence of dramatic activities that must be followed, there is usually a general progression from whole-group simultaneous participation to part of the group participating while others wait for their turn and are an "audience," to doing scenes for the class or some other small audience. Dramatic expression may take one or more of several forms: dramatic play, movement, pantomime, improvisation, scenes, and puppetry.

Dramatic Play

Dramatic play is most often seen in the early childhood years either at home or in the nursery school or kindergarten. Opportunities for this kind of experience should be offered to children in the primary grades—particularly in areas where children have had little opportunity for this kind of play. Dramatic play involves playing out situations and taking roles. Children may play doctor, house, grocery store, and so on. It is highly informal and not teacher directed, although a teacher may intervene briefly to reinvolve a child or to suggest a possibility that may continue the play. All that is needed is some space in the corner of the room and a few simple props or materials for costumes. In this kind of experience children learn to work with others to make the play more fun. They also have an opportunity to explore what roles various adults take and, in a very special sense, how it feels to be that adult.

Movement

This involves developing body-awareness as well as exploring differing ways of moving and expressing ideas through movement. It might be considered the forerunner of pantomime, although it is not as stylized. Children work on rhythm and moving to rhythms. They also learn about moving in various ways such as jumping, rolling, twirling, or gliding. An interesting book that may involve children in movement activities is *The Way the Tiger Walked* by Chaconas.[6] In this, a porcupine, zebra, and elephant admire the tiger and try to walk the way he does. And so the porcupine walks with a waddle and a bump, waddle-bump; the zebra with a clatter and a stomp, clatter-stomp; and the elephant with a rumble and a sway, rumble-sway.

Poetry, as well as prose, is a good source for experiences with movement. The spaghetti in "A Round" almost demands action as it "wriggles."

A ROUND[7]

Spaghetti,
spaghetti,
heaped in a mound;
spaghetti,
spaghetti,
winds and winds around;
spaghetti,
spaghetti,
twists and turns and bends;
spaghetti,
spaghetti,
hasn't any ends;

DRAMATIC EXPRESSION

spaghetti,
spaghetti,
slips and dips and trips;
spaghetti,
spaghetti,
sloops and droops;
spaghetti,
spaghetti,
comes in groups;
spaghetti,
spaghetti,
no exit can be found. . . . . .

Eve Merriam

Children can also develop skill in kinesics as they show through body actions and facial expressions various activities or feelings.

Pantomime

Pantomime is an outgrowth of movement although it is somewhat more formal. It involves postures and facial expression as well as body movement to communicate an idea without using words. Very young children have a great deal of difficulty refraining from using language as well as mime to express themselves, but older children often enjoy the challenge—especially if it can be done in a game situation at first. The class might be divided into small groups with each group selecting an action for their group (riding a bike, climbing a ladder, and so on) and a way of doing something (quickly, cautiously, intensely, and so on) to pass on to another group. The object of the game is to recognize the action and guess the -*ly* word they are demonstrating. Whole scenes may also be pantomimed with or without a spoken narration.

Improvisation

Improvisation is probably the central activity in dramatic expression for elementary school age children. It involves acting out events or situations without using a script and without rehearsing. It is an on-the-spot impromptu version of the events or the situation. Improvisations may be based on a familiar story or simply on a particular situation. Body actions and language are both used to carry meaning.

Scenes

Dramatized scenes are an extension of improvisation, involve some planning, and usually are more extensive in length. For elementary school children they are not planned to the point of becoming a set situation. Children should be free to use their own language and present their own arguments or reasons. The scenes are not show pieces; they still retain the flexibility and fluidity of an improvisation. The scenes may be based on a story that the children are familiar with or they may explore a concept or situation.

One group of fifth-graders who had been studying ecology did a dramatization of a concept. Their teacher set up the problem: a large manufacturing company has purchased several hundred acres of land in their area and wants to build a factory. Company representatives will meet with interested citizens to discuss the matter. Some children are school board members, some real estate developers, some represent homeowners groups, and so on. After choosing roles, the children spent a few days doing some research on the problem; then the town meeting was held. This dramatized scene involved the children in taking a wide variety of community roles as they created the various characters they portrayed. The preparation for the drama involved the children in meaningful research activities. The dramatization itself served as a good evaluation for the teacher in examining the students' knowledge about ecology as it was presented in their arguments for or against building the factory.

Puppets and Masks

Puppets and masks of various kinds are fun for children of all elementary school ages. In the earlier grades because of their egocentricity, the children working the puppets will sometimes speak as well as the puppets, but this in no way diminishes the fun or the learning for them. In the upper grades the shyer, more self-conscious children may find working with masks or puppets more comfortable. The teacher may want to provide some basic puppets which can be transformed into the characters needed, or the children can actually make the puppets they need. Facial masks can also be used. Another possibility is the "body mask" made from a

Children enjoy using puppets to dramatize favorite stories. (*Photograph by Charles Jones*)

A few teacher-made masks can be a starting point for children's dramatizations. Later they make their own, creating the necessary characters. (*Photograph by Charles Jones*)

large sheet of posterboard or a carton with cutouts for the face and arms—like the old-fashioned scenery boards for funny photographs at the beach. In any case, the puppets and masks do not have to be aesthetically beautiful. A simple cutout figure mounted on a stick or a stuffed paper bag will do as well as a complex *papier-maché* creation. A large refrigerator box with a cutout area will do per-

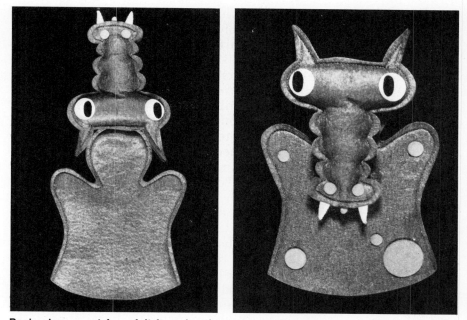

Basic shapes cut from felt for a hand puppet can be transformed into works of art. Children select from a variety of scrap pieces, then cut and stitch or paste them to create their own animal puppets. (*Photograph by Charles Jones*)

fectly well for a stage. The children should be involved in the planning and making. This is more important in the learning that comes from puppetry than having a professional looking stage or fancy puppets.

INITIATING DRAMATIC EXPRESSION

There are no hard and fast rules to follow that will guarantee success as you begin working with drama, but there are some general guidelines that should help you work effectively. The activities at the end of this chapter also provide specific examples of how to plan a story drama.

First of all, select stimuli for dramatizing—whether stories or situations—that have appeal for both you and your children. You should be genuinely enthusiastic, for your enthusiasm will be conveyed to your students. Heathcote, who has done extensive work in improvisational drama, speaks of the need to arrest students' attention.[8] She insists that drama should not be watered-down; it should not be fairies and flowers prancing around in leotards, but real situations and real problems to solve.

A second guideline is to start small. Begin with something simple, not a whole-class improvisation of an epic. In the primary grades, this might be some movement to music or very brief improvisations of scenes from a favorite book you have read to your class, or perhaps pantomimes similar to charades of events in the unit of stories they have just finished. In the upper elementary grades, you might start with improvisations of one or two favorite scenes from a book, or pantomimed actions and feelings described earlier in the section on pantomime, or stick-puppet scenes of the most exciting part of the library book they have read (instead of a book report). Be sensitive to what the children are comfortable doing, and try to make these early experiences a successful, satisfying contact with drama.

A third guideline is that you should do extensive planning of the dramatization even though what the children do will be spontaneous. Unless you have a great deal of experience with the theater and with dramatization, you need to do some careful planning to make the experience work for your students. You need to consider what arrangement of furniture in the room will be best, what warm-up or motivational activities might prepare them and make them more comfortable, what extra materials you may need such as music, fabric pieces for costumes, paper, sticks and paint for puppets. If you plan to have your students dramatize a story, you should analyze the story carefully as to possible scenes, characters, movement patterns, and appropriate motivational techniques. If you are working with the whole class in the story dramatization, consider how you can give each child an opportunity to have a part and participate in the dramatization. Selecting a story with a large cast, adding characters or scenes to stories with small casts, or repeating a scene two or three times with a new cast of characters each time would solve this problem. Although you would not take children through all of this process, you need to do it yourself. Even though the children may take a somewhat different direction than you expected, your plans can be adjusted and modified as you go along. The thinking-through that you experienced while planning will help you adapt to their ideas; when they need direction, you can be confident that you will be able to provide it.

Role Playing Experiences

Role playing familiar experiences is an ideal starting point for young children. It is one way that they can get to verbalize what has happened to them and to find out that some children have shared similar events while others have had quite different experiences. Family customs to the very young appear to be universal experiences, and at first it will be hard for them to believe that others do things differently. The role playing may begin with something that just happens in the classroom, or it may evolve from a discussion of a story or a picture.

Some situations which lend themselves to this kind of role playing with young children are birthday celebrations, going shopping, going out to a restaurant to eat, getting ready for Thanksgiving or Christmas, buying a new pair of shoes, having a new babysitter, meeting someone new who's moved into the neighborhood, planting a garden, and so on. The children should have experienced the situation themselves and the role playing should result from their familiarity with it. The role playing will probably need to be done in small groups since young children all want to participate at once in the dramatizing. The teacher may guide them by asking questions or proposing variations or complications to extend the dramatization.

With older children the situation for role playing should be somewhat familiar, but it need not evolve from firsthand experience. Some situations that might be appropriate for role playing in the upper elementary grades could develop from unfinished problem stories or from situations that they might face some time. The role playing could be such things as returning merchandise to a store, working in an office, selling products door to door, taking a job as a babysitter, taking a driver's license examination, or flying in a plane during an emergency. The role playing will need some discussion of the possible situation first, and again the teacher may intervene to guide the experience or extend it. There should be some problem involved in the role playing that needs resolution and that might be resolved in several ways. For example, if the group were doing something about a babysitting job, perhaps one of the children gets very ill or there are warnings of a tornado on the television or some friends drop in for a visit and break something. This is no time for preaching morals; it is a time for students to discover what alternatives there are in a situation and what the consequences of taking a particular alternative are. It is a way of exploring danger and reality in a safe situation.

Dramatizing Literature

Story dramatization is an exciting way to develop children's skill in exploring new ideas and at the same time reinforce and enhance the impact of a particular book or story. The first dramatizations you do may just be of one scene in the story that particularly interests your class, or some movement or pantomime related to something in the book. Think back through the general guidelines given at the beginning of this section on initiating dramatic expression and select something that appeals to both you and your class, start with something small, and do some extensive planning before you start to work with the children.

When you do get ready to dramatize the whole story, you still will need to do some motivational or warm-up experiences before the children are involved enough to lose themselves in the dramatization. These warm-up activities may involve heightening the children's awareness of the sensory environment through discussion: *Close your eyes. You are sitting on the bridge the three billy goats will cross. Reach down and feel the bridge. What is it like?* (wood, concrete, cool in the shade, warm in the sun). *What things can you hear?* (water running over the stones, boughs of trees scraping the bridge railings, a bullfrog down below). *What things can you smell?* (sweet grasses in the field nearby, apple blossoms, clover). It might involve pantomiming actions that will come in the dramatization or ones related to those in the story: *Without saying anything, see if you can be the smallest goat. How would you walk? How would you run? Now be the biggest billy goat! You are big and heavy. Your feet really clomp down.* The warm-up activities might include some dialog—or perhaps monolog. *Be the troll. Say what you would to the littlest billy goat.* Then move into pairs and one partner take the troll's part and one take the smallest billy goat gruff. *Now switch parts. The one who was the billy goat is now the troll, and the troll is now the biggest billy goat. Say what you think they should say.* These warm-up activities might involve moving to music or to a particular rhythm, developing the sensory environment, pantomime, monolog, or working on dialog with a partner. The extensiveness of the warm-up depends on the particular group of children and how easily they become involved in the dramatization. The warm-up activities need to be carefully thought out by you, the teacher, so that they build the children's self-confidence and prepare them for participation in the story dramatization itself.

Dramatizing Concepts

Rather than building a dramatization on a familiar story, you may choose to dramatize an idea within a situational context. One illustration of this was mentioned earlier in the chapter in which a class dramatized a problem in ecology. This kind of dramatization correlates very well with social studies.

A series of these dramatizations involving the whole class or a group within the class may explore universal themes. "Daring to Face the Unknown" might involve a dramatization of a Roman centurian off to face the fierce Pictish tribes in Great Britain or Columbus on his first voyage to America or a pioneer family crossing the United States to California in a covered wagon. "Decisions" might range from a contemporary of Louis XIV not wanting to participate in revolutionary activities, to Robert E. Lee resigning his commission in the U.S. Army to fight with the Virginia Militia, to someone in the late 1960s deciding not to accept his draft notice during the Vietnamese fighting.

The dramatization of the concept should present some sort of conflict that must be resolved. Although the children may need to search out some information on the topic, their speeches or lines are not planned. And if the dramatization is repeated with another group of children, a different argument may be presented. A minor character one time may become a major character another time. The drama may or may not be repeated depending upon the children's interest and enthusiasm.

As an early experience with drama, this kind of dramatization may be a bit overwhelming for both students and teachers. For most teachers it is more successful after the children have had some other experiences with dramatic expression of various kinds and feel more comfortable with the less structured situation.

CRITERIA OF DRAMATIC EXPRESSION

There are three major criteria of dramatic expression that the teacher can use as a general guideline in working with children: concentration, interchange, and involvement. These are key elements in the success of a dramatic experience.

Concentration

Children must be able to stay within the confines of the drama and not break out of the situation. They should feel as though the situation is real and they are the actual character being portrayed. They need to persist in continuing the dramatic experience. Concentration implies an intensification of feeling and a focus on the task at hand. The following questions may help you evaluate their concentration:

Are the students reacting to the drama as if it were real?
Can they continue the dramatization and extend it beyond a superficial level?
Are they beyond the point where minor distractions will interfere with the drama?

You will never be successful with drama if you permit some children to interfere with another child's interpretation of a role or situation. Laughing at someone will not only affect that person, but it will make everyone else reluctant to participate if they know they may be ridiculed. When this first happens, the teacher must firmly, but not punitively, stop the laughter.

Interchange

Drama cannot be a solitary experience. Dramatic expression in the classroom involves many children—whether a whole class or just a group of children. The participants in the drama must respond to each other in a meaningful way. This means cooperation is one of the key concerns of the teacher. As the children interact with each other, they participate mutually in the experience. In the interchange process they come to explore how they react in certain situations and how they respond to others. The verbalizing that goes on in the drama absolutely requires good listening and speaking skills. Since there is no script, there is nothing to fall back on. One must express ideas clearly and listen to what others say. It is at this point that listening and speaking skills develop. To evaluate interchange, these questions may assist you:

Are students working together in the dramatization, or is it one idea versus another?
Do the children listen to others and respond to what they have said?
Does one child pick up on what another has said and repeat or extend the idea?

The teacher may choose to intervene in a dramatization to clue children into an effective idea. This may be done by taking a role within the dramatization for a moment, or simply by making a quick suggestion. It is also possible to wait until the scene is finished, and then discuss a variety of ideas. Children may even decide to exchange parts and replay the scene.

Involvement

This is probably the keystone of all experiences with dramatic expression. If children are not really involved and committed to what they are doing, the whole experience becomes unreal. Dramatizing should provide a real learning experience for students. Dramatizing should not be just playing at being someone, it should be actually becoming that person. Of course it should be a pleasurable experience, but it should be more than just fun. Professional actors cannot really become this involved in a performance, because they must be concerned about conveying feelings to the audience. Children in classroom dramatizations do not have to worry about conveying feelings to an audience. The drama is done for their sake, not for someone else's sake. These questions should help you evaluate children's involvement:

Do you see changes which fit the character each child is playing or do the children retain their own personality and way of doing things?
Is there the quality of intensity, of becoming someone else, present during the dramatization?

If you continually find that quality of involvement lacking in the children's dramatic expression, it may be that the situation they're dramatizing does not seem right for them. Perhaps you are choosing stories or situations that are too superficial. It may also be that a particular group needs more motivational or warm-up activities before getting into the drama. Go back to basics and start doing some shorter, simpler dramatizations. Perhaps adding some costuming or props will help children become more involved. Try a different time of day or try working in smaller groups. Like so many other worthwhile educational experiences, dramatic expression is not easy and there is no simple formula for success.

SKILLS DEVELOPED IN DRAMATICS

Although dramatizing stories or concepts is usually an enjoyable activity for children, this is not the primary reason for including dramatics in the language arts program in elementary schools. Drama has a potential for developing language ability that is not paralleled by any other single language arts activity. It also offers possibilities for developing more general skills in the cognitive, affective, and psychomotor domains that few other activities possess.

Language Skills

One of the two main implications for teaching to come from the psycholinguistic theory of how children develop language is that they must need to use language in a variety of ways. Dramatizing stories or situations calls for just this kind of language use. Children must find language that is true to the character and to the situation they are playing. Through playing a variety of roles, students should experience the language that a variety of people would use. Their language in the dramatization becomes a creative oral composition. Even when the situation being dramatized comes from a story or book that they have heard or read, the language that they use in the dramatization is not taken verbatim from the original; they take the idea of what happened and create the language to fit it. Few stories actually require memorization of particular lines; and these lines should be chosen by the students rather than by the teacher. One student teacher whose group was dramatizing the *Three Billy Goats Gruff* tried and tried to get the child playing the troll to say, "I'm going to gobble you up!" He finally was able to repeat the line and the dramatization started. When the moment actually came, he shouted out in a frightening voice, "Hey, man, I'm gonna eat you up!" It was so right for him and for the rest of the children, and they were so involved in the dramatization that the student teacher just smiled to herself. When a situation arises that children think requires the exact language of the original story, they will either have it down pat or will ask for it. One specific case where this happens is in dramatizing the *Three Little Pigs*. The children want to say, "I'll huff and I'll puff and I'll blow your house down!"

Vocabulary development is another area of language that is increased through drama. In story dramatization there is a double occasion for this: the vocabulary presented through the story or book itself, and the vocabulary used in the dramatization. Children in drama feel the need to express just the right shade of meaning in the words they use. Thus, new words may be presented in the story in a meaningful context and these words or others may be used in the later dramatization. Meeting words in a meaningful context and then having an opportunity to use them immediately is an extremely effective way of building vocabulary.

The nonverbal elements of communication are also developed in drama as we use body movement, gestures, and space to develop the characters. "How can you show that Tommy is a young boy and Mr. Miacca an older man as they run? How close to Tommy would Mr. Miacca stand as he sized him up for the main course for dinner? How close to Mr. Miacca would Tommy want to be? Show us by your walk who you are; we'll try to guess."

All of these elements of language are developed through dramatization. They are the expressive part of oral language. The corresponding receptive part—listening—is also well developed through dramatization. Students need to listen to each other in the dramatization in order to respond meaningfully to each other. They need to extend the ideas or refute the arguments presented by others. In story dramatization, they also need to listen carefully to the story to be able to work with it later. Thus, the whole range of oral language skills is represented in dramatic experiences.

Cognitive Skills

In the hierarchy of cognitive skills outlined by Bloom[9] there are six major levels of development: knowledge, comprehension, application, analysis, synthesis, and evaluation. In drama, students can demonstrate their knowledge at various levels of complexity. They may perform accurately scenes from a story or book retaining the original material of their source, or they may extend the drama beyond it. In dramatizing concepts the children reflect their knowledge by using it or by using abstractions in a concrete situation.

At the knowledge level children can relate their knowledge of conventions or sequence. At the comprehension level they may interpret a story by reordering or rearranging the original material to present a new view of it. At the level of application they can show abstract ideas in a specific context. Synthesis involves producing a unique communication to show patterns that were not clearly there before. Although the sixth level (evaluation) may not be present in all dramatizations, in dramatic expression children are constantly judging the qualities of the original material against their perceptions of reality, truth, and justice. It seems clear that all six levels of the cognitive domain are involved in some way at some time in dramatic expression.

Affective Skills

The affective domain attempts to describe all the changes in interests, attitudes, and values as well as the development of appreciations and adequate adjustment. There are five levels of development arranged in hierarchical order: receiving, responding, valuing, organization, and characterization by a value or value complex.[10] Within this area in drama children can explore how they feel about various ideas and personalities and how others feel. In playing scenes several different ways, they can explore alternative emotional responses or attitudes. Through the make-believe element in dramatizing, children can see the consequences of certain behaviors as they take on various roles. They can see what it would be like to be someone else—to be treated differently than they are in reality.

The base level affective skill is receiving; this is developed through dramatic expression as children give controlled or selected attention to the dramatization despite distracting actions. At the second level, responding is a primary focus of dramatic expression. It involves all three sublevels of acquiescence, willingness, and satisfaction in response. The next higher level within the affective domain is valuing which involves beliefs or attitudes. In acceptance of a value children may use drama to indicate their desire to speak more effectively. In showing preference for a value, they can examine a variety of viewpoints through dramatizing. In making a commitment for a value, children may show their conviction through a deeper involvement within the drama. The last two levels involve bringing a complex of values into an ordered relationship in organization, and an individual acting consistently in accordance with internalized values in the level of characterization by value or value complex. Although these two are not worked on directly in dramatic expression, there is considerable evidence that these levels of affective skills may not be reached without a great deal of exploration at the lower levels of receiving, responding, and valuing. Drama can provide excellent opportunities for developing the lower skills so that children may reach the higher affective skill levels.

Psychomotor Skills

Psychomotor skills are those which pertain to movement and which emphasize an overt physical response. The hierarchical arrangement by Simpson[11] uses response complexity as the organizing concept so that the skill levels parallel the steps required to carry out a psychomotor act. The seven levels of skills are: 1.0 perception, 2.0 set, 3.0 guided response, 4.0 mechanism, 5.0 complex overt response, 6.0 adaptation, and 7.0 origination.

The whole area of perception, which includes becoming aware of objects, qualities, or relationships by way of the sensory organs, is heavily involved in dramatic expression. It is the primary aim of all of the movement and pantomime. Children respond to music or rhythm or to other sensory stimulation and relate their actions to the sensory stimuli in performing the physical movements. The second level of psychomotor skills is set, which is the preparatory adjustment or readiness for a particular kind of action and involves mental set, physical set, and emotional set. This occurs in drama when the body is positioned preparatory to acting out a situation or becoming a particular character. The third level, or guided response, has to do with performing as the overt behavioral act of an individual under the guidance of an instructor. The fourth level, mechanism, is closely related to the third and simply involves the action becoming part of the individual's repertoire of possible responses to stimuli without requiring guidance of an outside instructor.

The last three levels of psychomotor skills may be developed through drama as students develop more skill in the movements related to dramatic expression. A complex overt response involves skill in carrying out the movement smoothly and efficiently. Adaptation involves altering the motor action to meet the demands of a new situation which requires a physical response. Origination means creating new motor acts.

SUMMARY

An understanding of the skills—language, cognitive, affective, and psychomotor—which are developed through early and continuing experiences with dramatic expression seems to show clearly that dramatizing is more than just a "fun" experience. It offers opportunities for developing children's abilities in a multitude of ways. Every teacher at every level of the elementary school should consider dramatic expression a key area of language arts.

PRELIMINARY LEARNING ACTIVITIES

I. There are four main kinds of motivational or warm-up exercises which often help children get into the mood of the situation or story they are going to improvise. You will probably not want to use all four kinds each time you do some improvisation, but might use each of the four kinds at some time or other. These four kinds of motivational exercises are sensory exploration, movement to music, pantomime, and imaginary situations.

Below are examples of each kind of warm-up or motivational exercise that relate to a particular topic. Look at these carefully and then try to think of examples of your own on a second topic.

Downtown in the City

The following warm-ups are related to a topic of being in the center of a large city. They might be done before an improvisation of a story that takes place in the city or prior to improvising a problem dealing with living in a city.

1. *Sensory* Sensory exercises try to help children get a sense of the physical environment the drama will explore through discussing the various senses.

   sight   What buildings do you see?
             What other things? (buses, taxis, crowds of people) Any more? (a park, pigeons)

   smell   Close your eyes and tell me what you can smell in the city. (fumes from cars, smog)
             What good smells? (someone selling candied apples)

   taste   What can you taste? (bubble gum from a machine, hot dogs)

   touch   Sit down on that low wall near the building. What does it feel like? Hot or cold? Rough or smooth? Rub your foot on the ground below. What's there?

   hearing   What can you hear in the city? (horns, people's feet, pigeons cooing, sirens, the whistle of a police officer)

2. *Movement to Music* This kind of warm-up works on two things at the same time: setting the mood of the story or situation and working on rhythmic movement.

   (a) You walk across the street—wait at the corner for the light to change—now quickly cross the other way. Walk along with the crowd, stop to look in a store window.

   (b) Now you are an old man with a cane walking up to the corner.

   (c) This time you are a college student on the way to meet your date.

   (d) Finally you are a mother with a young child who has been downtown shopping for three hours—Wow! Do your feet hurt!

3. *Pantomime* Pantomime may be done simultaneously so that all the children are pantomiming the same thing at the same time. In doing this the children may show their

different reactions to the situation without the pressure of an audience watching. This motivational exercise—like any of the others—may be used alone as a dramatic activity or as a warm-up for something else. Pantomimes may also be done with small groups and, therefore, with some audience as the children appear to be comfortable with it.

(a) Simultaneous: a police officer directing traffic on a busy corner where there is no traffic light; someone walking a dog on a leash through the crowded streets

(b) Small groups: trying to get a taxi to stop for you; trying to get bus fare out of your pocket while your arms are loaded with sacks; a child in the back of an elevator trying to see what floor it is over the heads of the people in front

4. *Imaginary Situations* These are very similar to pantomime except that they may involve monologs or dialog. When members of the group are working on simultaneous situations, each member develops a monolog. In small group situations the dialog is loosely planned and the children would respond to each other.

(a) Simultaneous: asking directions of people who do not know or will not answer

(b) Small groups: a shoeshine boy or girl trying to get some customers; riding your bike on a busy city street; you have a flat tire on your car and it is in the center lane of traffic

Now that you have read some examples of things which might be done for each of the four kinds of motivational or warm-up exercises, try to suggest various kinds of warm-ups for an improvised story or scene involving the circus. Some possible answers are given so that you may compare your responses. Do not feel that you must have the same suggestions, however.

The Circus

1. *Sensory*
   sight
   smell
   taste
   touch
   hearing

2. *Movement to Music*
    (a)
    (b)
3. *Pantomime*
    (a) Simultaneous
    (b) Small groups
4. *Imaginary Situations*
    (a) Simultaneous
    (b) Small groups

Possible Answers for Motivational Exercises for *The Circus:*

1. *Sensory*
    sight   What colors would you see? What animals? What kinds
        of acts?
    smell   What good smells would you smell walking around out-
        side the main tent or building? What smells would be
        inside?
    taste   What might you taste at the circus? (hot dogs, carmel
        corn, candied apples)
    touch   If you were in your place sitting down to watch the cir-
        cus, what are you sitting on? Is it painted or not? You
        have a cup in your hand. How does it feel? Is it hot or
        cold? wet or dry? foam or waxed?
    hearing   What sounds do you hear? (people, animals, music)
2. *Movement to Music*
    (a) It's the grand parade at the beginning of the show. Be the
        drum major at the head of the parade. Now you're one of the
        people walking an elephant. . . .
    (b) You are the tall man walking on stilts. Take big, big steps
        and turn around.
3. *Pantomime*
    (a) Simultaneous: be one of the clowns, a bareback rider, and
        now someone walking the high wire with a balance pole
    (b) Small groups: you're a lion tamer with a whip; an acro-
        bat; a juggler
4. *Imaginary Situations*
    (a) Simultaneous: someone selling popcorn, peanuts, and cot-
        ton candy; now you're selling cokes and making change
    (b) Small groups: be one of the sideshow acts like the thin man
        or some Egyptian dancers, or a weight lifter; be one of the

main show acts like a bareback rider, a trapeze artist, an animal act, or the clowns all crowded up in the tiny car

II. Whatever warm-up activity or main dramatic activity you choose to do, it should be related to the main topic or story you have chosen. It should highlight and enrich the children's experience with the book and their response to it. Supposing that you did not want to do an entire story dramatization of the following two books, what dramatic activities might you do with each that is particularly appropriate for it?

1. *Briar Rose and the Golden Eggs* by Diane Redfield Massie. New York: Parents' Magazine Press, 1973.

   Briar Rose is a goose who gets into a lot of trouble by wanting to be like the Golden Goose she hears about in fairy tales. She is very unhappy in the chicken yard; in fact, she's bored by the chickens. She thinks she has solved her problem by finding a nice round stone and painting it gold until some robbers steal her and she must lay another golden egg or be put in the stewing pot. The farmer finally rescues her, but she is banished from her silk pillow back to the chicken yard.
   What movement to music or pantomime would you choose to do that relate to this book?

2. *Squaps, the Moonling* by Sita Jucker with text by Ursina Ziegler. New York: Atheneum, 1969.

   Squaps is the bravest moonling of all. He hides in the boot of an astronaut who had come to find out if there were any living creatures on the Moon. Squaps is discovered back on earth and goes to live with the astronaut's family. He is thrilled with water which he has never seen before, but becomes homesick. The children decide to give a party for him on the night of the full moon. That night he discovers that he can return to the moon all by himself. He leaves his moonstone necklace with his thanks and returns to the moon with a tiny pitcher of water using the power of the full moon to fly.
   What pantomime or imaginary situations would be appropriate for this book?

Here are some suggestions for activities that might fit each of the stories. You may have chosen others; that is fine as long as they relate to the story and have the possibility of making it more memorable for children.

1. For *Briar Rose and the Golden Eggs*
   This story is full of action and fun. It moves quickly and there are a lot of characters. The two kinds of dramatic activities that seem especially appropriate are movement to music and pantomime.
   (a) Movement to Music
       Briar Rose   walking around the barnyard unhappily;
                    painting some stones gold;
                    being admired by the farmer and friends;
                    being chased along by the robbers;
                    worrying about how to get a golden egg for the robbers to save herself
       the farmer   discovering the golden eggs;
                    telling everyone in town about his luck;
                    sending Briar Rose back to the barnyard
   (b) Pantomime
       Several small groups could act out one segment of the story for the other to guess.
       Briar Rose   nibbling tarts and cookies in the house;
                    watching the pot coming to a boil before being rescued;
                    pecking around in the barnyard after she is found out
       robbers   snatching Briar Rose from the house;
                    warning her about laying an egg for them
2. For *Squaps, the Moonling*
   This story has a more subdued tone. It is a bit more thoughtful and quiet, even though it deals with a most exciting idea—a moonling come to live with a family. For Squaps, some pantomime and imaginary situations seem especially suitable.
   (a) Pantomime (simultaneous)
       Astronaut   open the hatch, check around outside;
                   climb down ladder to the moon;
                   walk around in space suit;
                   collect some rocks and plant a flag
       Squaps   peeking out of boot at astronaut;
                   shaking hands with astronaut;
                   walking along in rain with umbrella;
                   playing in garden hose and sprinkler
   (b) Imaginary Situations
       Astronauts exploring the moon as they leave the landing module;

the reception crowd when the moonling first shows himself;
reporters interviewing Squaps at a press conference;
Squaps after the party getting ready to go back to the moon

PARTICIPATION ACTIVITIES

1. Choose a book that would be suitable to read to children and plan one or two dramatic activities as a follow-up. Try your lesson with a small group of children.
2. Make a list of five to ten books with a summary of each and brief notations of dramatic activities for each book that you could use with children of the age you plan to teach.
3. Take one of the books you have chosen above and write out full plans for dramatizing the entire story. Plan the warm-ups or motivational activities, the main scenes and characters for each, including your plans for each child to have a part in the dramatization.

REFERENCES

[1] James Moffett. "Acting Out." *A Child-Centered Language Arts Curriculum K-6: A Handbook for Teachers.* Boston: Houghton Mifflin, 1968, p. 35.

[2] Benjamin DeMott. *Drama in the English Classroom.* (Douglas Barnes, ed.) Champaign, Illinois: National Council of Teachers of English, 1967.

[3] J. N. Hook, Paul H. Jacobs, and Raymond D. Crisp. *What Every English Teacher Should Know.* Champaign, Illinois: National Council of Teachers of English, 1970, pp. 39–40.

[4] John Dixon. *Growth through English.* Reading, England: National Association of Teachers of English, 1967.

[5] James Moffett. *Drama: What Is Happening.* Champaign, Illinois: National Council of Teachers of English, 1967.

[6] Doris Chaconas. *The Way the Tiger Walked.* New York: Simon and Schuster, 1970.

[7] Eve Merriam. "A Round." *Finding a Poem.* New York: Atheneum, 1970.

[8] Dorothy Heathcote. *Three Looms Waiting.* Time-Life Films.

[9] Benjamin S. Bloom, ed. *Taxonomy of Educational Objectives: The Classification of Educational Goals, Handbook I: Cognitive Domain.* New York: McKay, 1956.

[10] David R. Karthwohl, Benjamin S. Bloom, and Bertram B. Masia. *Taxonomy of Educational Objectives: The Classification of Educational Goals, Handbook II: Affective Domain.* New York: McKay, 1964.

[11] Elizabeth Simpson. "The Classification of Educational Objectives in the Psycho-motor Domain." IN Robert N. Singer, ed., *The Psychomotor Domain: Movement Behavior.* Philadelphia: Lea & Febiger, 1972.

CHAPTER TEN

Written Discourse — Self-Expression and Communication

PREVIEW QUESTIONS

1 How do you determine whether a piece of writing is done primarily for self-expression or for communication, and does it matter what the purpose is?

2 What preparation for writing should the teacher make?

3 How can children's writing be shared with other children and adults?

4 What components make up a sequential program of composition?

5 How should children's writing be evaluated so that it promotes further skill development?

Although we often think only of stories and poems when we think of imaginative writing, all composition work involves the imagination. In composing stories or poems writers try to express their ideas and experiences in a unique and highly personal way. A well-written report or letter, however, also requires some of the same elements of imagination and creativity. Evidences of this are shown in the following story, note, and poem which were composed by elementary school children.

IF I WERE A STAR

If I were a star I would go to the moon or Venus or Mars and have a good time. But if I want to go to the sun, I would have to get a lot of sleep. But I do not want to—not me, not me. But I am not a star, so that's that!

February 20

Dear Mom and Dad,

Thank you for the nice valentine card you gave me. I liked it. It's just like me, especially when it says giggly. I love you and thanks for being my valentine.

Love,

_____

BIRDS

Birds fly while I try
To learn and read
Birds are show-offs!

PURPOSES FOR WRITING

Many adults have unpleasant memories of their own writing experiences in elementary school. Maybe you can remember a few? On the first day of school, you could count on writing about "My Summer Vacation." You could also be sure the teacher would red-pencil any spelling or punctuation errors. In this way students learned to dislike writing instead of finding it to be a way of communicating their ideas or expanding their imaginations. Today's teachers need to avoid perpetuating unpleasant and unproductive writing experiences.

The purpose for writing determines the ways that the teacher stimulates students to write and the kind of response that the student gets back. The authors of *They All Want to Write* suggest that writing serves at least two needs for the writer and the audience: that of artistic self-expression and of communicating functional ideas.[1] The first is personal, individual, imaginative, and highly perishable and is best kept alive by allowing complete freedom to experiment and complete acceptance of the piece regardless of its nature. The second is utilitarian, realistic, or intellectual, and needs the discipline of correct mechanics to be socially acceptable. Although a writer should observe certain conventions of spelling and punctuation as a courtesy to the reader, the teacher must realize that much ego involvement exists in communicative writing; and that it, too, must be handled very sensitively. When a child decides to share some of his expressive writing with others, it may be revised to meet conventions of writing. This should be the writer's decision with the teacher helping as an editor in an individual conference.

INDIVIDUALIZING WRITING EXPERIENCES

Just as children vary in their ability to read, they also vary both in their ability to write and in the experiences they have had to write about. An individual child may write easily and fluently one day, but spend much time thinking and experimenting the next day before starting to write. This indicates that the teacher should provide a multitude of experiences and stimuli from which children may choose, as well as the opportunity to go off in some independent direction in writing. It also means there should be some flexibility in time for writing.

Teachers may want to provide some group or whole-class experiences to talk about or dramatize before writing, but they should also be ready to make suggestions and stimulate independent thinking in individual conferences with students. A writing center somewhere in a quiet corner of the room with plenty of paper and sharpened pencils, a good dictionary, and some suggestions or questions to provoke thinking may aid in developing writing.

Writing should be primarily student-directed rather than teacher-directed. Materials which present a problem—something that challenges the imagination—lead a child to become a writer. Children need to learn how to express things in their own way, rather than in their teacher's way. They require reactions to their efforts, but these should come from other students as well as from the teacher. Too much composition work is done with the teacher as the only reader. In real life almost no one would take the time and effort that children expend to write something for only one other person to read. Children, as well as adults, must write for a real audience and get some kind of response from that audience.

Children do best when they experiment with their own ideas and are not confined by an assigned topic. One week they may want to write several things, and the next week they may not be in the mood to write much. Flexibility to pursue writing in these ways is inherent in the writing program suggested in this chapter. Flexibility, however, should not be interpreted as the right to choose never to write.

Writing is such a complex task that composition must be taught just as its complementary mode, reading. Composing or writing involves getting thoughts on paper for the writer or someone else to read later. It is difficult to convey in writing exactly what you want to say without any of the verbal and gestural cues used in speech. Yet, we probably give very little instruction to elementary school children in how to express their ideas or how to communicate in writing with others. This chapter explores various activities to help children start writing and information on teaching strategies to improve children's writing.

RESEARCH ON IMAGINATIVE WRITING

Research studies in imaginative or creative story writing are somewhat limited in both number and scope. The following reported studies correspond with authoritative opinion and theoretical views on stimulating children's stories or compositions. General trends in research, theory, or opinion can indicate procedures that are helpful for the individual teacher to follow.

A major study in stimulating writing at the elementary school level was conducted by Carlson[2] who sought to determine if special materials (as opposed to assigned topics) would provoke more original stories from fourth-, fifth-, and sixth-graders involved in the study. The experimental group which had the special stimulus materials wrote longer and more original compositions and used a more versatile vocabulary than the control group children who were writing on assigned topics. The research indicates that books, pictures, records, and toys appear to be better stimuli for writing than a single title.

The view expressed by Holbrook[3] is that actual objects, photographs, and news items are less likely to prompt "involved" creativity because they have too little unconscious content and symbolic quality. He contends that the examples that prompt creative work should be creatively symbolic in themselves—that is, pieces of music, poems, paintings, stories—rather than real objects or accounts of real events.

Research data on elementary children which examines frequent practice in writing and composition quality are not available, but two experimental studies explored this relationship using junior high school and senior high school subjects. Both the Burton and Arnold study[4] and the McColly and Remstad study[5] found that more frequent experiences in themselves did not improve the children's writing, but that functional instruction improves composition. Although we cannot apply these findings directly to elementary age children, they suggest that writing and more writing without instruction and positive feedback in the way of suggestions is of doubtful value. What is needed is a carefully planned program of instruction.

INITIATING IMAGINATIVE WRITING

In planning story writing for children, there are certain criteria that should be met. These are based on theory, research, and the experiences of teachers.

1. The basis for writing should be meaningful to the child.
2. The expectancy of success should be built into the activity.
3. The writing activity should permit full exploration of the child's ideas by minimizing any developmental limitations.
4. The experience should extend the child's response to the surroundings by touching the senses, emotions, or imagination.
5. An ongoing planned developmental program of instruction in composition should be a part of the language arts.

Consider these criteria as you examine the suggestions made here and in planning further writing experiences for children.

Dictated Writing

The very earliest experiences with composition should serve two purposes: communicating the idea and helping children realize that what they say may be written down for others to read. This means that the teacher, an adult, or an older child will print what children want to say—perhaps about a picture they have created or something they have made. It is important to transcribe exactly what a child says—the words and word order—using conventional spelling. From dictating titles or captions, the next step would be to dictate short stories. As the children begin to print, they may want to copy part of the message themselves. As the students become more capable of writing on their own, they may go on to writing stories by themselves or with a friend. The writing in pairs may be done completely by the children or they may want to decide together on their ideas and dictate the story to someone else.

Dictation, especially in the early stages of writing, is necessary because children just learning the mechanics of writing are not physically capable of getting down their myriad of ideas. Dictation, however, should not be limited to the primary grades. There are many older children whose ideas run far ahead of their skill in putting them down on paper. They might choose to compose a group story and share the writing chore as they have shared the inventing one. Here, too, is the possibility of using an adult to write for them or tape-recording the story for later transcription.

One primary teacher started children in composition by asking them to write about their friend. After the children had dictated the story, they illustrated it. These stories were bound into a book so that all the class could share them as they began to read. Here are two of the stories:

MY FRIEND

My friend is Toshay. We play house.
We play on the sofa because it's soft.

Kathy

MY FRIEND

Chris is my friend. I walk home with him.
He lives across the street from me. We play kickball
and cards. We play Go Fish. *We ride our big wheels.*

After studying about animals, another primary grade class dictated a story about the animal they would like to be. Johnny's story has a special imaginative quality as he tells his reason for wanting to be an elephant.

ELEPHANT

*I would like to be an elephant. An elephant is
big. I want to be big. I like peanuts to eat. My
brother couldn't beat me up any more if I was an elephant.*

Johnny Hall

Encouraging Children to Use Their Experiences

Although children become more capable of writing on their own,
they still need ideas to stimulate them. Their writing may be based
on a variety of experiences—personal experiences both outside and
within school, literature that enriches writing, and other creative
modes such as drama, music, or the visual arts.

Children bring a wealth of experiences with them as they bring
a wealth of language. The one piece of advice given beginning
authors is to write from what they know. This applies to children as
well. For primary school age children, early experiences with writing should explore further the world they already know. Most young
children have gone shopping, been to a party, ridden bicycles, or
been to a park or playground. Older children will have an even
wider range of experiences on which to base their stories. Capitalize
on these experiences and encourage children to write about what
they know intimately.

Making observations—careful and continued exposure to something interesting—often prompts children's writing. Wright includes two samples of writing from the same child who had had the
opportunity to make some careful, close observations of a pet iguana
who lived in a cage on his table.[6] The children had watched the
iguana, photographed it, and then wrote about it. Jon's first writing
is:

> *Creeping*
> *Crawling*
> *Walking down the sandy beach*
> *the green scaly iguana*
> *makes his way*
> *toward the forest.*

Several days later after he thought of the word *stoutly* to describe
the iguana's walk, he wrote:

As the iguana walks stoutly
small animals step
from his way.

The input of interesting things, such as animals and plants, and time to ponder ideas, leads to good writing.

Children need to become consciously aware of their senses and they should be encouraged to observe closely and accurately. Thus children become more alert to the subtle contributions made by one sense to another. On a rainy day we are often unaware of how much the sense of smell adds to that of sight; or when we are popping corn, we may be unaware of how our sense of hearing adds to the enjoyment of the smell. Developing more accurate and more sensitive powers of observation and perception contributes to the child's experience and thus to the process of imaginative writing.

Providing New Experiences

There are also ways to add new experiences or new ways of viewing past events. There are the kinds of experiences that explore things outside the classroom. These may be actual fieldtrips—to the water-treatment plant, to a nearby lake or river, or to a farm—or they may be informal explorations of nearby places such as a new department store, an area of the playground, the neighborhood, or the kitchen in the cafeteria. The new experiences may be objects brought into the classroom to see and touch, or a classroom activity such as making popcorn balls or nutbread, planting seeds, or making pinecone wreaths for candles.

Just having new experiences is not sufficient in itself as Lane and Kemp[7] point out when they say,

> The teacher will find it hard to provide stimuli for talking and writing . . . but she must seek regularly to do just this. She cannot continue to draw indefinitely on the capital of the children's haphazard experience of living; she must always feed in new experience to the child, which should be so presented as to affect him deeply and touch him through the life of the senses, the emotions, and the imagination.

In working with sensory stimuli, a teacher is attempting to refine and extend children's awareness of their senses as well as to explore the various senses in imaginative ways. How about darkening the room and then using a floodlight and a revolving color disk shining on an aluminum foil sphere fastened to the ceiling as background and stimulation for writing about space voyages? Add some eerie music, and get out the pencils and paper. A sequence of sounds may also suggest a story. For example, the sounds used for the story below are a door opening, a ripping sound, a police siren, and a scream. Colin Miller used this sequence in the first draft of his story.

THE MURDERING MUMMY

As Joe Wilson returned home he felt that somebody or something was watching him. He opened the door to get another pair of shoes.

As he bent down reaching for his shoes, something knocked him back. He saw that it was a whitish figure. The figure pounced on Joe. There was a sound of a dagger ripping through a man's body.

The next day the police were trying to identify the killer. They only found a piece of white cloth. This kept on happening until one day the thing got shot with a gun.

A policeman heard a scream. It was from a house on the other side of the road. He ran as fast as he could go. The lady was dead. The whitish figure kept on running across the yard. The policeman yelled, "Stop or I'll shoot."

The whitish figure fell. He walked over to the whitish figure. "Omigod," the policeman yelled. "A Mummy!"

The teacher must be careful not to overdo the stimulus or to structure it too tightly. The stimulus should serve as a springboard and not as an enclosure that limits children's creativity. Just saying, "Write a story" is not enough. Moffett suggests, "They need definite stimulants and frameworks that prompt the imagination. Their original stories are recombinings of familiar stories in more or less new ways."[8]

Structured comparisons are one way to break through clichés and stimulate the imagination. Two dissimilar things may be compared: a fire is like a snowstorm because . . . or, a paper clip is like a sweetroll because. . . . Another way of structuring comparisons is suggested in *Making It Strange*.[9] This set of materials is a four-book series in creative writing based on the conscious use of metaphor. One type of question posed is exemplified by the following: "Which weighs more—a cough or a sneeze? Which is louder—a smile or a frown? Which is thinner—day or night? Which is rougher —yellow or purple?"

Giving children an opportunity to be someone else can force them to look at the familiar with unfamiliar eyes. The teacher may start with objects in the room, classroom pets, or various animals. Each child can decide what he or she wants to be. The following are stories composed by a second-grader, a third-grader, and a fifth-grader.

I'M A LEAF

I'm a little leaf hanging on the tree all alone. I wish someone else would grow in spring. But everyone else is one the gound. I wish I'd fall, too! But I can't! Why, oh why can't I fall? I'm all different colors—red, yellow, and brown. It's atum now and I still haven't fell! All this time I still want to fall. Wish me luck!

Betsy's first draft

If I Was A Indian Girl

If I was a Indian Girl I would help do the cooking, washing, and other things around the village. But at night I would go hunting for [deer drawing]. The peple would say where did you get that [deer drawing]? Some weekends I would camp. I would camp |||[tent drawing]. I would [campfire drawing].

Myra's first draft

I'M SANTA CLAUS

I'm Santa Claus and I've got a lot of letters this year and I'll have to make a lot of stops. Here's a letter from a boy in Africa who wants a stuffed tiger. But oh dear how will I get there when my deer are used to cold. I'll have to send some magic pills that will make zebras fly. I'll tell him to send eight zebras to pull my sled.

So now don't be suprized if santas makeing zebras pull his sled. You proble want to know what I do with the deer. I still use them only in places where it's cold.

Denise's first draft

All of the stories show the ability to imagine being someone or something else. The children have used interesting details to make their "Being Someone or Something Else" stories their own.

Using Literature as a Basis for Writing

Literature that has rich language and is sensitive to children's interests can serve as a springboard to imaginative writing. Books present another view of life and experience to compare with "one's own sense of reality." Through literature one may also experience on a very personal level events, people, and times far removed in place or time from one's own lifetime.

Inductively the child can adapt or assume the form, style, or scheme of a particular piece of literature. This does not happen from a story heard once a week; it does not come from reading unimaginative or simplified books. It does result from daily exposure to excellence. The need to hear good literature does not end when the child can do some independent reading. It is just as necessary in the fourth, fifth, and sixth grades as it is in kindergarten through third grade.

Literature provides familiar stories to draw upon in imaginative writing, and can be important as a specific starting point for writing. Children may draw upon their familiarity with particular kinds of stories and write their own versions. Younger children may compose their own ABC or counting books after listening to others and looking at or "reading" some examples. An ABC book composed by some first-graders and illustrated by them has "Crayons begin with a C, Dog begins with a D, Easter egg begins with E, and Fence begins with F." Another group of first-graders did their book using a wide variety of fabrics, paper, buttons, etc. They even had a nickel on the N page. Older children may want to write accumulative stories patterned on *The House That Jack Built,* or *The Judge.*[10] They can write their own versions of *Chicken Soup with Rice*[11] using their favorite food and doing either months of the year or days of the week. Upper elementary children enjoy writing their own tall tales, parodies of fairy tales, and explanatory tales. One fourth and fifth grade group wrote their own Paul Bunyon stories in small groups with Paul solving the problem of a gigantic snowstorm. These are two of their solutions:

Paul told the mother snowstorm to tell the father snowstorm to tell the baby snowstorm on the ground to come home or he would spank him!

Paul ate up all of the pepper they had except for one plateful which he put under his nose. Then he sneezed and sneezed. He couldn't stop sneezing and he sneezed the snow away.

Preceding any such writing there should be extensive reading of the story and considerable inductive discussion of its form, format, or characteristics. Books may also inspire writing about a new character, a new adventure, a new event, or an ending to a well-liked story or tale. Some sixth-graders created a new character—"Snow White and the Seven Dwarfs" became eight as Wiggley joined the story. Another group was unhappy with the ending of *Dazzle*[12] because they thought the small birds were too nice to Dazzle who, in turn, had not been very nice to them. They wrote a different ending in which Dazzle served as their cook for awhile. These are very direct uses of particular pieces of literature; however, literature also indirectly influences children's writing as they become more familiar with many well-written and enjoyable stories.

Other Creative Media

Another way of developing both the senses and emotions is through opportunities to share new experiences, ideas, or feelings with others. We all view what we see and do through our own personal background of experiences, and sharing reactions with someone else gives us the ability to place a novel experience in perspective and to view other aspects of the experience.

Dramatic activities are also a way of dealing with new ideas. In talking about improvisation as a part of drama, Summerfield[13] suggests,

> It is a means of sharing one's own sense of the world, one's own sense of reality, with others and comparing with other's sense of reality. The imagining, the fantasy is made public, and once it's seen and shared by other pupils, the authenticity, the reality, the truth, the convincingness of an individual realization is something that can be assessed and discussed when the appropriate moment comes. . . . They can be observed and they can be extended and they can be refined and they can be rendered increasingly subtle, increasingly adequate, increasingly full.

Drama then becomes another way of talking about one's experiences, another way of sharing new ideas and new observations. Dramatizing an experience or extending that experience into the unknown but imagined in an unstructured drama may suggest a variety of ideas or avenues of approach to write about.

Just as drama is one way of sharing new experiences and making them personal, there are other ways of sharing. Music, painting, sculpture, and other creative media become both a way of viewing new insights and new experiences and a fresh foundation for creativity in composition. The creative arts can serve jointly with imaginative writing to express one's senses, emotions, or imagination, or they can serve as a stimulus for writing.

Many teachers have had success using music to motivate writing. Simply playing a record and asking children to write about what comes to their mind is usually not sufficient structure. Rousing march music might suggest a parade or a football game, and a few questions prior to the writing may provoke additional ideas.

The visual arts may be used as a stimulus for writing, and most children enjoy writing a story to go with a picture or poster. Pictures that present an element of strangeness or an apparent contradiction work well. Children do need to be able to select the picture they want to write about. They may also use their own pictures, prints, or crayon etchings as the basis for a story. One group of second- and third-graders painted large poster-type pictures of what they would like to be someday. Then they wrote about their paintings. Here are two of their stories.

I'd like to be a policeman because I'd patrol the area in search of crime. I'd tell the patrol what to do.

I'd like to be a preacher because I could tell the services and hypnotize babies.

One upper primary teacher had a large aquarium in her classroom. All of the children were fascinated watching the fish and snails move about. One boy drew a picture of his favorite fish in the tank and then wrote this story.

I am a fish and my name is Twish gurgle-gurgle. I like swimming through the weads because it tickles. I am a gold fish. It fils funny wene bubles hit me. The water is blue. people try to catch me but I am to fast for them. THE END

This unrevised first draft shows how familiar he was with fish, and at the same time exemplifies many elements of good writing and creativity. He has given the fish a perfect name, has used details about the weeds and bubbles to add a sensory impact, and has included a clever ending.

Vaneta drew the picture below and then wrote a story about dressing up—a familiar experience for many children. The story has been edited for spelling and punctuation.

THE BIG HAT

Hello, my name is Cindy. See my hat. Well, it's not mine; it's my mother's. I'm just playing house and dress-up in one. I'm the mother. The hat swallows me whole. It's so big Mother has to tie it. I found it in our cedar chest. I think I'll find another hat to play with that doesn't stink like cedar. Bye now!

Pictures that are used as a basis for writing should be somewhat unusual; they should pose a problem for the writer to solve. This kind of picture can often be found in advertising which uses the unusual to attract attention. Advertisements that have been successful are an elephant carrying a typewriter, a dining room table set with china and crystal in the center of a busy street, a sweet grandmotherly woman sitting on a sofa holding a rifle, and some Madison Avenue types in business suits flying kites in Manhattan.

An unfinished line drawing may also stimulate some children to write. They can finish the drawing and make anything of it they want and then write about it. A drawing like this is included at the top of the next page. Some of the things the children made from this and wrote about were a six-million-dollar robot, an ice cream cone machine, a man shouting for help, a drum major, and an automatic room cleaning and bed-making machine.

Many middle and upper grade children love comic books and these may be used by a teacher to facilitate story writing. They are particularly good for developing plot structure and the conversation or dialog in children's stories. You can begin with simple figures with a number of empty balloons for the children to complete.

Make something of me!

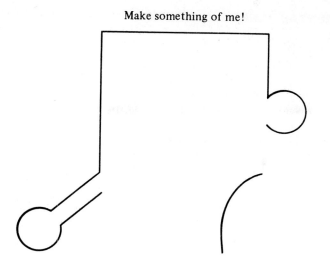

Another step is to give a series of empty frames with some indication of what might be happening—something very open-ended. Maria worked on a four-frame strip like this which had the following suggestions: The zooger is king of the world, he sees a strange object, he goes after it, and he gets rid of it. Two of her frames are shown below along with a story developed from her ideas.

>*The zooger who was king of the world loved to sing to his world. Then one day he looked out and saw a very strange object.*
>   *"I'm going to catch that thing!" he said, and he did catch it.*
>   *"M-m-m! What good coffee," he said. And from then on it's been a coffee cup and a saucer for King Zooger.*

It is much easier to make the transition from the balloon wording into quotations and from descriptive captions into descriptive paragraphs once the ideas have been clearly established through the cartoon.

DEVELOPMENTAL TRENDS IN WRITING

This section will examine some of the developmental trends that one finds in children's writing. Before looking at some of these trends, it should be made clear that there are no "stages at certain ages" associated with imaginative writing. The trends in the use of language in writing and the development of conventional story technique do not follow a pattern of particular items at particular grade levels. They indicate, rather, the progression that most children follow in development, and children at any one grade level will vary greatly.

Language in Writing

The two most general trends in written language are from the simple to the more complex and from the more general to the more specific. These trends are manifested by increasing sentence length, changes in structure from simple sentences to more coordination to more subordination and embedding, increasing use of a variety of pronouns and synonyms, increasing precision of words used, and greater fluency and overall length.

Development of Conventional Story Technique

Analysis of children's imaginative writing reflects the same two general trends of increasing complexity and specificity: a change from basic description to the development of events, movement from the view of self to the view of others, development from single to multiple events, increasing use of dialog, increasing use of details, and the addition of minor events and explanations.

Perhaps it would clarify the trends suggested above to examine some samples of children's stories written about the same picture.

A FIRST-GRADER'S STORY

I have a Siamese cat. I like my Siamese cat. I like butterflies. They are pretty. Leaves are pretty too. I like them. Sometimes they are brown. I like them. I love animals. I have blue eyes. I have red hair. I like looking at butterflies. I like to catch them. My cat likes to eat them. My cat likes to catch them. Sometimes I catch them. I put them in cages sometimes.

A SECOND-GRADER'S STORY

It has big green leaves, and the girl is looking at the big butterfly, and the cat's looking at it, and the girl has red hair, and the cat's brown, and it has big blue eyes. It looks like the cat is trying to get a butterfly.

A THIRD-GRADER'S STORY

Once there was a girl with long red hair and big blue eyes. She was walking through the forest with her Siamese cat. When she saw a big red and black butterfly, she stood there looking at him. She was thinking it was pretty. Her cat was thinking, "Boy would I like to catch him!" All of a sudden he ran after the butterfly. The girl decided to walk back out of the forest because the butterfly was gone.

A FOURTH-GRADER'S STORY

I have red hair and blue eyes and a pet cat, and I like to go in the woods and look at butterflies and try to find out what kind they are, and try to find out what kind the leaves are and collect the leaves and look at other animals. One day when I went along with my cat, I saw a butterfly with orange and brown spots; but it flew away, and I never saw anymore like it. One day I saw one almost like it, but it had red spots. But it flew away too. One day I got a butterfly that had all different colors in it, and I kept it for a pet. One day it flew away, but I knew it was happier there with other butterflies so I wasn't too sad.

A FIFTH-GRADER'S STORY

There was once a girl who was lost in the woods and couldn't find her way out. She had a pet cat who followed her in the jungle, and the butterfly showed her the way home. After that she made a little place in the woods where the butterfly showed her the way home. When she got older, she lived in this place where the butterfly lived. When winter came, the butterfly had to fly down to Florida; and the girl was sad because he had to fly down south, and she didn't think it would fly back. After winter was gone the butterfly flew back. Then they decided to move to Florida so the butterfly wouldn't have to fly away, and that's where they lived from then on.

A change from basic description to the development of events. Both the first and second grade stories are entirely descriptive. In the third grade story, the cat chases the butterfly and the girl leaves. The fourth grade story is similar in the sense of the butterfly leaving, but its author adds other butterflies to the story. In the fifth grade story we see the development of a crisis when the butterfly goes to Florida for the winter and the girl fears she won't see him again. Happily the butterfly does return and they move south so they can be together.

Movement from view of self to the view of others. The first grader uses the first person, but more importantly many personal notes are added as "I" becomes the central character. "I love animals," "I like them (leaves)," or "I put them in cages sometimes" all appear to be the author speaking. The second, third, and even fourth grade stories may use first or third person, but seem to involve the author as a participant in the stories. In the fifth grader's story, there appears to be a story from the viewpoint of a disinterested person; certainly there is less involvement of self.

Development from single to multiple events. In the first two stories, the events are not developed. The third grade and fourth grade stories suggest a single and similar event—the butterfly goes away. In the fifth grade story, there is the butterfly leaving, but upon return, they all go south to be together.

Increasing use of dialog. Unfortunately for illustrative purposes, only one of the stories uses dialog—the third grader's story. In order to use some dialog, the story must be viewed as separate from the storyteller and this is not typical of the early primary grades. It could well have been added to the fourth or fifth graders' stories, but was not. This may be an individual developmental item, or the result of infrequent opportunities to tell or write stories.

Increasing use of details. In the first grader's story about the only descriptive details used were the use of "pretty" and of colors. In the second grader's story, there are additional details—"big, green leaves" and "the cat's brown, and it has big blue eyes." The third grader's use of details is more frequent and more extensive with "long red hair and big blue eyes" and "A big red and black butterfly." Both the fourth and fifth graders do use descriptive adjectives, but they more frequently supply details in other ways. The fourth grader adds, "I like . . . to find out what kind they are," "I never saw anymore like it," and "I knew it was happier there . . . so I wasn't too sad." The fifth grader adds similar details such as "a girl who was lost in the woods and couldn't find her way home," and "made a little place in the woods where the butterfly (had) showed her (the) way home."

The addition of minor events and explanations. This is closely related to the use of details discussed above. We see in the third grade story an example of the addition of explanations as we find out what the girl and the cat were thinking. In the fourth grader's piece, there is the idea of the girl as a scientist looking at butterflies and other animals or leaves to identify them. There is also the addition of other butterflies previously seen, "a butterfly with orange and brown spots" that flew away and "one almost like it, but it had red spots" and it flew away too, and finally a butterfly with "all different colors on it, and I kept it for a pet." The fifth grader adds a series of events as the butterfly shows her the way home; she builds a place in the woods; when she is older, she lives in that place; winter comes and the butterfly goes to Florida; after winter, he flies back; and finally they move to Florida so he won't have to fly away in the winter.

The trends toward more maturity in the development of story technique and in the language used in writing really need to be examined in multiple samples of children's writing. They indicate the pattern of development, and maturity will be most evident in the older or more mature children's writing, and with those who have had a fine composition program.

EVALUATION OF IMAGINATIVE WRITING

In evaluating children's writing of any kind, and particularly story writing, the thrust of the evaluation should be to look for value. The emphasis in evaluation should be on the positive, on what was beautifully conceived or expressed. Measurement in the sense of making comparisons with others or with some set standard are completely inappropriate. Evertts[14] states that stories are "not exercises to be corrected, scored, rewritten or graded. (NEVER graded! Who can grade imagination, especially that of a young child with a lifetime of growing to do?)"

The legitimate purposes of evaluation are twofold: to express to the child what you value in the composition, and to seek what is valuable to use as a basis for future growth. Because imaginative writing is so intimately tied to one's own personal experiences and views of reality, it is very painful to be criticized by someone else. Future improvement and growth come from the basis of what is done well or expressed well. The teacher's evaluation should be confined to two purposes: communicating to the child what is good about the writing and using observations of the child's work to plan helpful writing experiences.

Evaluation, then, involves looking for what is valuable in children's work and communicating this to them to foster future development. The teacher must be very specific in communicating what is successful to the author. Was it the idea itself or an interesting event or explanation? Was there an interesting beginning or a particularly effective ending? Did the child use details well to build an effect, was there some unique touch that made it personal, or was there some humorous aspect that gave it life? Was there some interesting dialog or were some especially effective words used? These are some values in a child's writing that can lead to more exciting, more unique, more effective writing.

Evaluating children's writing on the basis of what was well done does not mean that the teacher should ignore conventions of written language, such as spelling, punctuation, capitalization, and so on. Problems in the supportive writing skills should be noted for future instruction. Some writing will be corrected completely in conference with the teacher and other pieces will remain as uncorrected first drafts. This whole area of conventions of writing and revision is discussed later in the chapter.

Elements of Creativity

Checking the mechanical aspects of children's writing is a relatively simple task, which is perhaps the reason it is so frequently used as the prime evaluation criterion. It is more difficult to judge structural elements such as sequence of ideas, an interesting beginning or ending, the use of descriptive details, or the use of dialog. Creativity in writing is an even more obscure quality. Some of the qualities that a teacher might look for in imaginative story writing are suggested by various originality scales developed for rating compositions for use in research or by teachers.

Yamamoto developed such a rating scale with six major parts: organization, sensitivity, originality, imagination, psychological insight, and richness.[15] Sample subdivisions listed for imagination are: richness of imagination, fantasy, abstraction, identification, and reasoning. This scale was supplemented by Torrance in a two-section rating for evaluating originality and interest.[16] The originality section includes picturesqueness, vividness, flavor, personal element, original solution or ending, original setting or plot, humor, invented words or names, and an unusual twist in style or content. The section on interest includes naturalness, variety of kinds of sentences, personal touches, questions and answers, conversational tone, use of quotations, and humor.

Another scale for evaluating originality in children's writing was developed by Carlson.[17] This scale has five main divisions: story structure, novelty, emotion, individuality, and style of stories. Then each of these is subdivided into numerous items. Story structure, for example, has five subsections: unusual title, unusual beginning, unusual dialog, unusual ending, and unusual plot. The section on novelty has sixteen divisions, some of which are novelty of names, new words, new objects created, picturesque speech, unusual related thinking, and quantitative thinking. The *Carlson Analytical Originality Scale* was developed after extensive sampling of children's stories and has a six-point rating scale for each subitem. Four of the six points for each are illustrated with samples from children's writing. The main sections and subsections are appended to this chapter.

Kantor suggests that we may find some realistic guidelines for criteria to use in evaluating creative writing in the psychological literature on creativity.[18] The first concept of creativity, divergent thinking, is suggested by the Guilford study. A second concept which comes from Freudian theory is playfulness and fantasy. The third quality that may be found is risk-taking and skepticism about convention. The fourth category is openness to experience which is described by various theorists such as Carl Rogers or E. G. Schachtel. It involves the inclusion of original concrete details, perhaps in unusual combinations with each other. The fifth quality suggested comes from Jerome Bruner—effective surprise, a shock of recognition caused by connections between previously unrelated realms of experience. The last quality is that of symbolic expression which involves using the metaphor to suggest deeper relationships. Kantor adds a final caution that seems particularly appropriate here. "In adopting these concepts of creativity as guidelines for evaluation, we run the risk of bringing about a regime as rigid and dictatorial as the old one. In short, if students begin to write more imaginatively solely to satisfy the teacher's expectations and not because they find it personally worthwhile, then we haven't come very far."[19] It seems clear that we must help our students find more pleasure in their own writing and provide them with opportunities for a real audience as an alternative to the teacher as the sole audience for writing. The scales and concepts of creativity should indicate to the teacher some of the aspects of creativity that may be found in children's writing that need encouragement. They may serve to help the teacher specify precisely what a child did well in a piece of writing so that the child can apply the learning in additional stories.

Improving Mechanics in Story Writing

The first thing the teacher needs to do is to become convinced that the purpose for the writing determines what should be done about editing or correcting any mechanical aspects of writing. A general rule of thumb would be that if the child or the teacher is going to share the story by reading it, there is no need for correcting mechanical errors. If others are going to read it and would have difficulty, it should be corrected as necessary. Editing or correcting for no real purpose does not teach correct mechanics nor does it advance imaginative writing.

The second thing that the teacher should do is to help the child avoid making as many mechanical or spelling errors as possible. Then correction becomes less necessary and less frequent. A good program of instruction as outlined in the chapter on supportive writing skills should gradually reduce difficulty with conventions in writing. In the meantime, there are two main ways of making corrections less necessary and less frequent: dictating imaginative writing and helping the children while they are writing. Burrows[20] reports that research plainly indicates that young children should be given plenty of opportunities to dictate stories, reports, verse, titles, questions, plans, and other forms of composition. She adds that research also indicates that "it's more desirable to cherish fluency and uniqueness of expression than complete correctness."

As children begin to become independent writers, they still need someone to transcribe part of their story before they make additions to it or finish it. Children in the upper grades also need opportunities to dictate stories from time to time. Various people may take the dictation—parents, aides, and older children as well as the teacher —or the dictation may be tape-recorded for later transcription.

Spelling errors are frequent problems in children's writing, but there are a number of ways they can be avoided. Children should be encouraged to keep a separate sheet of paper nearby when they are writing to note any words they need to know how to spell. Then they leave a blank space in their writing for that word to be added later. If you circulate around the room where the children are writing, you can supply the spelling for these words. The children should also have a personal word dictionary with one or two pages for each letter. Then as they obtain the spellings for the unknown words, they can write them in their personal dictionary for later use. It's amazing how children learn to spell the words they look up frequently. If children are writing about a similar experience, the teacher may put some of the words they think they may want to use on the board. A caution here is that this kind of group listing may limit the ideas which the children use in their writing if they feel confined in any way to the words on the board. There is also the possibility that children may ask someone else near them how to spell a word or they can simply go ahead and write the word the way they think it is spelled. If the piece of writing is going to be shared orally, there may not be a need for correct spelling. Burrows[21] suggests that this kind of writing needs to fulfill only the child's desires, except upon those extremely rare occasions when correct form is necessary out of consideration for others or when the product is to be permanently preserved.

When it is necessary to put imaginative writing in correct form, the teacher should edit the writing with the child in a person-to-person conference. At this time, the teacher can supply the corrections while explaining what the revision is or by asking how the child wants to solve a particular problem.

The most important way for a teacher to help improve children's imaginative writing is by truly appreciating and cherishing what they write. If the teacher delights in children's ideas and is not dismayed by their form, the children will freely use their imaginative and creative powers and write. Moffett suggests[22] that "children should begin their careers thinking of the class as more the audience than the teacher, who should avoid making himself the source of evaluation."

One teacher shared some imaginative writing about Thanksgiving with the parents of the children in her room without any editing changes. Along with the publications of their writing was the following note,[23]

> I would like to take this opportunity to pass on to you a sampling of our creative writing. The results this week have once again shown me that there is always thanks in the hearts of children.
>
> Let me tell you about creative writing. It is not natural or spontaneous for some children. The mood must be set and the child must be led carefully and skillfully to express himself. All children have deep thoughts and feelings, but the difficulty lies in getting these thoughts and feelings from the minds and hearts to the paper. If a child knows that every incorrect word is going to be circled in red—he will not write! I did not change these stories because to tamper with the form is to destroy the spirit and charm which the author intended.
>
> Read the following with humor and taste and the knowledge that you have had a rare opportunity to look (for a few seconds) into the minds and hearts of these beautiful children.

How could anyone fail to enjoy these children's writing? They were second-graders, and much of their spelling reflected good second-grade-style guessing; but the warm reception of their teacher was reflected in the enthusiasm with which they wrote.

If the teacher is to become a source of improvement for students, there must be accurate diagnostic records of each child's writing. The teacher must look at both the growth of individual children and that of the entire class. One way of keeping records is through anecdotal notes. As the teacher circulates around the room when children are writing or when they share their stories, he or she may note particular strengths or particular problems that the children are having.

Another way of keeping track is for teachers to develop a checklist. Then they can keep one for each child—recording and diagnosing each story written—or they may use such a checklist for the class on particular pieces of writing in order to select children for small-group instructional purposes. In the vertical columns teachers would list the particular aspects of structure and originality they are looking for. These might be such things as development of an idea, effective beginning or ending, use of vocabulary, use of dialog, novelty or ingenuity of ideas, variety of sentences, and humorous incidents or touches. In mechanics one might examine spelling, punctuation, usage, capitalization, and sentence form. Then in that column opposite the name of a particular piece or an individual child, one would indicate the diagnosis by a comment or by a symbol.

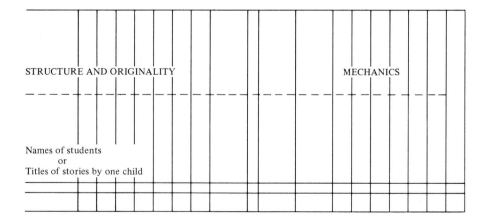

STRUCTURE AND ORIGINALITY

MECHANICS

Names of students
or
Titles of stories by one child

Once the teacher has had an opportunity to examine several pieces of imaginative writing from the children in the class, a brief look at the checklist will show if there are several children with a similar problem. These children may be grouped for instructional purposes to work on this specific area.

The key point in any discussion of mechanics or spelling in story writing is that the teacher should look for and respond to improvement in the imaginative quality of the writing and not emphasize the correctness of the form in which it is written. Form may be dealt with separately. Imaginative writing is not reserved for just a few children in the class. Moffett points out that creative writing is a staple of learning for all children, not just Friday afternoon fun for advantaged children who are mastering the basics on schedule. "The testimony is ample from many hard-working teachers in urban ghettos that deprived children can learn 'basics' only *after* they have become persuaded that the world of letters has something in it for them."[24] Imaginative writing is a vehicle for children to use in dealing with their ideas and their fears—their own personal reactions to their world.

WRITING POETRY

Poetry is another kind of imaginative writing that should be an important part of every child's elementary school experience. It should be an alternative way for children to express their personal reactions, feelings, and observations. Interest in poetry and interest in writing poetry needs to be developed and expanded during these early years.

There are two main factors involved in developing children's interest in poetry: increasing familiarity with various kinds of poetry and extending responses to poetry. An important part of stimulating children to write poetry is to increase their familiarity with all kinds of poetic expression by reading a wide range of poems to them.

Increasing Familiarity with Poetry

Anthologies will certainly provide some material, but these often contain older, traditional poems and only rhymed, metered poetry. Because of copyright laws, the anthologist is somewhat limited in the selection of poems which are available and financially feasible to include. The major source for modern poems is the individual collection written by a particular poet. There are any number of these collections available now—beautifully illustrated and comprised of the best of the poet's art.

Children need to have a variety of books of poetry available to read and examine. Special favorites may be displayed in a class-bound book or on a special bulletin board. Teachers should make a point of reading poetry to children frequently. If teachers keep and organize copies of poems they may want to read to their class, they can easily find the one about dandelions on the very same day these bloom outside. A sharing time report of fixing breakfast could trigger the teacher's reading "Mummy Slept Late and Daddy Fixed Breakfast."[25] Poetry should never be just "the words we copy from the board for handwriting practice." Poetry should become an integral part of talk and response in the classroom. Children need to know that poetry is a way of reacting to something very real in their lives, and that it is a meaningful response.

Extending the Response to Poetry

Children's response to poetry may be enlarged by various activities that encourage the children to become more involved with a particular poem. Some of these activities are making media presentations of poems, choral reading experiences with poetry, and setting poems to music.

Media presentations of poems are a way of visualizing the poem in one of the graphic arts. Children may select a poem they particularly like and illustrate it in some way. Chalks, finger paints, crayon and crayon engravings, mobiles, clay sculpture or soap or paraffin carvings, dioramas, models, murals, collages and mosaics, torn paper illustrations, or homemade slides—all of these media presentations help make the poem more meaningful to the child who creates them. Directions for making your own slides are as follows:

1. Place transparent contact paper over a 2" × 2" color (clay base) picture from a magazine.
2. Rub contact paper with spoon until picture is clear.
3. Cut out.
4. Put in warm soapy water and peel off paper that originally had picture on it.
5. Place between slide frames.
6. Iron or glue frame closed.

If children are allowed to select a poem to read chorally and plan how the lines will be read, there is a great deal of learning and involvement in the activity. Groups of three to five children can work together in planning the readings which may be tape-recorded or given orally. In the process of planning the reading, deciding which lines should be emphasized and how gives children a lot of insight into the poem.

Setting poems to music is an additional way of extending the mood or feeling of the poem. Children may make up their own musical accompaniment and play it while the poem is being read, or they may choose some professionally recorded music as a background for their reading. Rhythmical instruments rather than a full musical background may be more appropriate for some poems.

Research on Children's Interests

Children's interests in poetry—the kinds of poems or qualities in poetry that they prefer—have remained surprisingly stable over the years. A recent study by Terry examined children's interests and preferences in listening to poetry.[26] She analyzed fourth-, fifth-, and sixth-graders' responses to over one hundred selected poems and found the following characteristics in the poems liked and disliked by the children in this national survey.

Characteristics Liked	*Characteristics Disliked*
humorous poems	sentimental or serious poems
rhythm, rhyme, sound	imagery and figurative language
enjoyable familiar experiences and animals	unenjoyable familiar experiences
contemporary poems	traditional poems
familiar poems	free verse
narrative poetry	haiku
limericks	

There appear to be several important implications from Terry's study that relate to children's writing poetry. One of the things that children liked to hear was familiar poetry. Unfortunately, this same study revealed that three-fourths of the teachers read poetry to their classes only "occasionally" or "once a month." Writing poetry was not a common practice in these classrooms, as over ninety percent of the teachers in the study had their children write poetry only "occasionally" or "very seldom."

Two other studies just over forty years apart relate to children's interests in poetry and to what teachers read to children. Coast[27] in 1928 examined the poems that a group of teachers most enjoyed teaching and the poems that children in these classrooms preferred. She concluded that the poems which teachers prefer are the ones most frequently chosen by children. Tom[28] conducted a survey in 1969 to determine what poems were read to children in the fourth through sixth grades. Almost six hundred questionnaires from five states showed that the majority of the forty-one most popular poems were in narrative form, and that all but four of them were written before 1928. The poems most often read by teachers were: "Paul Revere's Ride," "Stopping by Woods on a Snowy Evening," "A Visit from St. Nicholas," "Casey at the Bat," "Little Orphan Annie," "Fog," "The Village Blacksmith," "My Shadow," and "Hiawatha." Unfortunately, many of the poems represent the traditional poetry that Terry found children dislike and frequently do not understand.

Children's overall interest in poetry decreases in the upper elementary grades, perhaps because we are not capitalizing on their perferences for poems about familiar well-liked experiences and for contemporary poems. It is also difficult to determine if their preference for rhymed metered poetry is a reflection of what they think poetry should be because of the poems they have been exposed to or a preference which is independent of previous experience with poetry. We also need to distinguish between what they enjoy listening to and what they enjoy and are capable of writing.

POETIC FORMS

Children need many experiences as a base for writing poetry. They need to play with words and with sounds and images. Typical of this is the seven- or eight-year-old who leaned out over the swimming pool watching a bug on the water and made up a word-play poem which he repeated over and over.

> *Bug off, bug*
> *Go away*
> *Who needs you*
> *On a sunny, summer day?*

Another example of this fun with wordplay and with sounds of words that younger children enjoy so much occurred while children were working on a task of combining two simple sentences into a single sentence. The children, a second grade group, were shown these two sentences: *My hat is blue. My hat has flowers on it.* One child, after hearing the sentences read, responded immediately, "My hat is blue, my hat just flew, up in the sky so high."

The starting point of poetry is developing experiences—direct experiences that create an impression on children and also a need to say something about the experience. Another part of stimulating children to write poetry is providing them with a rich and varied background of knowledge about poetry by reading a wide range of poems to them. The third part of getting children started in writing poetry is to have reasonable expectations of their abilities and introduce poetic forms that enable them to be successful. There should, of course, be a feeling of willingness to try new or different things because the teacher has set up a warm and responsive climate in the classroom in which children can experiment and take risks.

Children's first attempts at writing poetry are far from being really fine poetry. Before they reach this point, they need frequent opportunities to express themselves poetically. The following suggestions for writing free verse, concrete poetry, invented unrhymed forms, and simple rhymed forms are beginning points in writing. The final objective is the ability to use poetry—rhymed or not—as an alternative to writing prose for those ideas that are especially suited to poetic expression. An ongoing writing program can produce poetry such as David's "Year In Year Out" written in the fourth grade.

YEAR IN YEAR OUT

School is in, summer is out.
All the children start to pout.
Until Halloween, they're mean;
Then after that, they're sort of fat
From the candy that they've eaten
After going trick-or-treatin'.

Some child might have a sticky thumb
From playing with his bubble gum.
Another might have a stomach ache
From eating too much chocolate cake.
The child with the monster suit
Got more than his share of candy and fruit.

Before the jack-o'-lantern starts to rot
My mom boils it inside a pot.
Then my brother begins to cry,
"Mom, please make a pumpkin pie!"

The season is fall and as a rule
The temperature gets rather cool.
It gets in the forties, it gets in the thirties,
And then you don't see any more birdies.

The birdies! The birdies! Where do they go?
They go someplace to avoid the snow.
They go down south below the equator
And they won't be back 'til several months later.

Hooray! It's time for winter vacation,
Hanukah, Christmas, and relaxation
Without any homework aggravation!
It is a season for gifts and play.
The children are happy, excited, and gay.

It's time for New Year's Eve, that's fine!
We'll have wine, and dine, and sing "Auld Lang Syne."
Then quick as a wink our vacation is done. . . .
I must admit, we had lots of fun!

The first day back in school is tough.
In my opinion, I've learned enough.
Still I must go to school, for it's sad but true,
There ARE many things I must learn to do.

There's a long spread of time that is not in this rhyme.
Soon it's February 14th—who's YOUR Valentine?
Then in blows March with winds so strong
That as you walk they push you along.
Those who like to fly kites could be young or old,
Big or small, timid or bold.

Passover and Easter come in the spring
With all the joys the season can bring.
These are wonderful holidays
Which we celebrate in many ways.

Of all special days I think the worst
Is the one that occurs on April the first.
I really don't like it when I am picked
To be the one who gets fooled and tricked.

Then after April with all its showers
Comes the month of May, with beautiful flowers.
We can hardly wait for the very last day,
For beginning in June we can sleep late and play.

Vacation is in, school is out!!
All the children laugh and shout!!
Hope we go on a trip, and that it's quite far. . . .
Do you think we will go by boat, plane, or car?

On the Fourth of July, Independence Day,
We'll go on a picnic, and after, we'll play.
In July and August we get lots of rest
And do all the things we like to do best.

Some go to camp, and some stay home.
Some go to AstroWorld, some go to Rome!
Our holiday is fun, we play in the sun,
We jump and we run. . . . but now it's all done.

School is in, summer's out.
It wouldn't do any good to pout.
We see old friends, but there's little play
And a whole lot of study . . . . SO WE'LL MAKE AN "A"!!

David Stark

Free Verse

The first writing by children should be very free—something we might call word pictures. An example from a first-grader is a poem about time.

THE CLOCK

The clock tells time
  Bedtime
    Suppertime
      Playtime
The best time of all.

Barry Page

This kind of writing, as it develops, becomes the kind of free verse written by a seventh-grader.

The sky never ends
up and up forever high
reaching for the top

Darkness spreads like ink
Till the stars shyly peep through
And extend their light

The morning comes thin
and pinkish paint soars the sky
The sun wakes us up

Christine Jenkins

Concrete Poetry

A kind of poetry that may appeal to children throughout the elementary grades is a special kind of picture writing. In concrete poetry the words either outline a visual picture of the topic or form a more solid picture of the idea of the poem. Mark Davis's poem about birds is a fine example of concrete poetry.

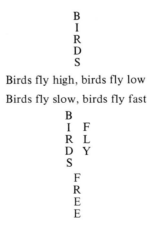

Chris, a third-grader, contributed the following concrete poem about going up a hill.

The Hill

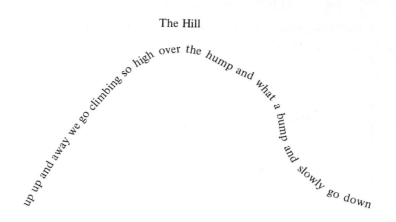

up up and away we go climbing so high over the hump and what a bump and slowly go down

Concrete poetry can be one of the easiest kinds of poetry for young people to write because there is so much appeal inherent in the visual picture and because there is so little structure that is predetermined. Since the poet sets the pattern of the concrete poem, it may also have a very complex form and be a most demanding kind of poetry to write.

Invented Unrhymed Poetry

Several of the invented forms of poetry that do not depend upon rhyme give children some structure for composing without being too difficult to use. After seeing several examples of a particular kind of poem, students can compose their own poems without knowing the technical names of the parts of speech. An easy form of poetry is the cinquain. This is a five-line poem: line 1 is the name of something or someone; line 2, two words that describe; line 3, three *-ing* words that show an action like *running* or *shaking*; line 4, a four-word comment or feeling; and line 5, one word which is either a repeat of line 1 or a synonym for that line. Betsy's cinquain is about a candle.

> *Candle*
> *Bright, light*
> *Glowing, shining, sparkling*
> *Such a pretty sight*
> *Fire*

A group of first-graders dictated the following poem about a cat.

> *Cat*
> *Furry, cuddly,*
> *Walking, meowing, scratching*
> *Likes people petting him*
> *Kitten*

Another group of children decided to make an even smaller cinquain and came up with the following poems about some fish in their room.

Fish
Big, little
Swimming, eating, hiding
In water
Blurp!

Fish
Big, small
Swimming, floating, eating
Sliyme things
YUK!

The rather unconventional spelling of slimy doesn't really detract from the poem; in fact, it makes it seem even slimier.

Another invented form which is a bit more difficult is the diamante, so called because of its diamond shape. The first three lines follow the cinquain pattern. Line 4 has four nouns which start to form opposite between the second and the third. Then line 5 is like line 3, line 6 is like line 2, and the seventh line is a noun which is the opposite of line 1. Carolyn, a sixth-grader, wrote the following diamante:

> *Enemy*
> *Strange, untried*
> *Challenging, teasing, ignoring*
> *Opponent, competitor—teammate, pal*
> *Playing, sharing, giving*
> *Nice, new*
> *Friend*

Shay has taken a few liberties with the fourth line, but his poem certainly makes his own comment:

Flag
Stars, stripes
Waving, flapping, symbolizing
Expressing leadership—battle torn
Decling, splitting, weakening
Fight, die
War

Children may also enjoy making up their own invented forms of poems. They can vary the number of words in various lines, use certain kinds of words, color words, action words, *-ly* words that describe like *slowly* or *cautiously,* and so on. They might enjoy working on these poems with a partner at first. One group of fourth- and fifth-graders who were studying about their state wrote the following poem in their own invented form:

Georgia
Pines
green and brown
waving, rustling, murmuring
Earth
orange and red
warming, feeding, encouraging
Growth

Rhymed Forms

When you begin to introduce writing rhymed poetry, you should begin with very simple forms. One that has had special appeal and considerable success is terse verse. These poems consist simply of two rhymed words with a rather long explanatory title. Start with the pair of rhymed words and then add the title to it. Children throughout elementary and middle school or junior high school have had fun and success with terse verse. Lee Nichols wrote:

What the girl said to her mother in the springtime—
Green
Scene.

At Christmas time Angela Kentonicks wrote:

What Santa said to the elves—
Toys
Boys

and Darren Gates wrote:

> What the Reindeer said to Santa Claus—
> *Weird*
> *Beard!*

Another form of rhymed poetry which children have enjoyed is the clerihew. Clerihews are four-line poems; line 1 is a name and rhymes with line 2, and then lines 3 and 4 rhyme. These poems are considerably more difficult than terse verse, however; and when they are introduced to children who have had little experience with poetry, the result is often loss of meaning or convoluted word order. In the attempt to meet the rhyme scheme, the children alter their normal language patterns or come up with nonsense verse. This is one important reason for introducing unrhymed poetry to children. You will also want to caution students about substituting rhyme for meaning in their poems. The following are two clerihews written by children who have had some experience with poetry and who were not restricted by the rhyme scheme.

Casey Jones	*Santa Claus*
Broke all of his bones	*Had to pause*
He did it fast	*Bringing toys*
Before he crashed.	*To girls and boys.*
Tammie	William

Another rhymed form of poetry is the triplet, or three-line rhymed poem. Again these are a bit more difficult because of the need to come up with three rhyming words that make sense together at the end of the lines. Here are two written by a group of ten- and eleven-year-olds who succeeded quite well:

As I sat under a tree	*There was a bear*
Along came a bee	*Who had a lot of hair*
And said, "Hi" to me.	*But he did not care.*

There are, of course, additional forms of rhymed poetry with various patterns of rhyming lines. As children become more at ease with poetry, and as they develop a larger vocabulary, they are more able to write rhymed poetry.

We have not included the oriental forms of haiku and tanka in this section although they are often recommended as forms of poetry

for children. Both haiku and tanka, which are syllabic arrangements, make a comment on life in such a way that the whole poem
is really a metaphor. Since we have considerable evidence that
children have a great deal of difficulty understanding metaphorical
language and since writing haiku and tanka calls for making a
seventeen- or thirty-one-syllable metaphorical comment on life, we
feel that both of these forms are too abstract and may be far too
difficult for many elementary school children. Also, accepting any
seventeen syllables arranged in five-seven-five syllable lines without the additional characteristics of the haiku seems to be cheating
children by letting them think they have written a haiku when they
really have not.

THE WRITING PROCESS

Before children actually begin writing poetry there are a number of
things a teacher can do to facilitate matters. Children need to have
a wide background of experience from which to write. A teacher can
make various experiences in school and out of school more meaningful by asking questions that challenge children's thinking and
that help children relate new experiences to familiar ones.

Children also need to have another kind of experience—real
familiarity with poetry of all kinds. They need to hear poetry of all
kinds: poetry that is metered and rhythmical; poetry that is free and
unstructured; poetry written by professional poets and poetry
written by other children or by their teacher; poetry that touches
children's everyday experiences and poetry that stimulates their
dreams; poetry that tells a story and poetry that describes a mood,
a feeling, or a place.

Because poetry is so highly condensed, every word is very important. Teachers can help children write by helping them enlarge
their own vocabularies and by aiding them in seeing various shades
of meaning. Discussing an experience the children have had and
asking children to make close observations helps with this process.
If there is an aquarium in the room, what words could describe
how the various fish move? The small ones *dart* or *dash* or *spurt
about*. The larger ones may *float* or *glide* or *slip from weed to weed*.
The catfish on the bottom may *laze along* or *drift* or *hover about*.
They don't just *swim!* Having the range of words to express just
the right feeling or picture helps children with writing poetry, in
fact, with any writing.

Selecting the right kinds of form to introduce to children, while
still allowing them to use whatever form they like or whatever

seems right for their ideas, is an important part of the teacher's job. A certain amount of form or structure may help children write, but too much demand for meter and rhyme is frustrating and may destroy children's enthusiasm for writing poetry. Sometimes children may be anxious to share their writing—at other times they may appear uninterested. This should be their decision. There should be opportunities for sharing with the teacher or another adult and opportunities for sharing with other children. Some poems may be copied in edited form in individual or classroom books, bound and kept to share with others. You want children to develop an interest in reading and writing their own poetry. The long-range goal is for students to freely express their thoughts and feelings through poetry without the help of motivational devices.

Group Poems

In the primary grades children have many more wonderful ideas than they are capable of writing down. This is a good time for group compositions where everyone can add ideas and feel they have shared in the writing of the poem. One child's contribution often will stimulate another child to add a really special touch. In addition, it gives the children the knowledge that poetry is not something lofty and untouchable, but rather that it is one way to share ideas and experiences with others.

Group writing is also a good way to introduce children to poetic form. After seeing and discussing many examples of the form, the group can write several poems together. Group writing may also mean pairs or trios of children writing together without the teacher's direct supervision or help. Some children really enjoy this kind of experience and feel less self-conscious about their own contributions. In the process of writing together, the discussion of what words to use, which order of ideas is best, or which form fits the idea, leads to new knowledge and increased interest in writing.

One of the most important things for the teacher to recognize is that no one can simply turn on creativity. Creative writing of stories or poems can not be done in thirty minutes neatly scheduled for Friday afternoon. Giving children longer periods of work time with a variety of activities to choose from is much more productive. There will be some children who will nearly always choose to write alone, and others who will prefer some kind of group writing. That's just part of the individuality of children. Sometimes children will get very excited about writing and produce a great deal; other times, they may write very little or nothing. That, too, is being an individual.

Found Poetry

Found poetry may be a kind of poetry that children will enjoy discovering. Found poetry comes from prose—a segment of prose that can be rearranged into poetry. You can find poetry in any number of types of prose—advertising, descriptive writing, stories, and so on. The piece of prose, when rearranged in some format, may take on a shape much in the same way concrete poetry does or it may be set out like free verse.

Here is an example from an article by William F. Herrnkind about the "Strange March of the Spiny Lobster" for the June 1975 *National Geographic*.

> A prickly forest of legs and feelers seethes under a rock ledge 25 feet down in the warm Gulf Stream washing the Great Bahama Bank. Spiny lobsters—hundreds of them—cram a single den no bigger than a pool table. Slowly, several leaders emerge, drawing others into bustling podlike clusters. Gradually the pods string out into lengthening files. . . .
>
> Then it begins: a relentless head-to-tail march, a mysterious impulse that drives these crustaceans day and night for miles along the sandy, unprotected shallows.

This might be arranged into a free verse poem by selecting certain phrases and rearranging them into a poetic form.

> *A prickly forest*
> *of legs and feelers*
> $ee^{h}e_{s}$
> $s_{t}s$
> *under a rock ledge.*
> *Spiny lobsters*
> *cram*
> *a single den.*
> *S l o w l y*
> *several leaders emerge.*
> *Then it begins*
> *a relentless*
> *head-*
> *to-*
> *tail*
> *march.*

With a shorter passage, the entire portion of prose might be used as a found poem.

Working with found poetry is good experience for many children. It may make them more aware of writing styles and phrasing, and also be a good introduction to poetry that says something that is not about trees and flowers and fairies. For children who are unsure of their ability to write poetry, found poetry may be an intermediate step to original writing.

Evaluating Children's Poetry

Evaluation of poetry is a particularly difficult task for anyone, and it is especially important for the teacher not to impose adult standards on children's writing. One practice that might help in guiding and evaluating children's progress in writing poetry is for the teacher to write. Also, as in story writing, emphasis on valuing in the evaluation process (instead of on grading) is a way to heighten interest and ability.

The following guidelines may help in indicating the kinds of things teachers may look for and appreciate in children's poetry.

An awareness of an experience: The sense that the child has written about an event that meant something.

Sincerity of feeling: The impression of honesty and genuine expression.

Appropriate and natural language: The words are the child's own and fit the topic; there is no obvious straining of sentence structure to make a rhyme; the words are precise without seeming unnatural.

Creation of a response in the reader to the poem: The reader of the poem is somehow touched, amused, or made conscious of something new because of the poem.

Responding to children's poems by telling them what you particularly liked in the poem and having other children hear and read their poems and tell what they liked stimulates both an interest in writing poetry and growth in writing. Responding with encouragement does far more good than any grading scheme or evaluation system.

INFORMATIONAL WRITING: RECORDING AND REPORTING

One of the most difficult tasks for children in elementary school is that of writing an informational report. Part of their problem is that reporting calls for a more formal key or style of language than they are accustomed to using, and another part of the problem is that they are told to write a report without being given enough help in how to do this. What too often happens is that they look up information in an encyclopedia or other reference books and then copy whole paragraphs or sections for their report. We would like to suggest that there is an earlier kind of informational writing that should precede report writing—recording. In written recording children begin to develop the skills necessary for more formal reporting.

DEFINING RECORDING

Written recording involves some kind of data gathering on a first-hand basis and then converting the information in these data into written sentence or paragraph form. As a beginning step in informational writing, the information that the children use is something they themselves have observed and recorded or something they have found out personally by surveying, measuring, and so on. Since we know that children of elementary school age do not learn from abstract sources, it is particularly important to involve them in collecting the information they will be writing about.

The observations or survey results should be categorized by the children on some type of chart or graph. This grouping or categorizing helps to consolidate the information they have gathered into a manageable form. Then they are ready to write sentences or paragraphs about their observations.

Learning to record is an important process for children. They learn how to use information and how to organize and write their observations on paper. Not until they have had a lot of opportunities to use the recording process are they ready for written reports which involve library materials and other secondhand sources for their information.

Written recording is an appropriate activity for children in all grades, but is especially valuable for older children who have not had previous experiences with recording. It should be a regular part of the writing program for younger children who need many experiences with written recording before moving into report writing.

CLASSROOM RECORDING EXPERIENCES

The kinds of recording experiences that children have should be related to the other activities they are doing rather than unconnected exercises intended for practice. Recording relates very well to science and social studies where children are observing, comparing, and surveying anyway.

Comparisons

Young children are very perceptually oriented, and the teacher can capitalize on this by challenging them to compare two items. These might be two shells, two rocks of different types, or two plant cuttings. More mature children can compare three or four samples, looking for similarities and differences. An occasional question or suggestion from the teacher may help them make finer distinctions among the items they are comparing.

In comparing plant cuttings, the children will quickly notice the colors of the leaves, their general shape, and perhaps whether they are fuzzy, smooth, or waxy. They may not notice if the leaves grow opposite one another or if they alternate, whether the stem is round or square, and whether the plants have a distinctive odor or not. These are the kinds of cues the teacher may suggest when the children appear to have finished their comparison.

Observations

There are many, many observations that children make that can be used for experiences with recording. These may involve observations of the living things in their classroom or on the playground. They may involve observations about the experiments they are conducting in science. As children observe, they should keep some type of log, journal, or chart. If they are recording an event over a period of time, the observations need to be made at regular intervals.

One group of second-graders made observations about changes that took place during the fall season. They each took a particular tree on the playground area and went out every two weeks to see what changes were taking place. Some others kept track of the average daily temperatures and amounts of rain during those same two-week periods. By mid-November they were ready to put together their observations and write about the changes that take place in the fall.

A group from a fourth-grade class made daily observations of the baby gerbils born in their classroom. They recorded the growth of fur, when the eyes opened, when they began to eat independently, how much they weighed, how well they walked, etc. After five weeks the gerbils were grown, and the children wrote their description of the growth of the baby gerbils based on their recording.

Surveys

Occasionally a disagreement over something or the mention of a favorite program or pet may lead children to take a survey of some kind. Any number of things may be surveyed—favorite sports, foods, colors, television shows, birthday months, transportation used in getting to school, or state capitols visited. The results of the survey can be easily graphed and written about.

Taking a survey is the beginning of interviewing and is an important way of gathering information for reporting. At first the children can make the survey within their own room; later, they may survey children in other rooms, the teachers or other school personnel, or people within the community.

Measuring

Still another kind of recording experience involves taking measurements of various kinds and recording the results. Children may compare standard measures (foot, cup, inch) against nonstandard measures (span of a hand, a glass, a piece of yarn). They may work with various standard measures—cup, pint, quart, gallon—to find out for themselves how many cups are in each of the others, or how many pints in the quart, gallon, or half-gallon. Their measuring could involve comparisons between measures in use now in the United States and metric measurements.

Any number of regular activities that children do can be used as a basis for recording. Children need many experiences with recording as a basis for the more formal written reporting that they will be called on to do later. If they can learn to depend on their own observations and ideas in the early stages of reporting, they will not be as prone to copy pages and pages from encyclopedias. Also, some children are much more oriented toward the realistic than toward the imaginative. They need opportunities to write in that vein as well as opportunities to write stories and poems. The kinds of close observation used in recording form a solid basis for descriptive writing.

MOVING INTO REPORTING

There are several ways of easing the transition from informal recording activities into more formal reporting. The first written reports might involve topics closely related to the children's interests which could be easily illustrated. The main part of the information could be conveyed with a series of illustrations or a display of some kind. The children could set up a model or diorama or collection on a table display or a series of illustrations on a bulletin board. The labels or explanations along with the illustrations would constitute their report.

The first uses of reference materials might involve informational books which could be shared. Too often we think only of encyclopedias or similar reference books for reports when there is a wide variety of well-written illustrated informational books with a range of reading levels. The first reports that children write might be a review or summary of one of these informational books.

DEVELOPING REPORTING SKILLS

There are three major skills involved in writing reports: taking notes, organizing ideas for writing, and using reference materials. These skills need to be taught. You can not just send children to the library with a topic for a report and a set time period and expect them to be able to write a good report. Each skill needs to be taught before the children are required to use it.

Taking notes Much of the problem with copying portions of encyclopedias and giving them as reports starts with children's inability to take notes in their own words. Although selecting the main idea from a paragraph or even a larger portion of material is a reading skill that is tested throughout the school years, much of the time the main ideas are chosen from a predetermined set of choices. In order to prepare children for stating the main idea from a range of materials in their own words, a great deal of preliminary work needs to be done.

One workable way to do this is to write out on chart paper or on a transparency a paragraph of material from a source similar to the ones they will be using. Have the children read through the paragraph carefully, then remove it from their sight and ask them to write down one or two of the main ideas that were in the paragraph. The instruction may be more effective if done in small groups. When they have finished writing (or nearly finished), ask them to take another look to fill in any details or ideas they missed. Discussion is very helpful. You will want to talk about the main ideas and the details that are important to include.

When they have become proficient at selecting the main ideas from materials that you control, they are ready to work with duplicated materials on their own. This is a critical time to make sure that they are not reverting to copying whole sentences from the printed information, but rather formulating the ideas in their own words. After they have mastered the skill, they are then ready to take notes independently from library sources.

Organizing ideas There are a number of ways to organize the material collected for writing—many of them highly individualistic. We will suggest one way of pulling ideas together so that they form a kind of rough outline. Mature writers may not need to go through this kind of process as they are more able to handle abstractions and organize mentally without resorting to paper and pencil.

This process of organizing material before writing has four main steps: listing ideas, grouping ideas, ordering the ideas within groups, and then ordering the groups of ideas. At first the child lists all of the ideas to be included in the report (each one in a word or short phrase). Then the child groups together the ideas that somehow go together. After this, the ideas within each group are put in sequence for writing. The final step in organizing is to decide which group of ideas will be dealt with first, second, third, etc. When that is finished, the child has a rough outline of the report. At any time in the process, a particular idea may be discarded or changed to another group.

Teachers may want to go through this process several times before expecting children to be able to do it independently. The first two steps are really categorizing, and are most appropriate activities for younger children to do simply as a way of organizing information.

Using reference materials Before starting to use reference materials independently in the library, children need some help in knowing what kind of information is in what kind of book and how to find out whether a particular book covers the topic of interest. If you can obtain a small collection of reference materials in the classroom, you can help your students learn to use an index and table of contents. Skimming is an important skill in working with reference materials, especially skimming through a segment and reading only the titles and subtitles of the various sections. If you have a school librarian or can locate a parent, high school student, or aide who is familiar with library research procedures, they can be of immeasurable help.

EVALUATING INFORMATIONAL WRITING

Report writing and recording are primarily informational and not particularly personal or emotional in nature, so that the teacher is somewhat more free to suggest revisions and help with editing. The general purpose of the report or recording is to communicate information to others rather than to express individual ideas. Because of this, it should be easily read by others. Conventional spelling, punctuation, and mechanics aid the reader and should be correct as a courtesy to the reader.

Marking the report with *Sp.* (for spelling errors) or *P* (for punctuation errors) is not a very helpful way to go about making the child's report better mechanically. Corrections should be made in individual conferences with students. One idea that may help your students accept the idea of correcting their reports, is to always refer to their first writings as the "first draft." If one knows from the beginning that there will be revisions and corrections—that one is writing a first draft instead of the final copy—it is much easier to revise and rewrite.

Keeping some kind of record of the kinds of problems particular children are having will help you group for instruction. You may want to keep their first drafts in a folder for future reference. However, attaching a note of items for instruction may save time in the long run. A columnar chart similar to the one suggested earlier for recording children's work may be even more helpful. As with any kind of writing, pointing out what the children did well does help improve the quality of recording or reporting. It also may serve as valuable information for others in the class.

PERSONAL WRITING

Personal writing includes all of the kinds of writing that might be called social correspondence in etiquette books as well as the writing one does for oneself—reminders, journals or diaries, and messages—and personal notes. Because most personal writing is very private, it presents special problems for the teacher. What writing of this kind should be checked and what should be private? How do you encourage children to freely express themselves in writing, much as they would in an intimate conversation, without being an intruder? How important *is* form? Perhaps two samples of letters written to an author will clarify the issue.

November 15, 1975
Dear Mr. Burch,
Our teacher read Queenie Peavie *to us. It was a nice book. Thank you for writing it. We liked it.*

Sincerely,
Julianne

Dear Mr. Burch,
Our teacher read us the story you wrot about that girl who was so mean and I wanted to tell you that lots of girls are that way cause the boys are so mean to them that they half to be that way. You just made it seam so real that I could believe it.

Your friend,
Julianne

If you were Mr. Burch, which letter would you prefer to get? Letter number one is in perfect form, and probably that student could name the parts of the letter: the heading, greeting, body, and closing. The second letter has a few spelling errors, no date, and some other mechanical errors, but it certainly lets one know that the child has been touched emotionally by the story, that she really did like it.

Certainly proper form does need to be learned, but not at the expense of individuality and ideas. Acquiring form may be a slow process that takes place over a number of years. Provide children with a sample of the form, and let them emphasize individual ideas. The form becomes an instrument like the sample letters in manuscript or cursive writing over the chalkboard, something to refer to when needed. It should not be the whole focus of the experience.

PROVIDING REAL EXPERIENCES FOR WRITING

The most important thing that children have to learn about letter writing, personal notes, invitations, announcements, or messages—all of the kinds of personal writing that will be sent to someone else—is that one can communicate ideas through writing. Writing can get something done, can get an idea across. This means that writing these kinds of things for practice—just for practice—is self-defeating. Writing needs to be real.

Letter writing Both personal letters and what might ordinarily be termed business letters may be somewhat informal during the elementary school years. If children are writing for information of some kind or wish to order something, you will need to remind them to put their addresses and their full name in the letter, suggesting the proper placement. You may offer to check over the letter if they would like you to, and to help them with spelling as they are composing it. However, probably the most important thing that you can do is to use meaningful situations that call for writing a letter.

You may be able to establish pen pal relationships with a class in another city or a different part of the country. When one of the children or a group has enjoyed a particular story or book, suggest that they write to the author. If you need some "free or inexpensive" teaching materials, recruit some of the children to order them for you. Keep the addresses of children who move away during the year so their friends can correspond with them. Adopt some patients in a nearby veteran's hospital or nursing home. You can encourage the children to write to the subject or author of articles (in the children's magazines they subscribe to, in "TV Guide," or in your local newspaper) in which they seem particularly interested.

Personal notes Instead of being upset by children writing notes to each other, capitalize on their interest and channel it into good practice in writing. Set up mailboxes for each child somewhere in the room, where they may put notes for one another and where you may also put notices, reminders, or notes for them. A special note from the teacher once in a while may be cherished, and writing only two or three a day does not take much time. It's a nice way to compliment someone who does not often get compliments.

Invitations Children of all ages can help write invitations to others asking them to visit the classroom for something special. If they are too young to write the invitation in letter form, compose some that they can complete: Please come to _____, Where _____, Time _____, etc. Even beginning first-graders can copy in the necessary information and make the decorations for the covers. When the children are older, they can write out the full invitation. You will need to remind them of what information is needed, but they can do the actual wording themselves. Perhaps there should be a writer or secretary on the "Helpers" chart each week to take care of invitations and thank you notes. Be sure to give the secretary something to write during the week, even if it is a thank you note to the cooks for an especially good lunch.

Announcements and messages Children need to be able to make announcements and take down messages in written form. The key is providing opportunities for them to have real practice in doing this. However, be sure to have alternative plans for those really crucial pieces of information until your children have had enough practice to be completely reliable.

KEEPING A DIARY OR JOURNAL

Keeping a diary or a journal which is completely private or one that may be shared is a valuable experience for upper elementary school age children. In this book they can keep notes for themselves about something interesting they have observed, a new word or phrase they like, an idea for a story or poem, something they have wondered about and would like to check later, or just how they felt about the day or what they did.

The journal may be completely private; if so, perhaps you can provide a file drawer or other locked closet or drawer where they may be stored. If they are not so private, the children may wish to keep the journal at their desk or storage spot. Sometimes a diary with space for every day for a whole year is rather intimidating. Instead, they could make their own bound book and fill in the days or dates as they have something to write. They might like to try out the idea first just for one month, and bind a booklet with the days and dates for that month.

At the end of a week or a month, you might like to take some time with them to talk over the good times and the bad times you have had as a class. Their journals can serve as a reminder and also as a chart of their growth. They will need time, though, to write in their journals. Some teachers who have blocks of time for a variety of activities find that the children can take care of this writing during that time. Others with a more structured schedule like to take a quiet time at the end of the day for the children to make their journal entries, get homework assignments, and generally catch up on the day before the bus leaves or the bell rings.

EVALUATING AND IMPROVING PERSONAL WRITING

The main key to improving personal writing is giving children ample opportunities to use this kind of written communication. A secondary factor is your availability to help when help is needed.

This help may be in the form of individual consultation or it may be providing sample formats and suggesting possibilities for content. A quick, "Be sure to tell Tim about the softball game" or "I think Sally would be interested in what we learned about quilting from Mrs. Sommers" really helps children with ideas to use in their letters. If you do not know the individuals your class is writing to, you may suggest some more general ideas about things you have done as a class and then ask the children for further ideas. Encourage them to write their letters and their journals as though they are telling someone about their experiences. This kind of writing is the closest to "talk written down" that exists.

As far as evaluating personal writing, the evaluation must really be done by the writer and not by the teacher. Asking them to write one thing they have done well and one that they need to work on may help them examine their own strengths and weaknesses.

DEVELOPING A WRITING PROGRAM

Composition should not be a hit-or-miss portion of the elementary school experience. Just as reading skills are carefully developed throughout the elementary grades, so composition skills should be developed. We have suggested in this chapter some writing experiences of each type that are appropriate for all of the various age groupings of children.

One of the two main things to consider in planning a writing program is to provide a balance of writing experiences. Children need many opportunities to write stories and poems, record or report, and undertake a variety of kinds of personal writing. There should be some kind of sequence that will ensure variety in the writing program. Just as they should not hear the same book read to them each year, no matter how much their teachers may enjoy reading it, they should not write just cinquains or terse verse year after year. Teachers also need to provide for individual children's abilities and growth. Some children are ready to move into more formal aspects of writing earlier than others; options and choices need to be provided along with guidance from the teacher.

We have not set up a sequence of writing activities on a grade by grade basis because there is so much variation from one classroom to another and from one child to another within an individual class. Children do not have to write one story every week and one poem and one report and one letter. They do, however, need meaningful opportunities to write each of these kinds of compositions sometime during a larger block of time.

The second factor to consider in developing the writing program is that much of their writing can and should be integrated with other aspects of the language arts program and with other content areas. Their individual interests and preferences come into consideration here. If the teacher is alert to the possibilities for writing inherent in other content areas or those associated with the units of stories in the basic reading program or the books children are working with in an individualized reading program, it is easy to structure a variety of writing experiences that may be integrated with other work and with children's interests.

Our obligation to the children we teach is to make them not only competent writers, but also adults who find pleasure in writing and who can easily communicate in writing.

PRELIMINARY LEARNING ACTIVITIES

1. In each of the dictated compositions below, suggest two specific things the child did well.

   WHAT I WOULD DO IF I WENT TO THE MOON

   If I went to the moon, I'd take a friend and we'd jump over the craters and we'd eat cheese and crackers and drink cokes. We'd visit the stars and jump over their points. We'd sleep in a rocket and go back to earth.

   THE ROAD TO GRANDMA'S HOUSE

   One morning we were on the way to Grandma's house and we always liked to sing songs on the way. And sometimes when we come to a big bump, we take off our seatbelts and go flying in the air. And you can look up in the sky and look how blue it is. And there's a bunch of green trees along the way.

   We go riding on a horse at Grandma's house and in the night-time Grandma tells us stories about people who lived in the house before they did. And how they killed wolves who got in the back door. And once my brother had to go to the outside bathroom and when he came out, he got chased by a lion. And Mom didn't believe it!

2. What elements of originality do you see in the following unedited stories? List the original elements and write out a brief note to the child-author of each piece.

SAVED

One day I was camping out in back of my yard. Suddenly it turn night. I was afraid of the dark and so I went to sleep. I heard creeping noises and the wind blowing. Then I heard footsteps. And suddenly I saw something on the ground. It was a dead body. Then I turnn into a detective. I heard the footsteps again. I saw green man from Mars, but he didn't see me and I shot him with my 22, 38, 49, 50, 58 shotgun. And thats how I solve my mystery.

JUNIOR

Junior is a bug with eight legs. He's a very nice bug and likes to climb trees. and he bites them too. But one day there was a man standing very still. Junior thought he was a tree and bit hem. It hurt so bad, the man jumped, and through Junior off! That taught Junior a leson. Allways check good before you bite.

3. Give examples from the stories at five grade levels of the developmental trends in children's writing that pertain to language development.

4. Draw up a chart similar to the one suggested in the section on evaluating children's story writing and check off or record what you think should be recorded for the story below.

LISANINEING SECRETLY

Once a pome a time a hippo was liveing in a zoo. He was tired of hearing the same old thing (Hot Dogs) (Hurry folks step right up.) It was makeing him sick. So he decied to run away from the zoo. that night he herd strange noisees! He said, (Who goses there.) So the next day was almoset here! he had to hurry if he was going to run away. the next day, the zoo keeper was going to hippo's cage. Hippo wasen't there! He left a note the note read,

> *Dear Zoo,*
> *I was tired of hearing the same old thing. So I ran away.*
> *Hippo*

He found lots of new things to hear a policeman's wishle, Beeps of cars, oh just lots of things! But he missed all the people watching him, splashing all day. And even the loud noeises! So he said, the zoo is my home, I miss it there. So he went to the zoo. All the people was glad to see him! But he relised that after you are use to someing you will miss it if you leve it!

> *the end*

5. Suggest a children's book for K-second, one for third-fourth, and one for fifth-sixth grades that you might use directly in an imaginative writing experience. Indicate also how you would use each of the three books and what discussion or dramatization might precede the writing.

6. Try writing some poetry using three or four of the different kinds of poetry forms. Then indicate what kinds of problems they might present to children trying to use them.

7. Conduct a recording experience by making some comparisons or observations, taking a survey, or doing some measuring. Put your results into some kind of chart or graph and write the results in a paragraph to two.

8. Start keeping a journal that you might share with your class when you start teaching.

PARTICIPATION ACTIVITIES

1. Have some children dictate or write some stories using a variety of stimuli, and evaluate them to see which stimulus prompts the most creativity and involvement on the part of the children.

2. Try teaching (inductively) one of the poetic forms that is appropriate for the children with whom you are working. Do some group compositions, and encourage children who would like to try writing some on their own.

3. Set up some comparisons or experiments related to what the class is studying in science and have the children record them. After the children have set up their chart of observations or similarities and differences, have each small group write what they discovered in paragraph form.

4. Have the children do some kinds of personal writing—diaries, journals, etc.—whatever is appropriate considering other classroom activities.

CARLSON ANALYTICAL ORIGINALITY SCALE

I. **Story Structure**
   1. Unusual title
   2. Unusual beginning
   3. Unusual dialogue
   4. Unusual ending
   5. Unusual plot

II. Novelty

1. Novelty of names
2. Novelty of locale
3. Unique punctuation and expressional devices
4. New words
5. Novelty of ideas
6. Novel devices
7. Novel theme
8. Quantitative thinking
9. New objects created
10. Ingenuity in solving situations
11. Recombinations of ideas in unusual relationships
12. Picturesque speech
13. Humor
14. Novelty of form
15. Inclusion of readers
16. Unusual related thinking

III. Emotional Aspects

1. Unusual ability to express emotional depth
2. Unusual sincerity in expressing personal problems
3. Unusual ability to identify self with problems or feelings of others
4. Unusual horror theme

IV. Individuality

1. Unusual perceptive sensitivity
2. Unique philosophical thinking
3. Facility in beautiful writing
4. Unusual personal experience

V. Style of Stories

1. Exaggerated tall tale
2. Fairy tale
3. Fantasy turnabout of characters
4. Highly fantastic central idea or theme
5. Fantastic creatures, objects, or persons
6. Personal experience
7. Individual story style

REFERENCES

¹ Alvina Treut Burrows, June D. Ferebee, Doris C. Jackson, and Dorothy O. Saunders. *They All Want to Write.* New York: Prentice-Hall, 1952.

² Ruth Kearney Carlson. "Recent Research in Originality," *Elementary English,* vol. 40, October 1963, pp. 583–589.

³ David Holbrook. "Creativity in the English Programme" IN *Creativity in English* (Geoffrey Summerfield, ed.). Champaign, Illinois: National Council of Teachers of English, 1968.

⁴ Burton and Arnold. *U.S. Office of Education, Cooperative Research Project No. 1523.* Florida State University, 1963.

⁵ McColly and Remstad. *U.S. Office of Education, Cooperative Research Project No. 1528,* University of Wisconsin, 1963.

[6] Evelyn Wright. "Wishes, Lies and Dreams: Pedagogical Prescriptions," *Elementary English,* vol. 51, April 1974, p. 553.

[7] S. M. Lane and M. Kemp. *An Approach to Creative Writing in the Primary School.* London: Blackie and Son, 1967, Preface.

[8] James Moffett. *A Student-Centered Language Arts Curriculum, Grades K-13: A Handbook for Teachers.* Boston: Houghton Mifflin, 1968, p. 118.

[9] Teacher's Manual, *Making It Strange.* New York: Harper & Row, 1968, pp. 33–34.

[10] Antonio Frasconi. *The House That Jack Built.* New York: Harcourt, Brace, 1958; AND Harve Zemach. *The Judge.* New York: Farrar, Strauss, 1969.

[11] Maurice Sendak. *Chicken Soup with Rice.* New York: Harper & Row, 1962.

[12] Diane Redfield Massie. *Dazzle.* New York: Parents' Magazine, 1969.

[13] Geoffrey Summerfield. "About Drama in England," *Elementary English,* vol. 47, no. 1, January 1971, pp. 20–21.

[14] Eldonna L. Evertts, ed. *Explorations in Children's Writing.* Champaign, Illinois: National Council of Teachers of English, 1970, pp. 86–87.

[15] K. Yamamoto. *Scoring Manual for Evaluating Imaginative Stories.* Minneapolis, Minnesota: Bureau of Educational Research, University of Minnesota, January 1961.

[16] E. Paul Torrance. "Supplementary Scoring Guide for the Evaluation of Originality and Interest" IN *Scoring Manual for Evaluating Imaginative Stories.* Minneapolis, Minnesota: Bureau of Educational Research, University of Minnesota, January 1961.

[17] Ruth K. Carlson. "An Originality Story Scale," *The Elementary School Journal,* April 1965, pp. 366–374.

[18] Ken Kantor. "Evaluating Creative Writing: A Different Ball Game," *English Journal,* April 1975, pp. 72–74.

[19] Ibid., p. 73.

[20] Alvina T. Burrows. "Teaching Composition," IN *What Research Says to the Teacher* (Sidney Borrow, ed.), no. 18. National Education Association, 1959, p. 11.

[21] Burrows, Ferebee, Jackson, and Saunders. *They All Want to Write.*

[22] Moffet. *A Student-Centered Curriculum,* p. 126.

[23] Mrs. Blazer. *Madison Local School District.* Columbus, Ohio.

[24] Moffett. *A Student-Centered Curriculum,* p. 242.

[25] John Ciardi. "Mummy Slept Late and Daddy Fixed Breakfast," *You Read to Me and I'll Read to You.* Philadelphia: Thomas Y. Crowell, 1962.

[26] Ann Terry. *Children's Poetry Preferences: A National Survey of Upper Elementary Grades.* Urbana, Illinois: National Council of Teachers of English, 1974.

[27] Alice B. Coast. "Children's Choices in Poetry as Affected by Teacher's Choices," *Elementary English Review,* vol. v, May 1928, p. 145.

[28] Chow Loy Tom. "What Teachers Read to Pupils in the Middle Grades" (unpublished Ph.D. dissertation). Columbus, Ohio: Ohio State University, 1969, p. 194.

CHAPTER ELEVEN

Supportive Writing Skills

PREVIEW QUESTIONS

1 When should children's writing be corrected or revised?

2 How can instruction in mechanics of writing, spelling, and handwriting be taught within a meaningful context?

3 In what ways can spelling instruction be more individualized and meaningful?

4 How can one improve handwriting instruction in both initial instruction and skill development?

When we talk about supportive writing skills, we are referring to capitalization, punctuation, spelling, and handwriting. Our effective use of these skills enables others to read easily and understand our written language.

Stop and think what would happen if the spelling of words was not standardized. What if we were all responsible for developing our own spelling system? We might pick up the newspaper one morning and see: WUMUN PHALLS PHROM TOUER. And in the evening paper we might read the same headline, but the words would be spelled differently: WUHMUHN FALS FRUHM TAUR. How mind-boggling! If individual systems prevailed, we would continuously be learning and adjusting to new systems. Reading material without capitalization and punctuation items would produce similar frustrations. Can you imagine reading a recent best selling novel in which all punctuation was omitted? It could be the "longest" book that you have ever attempted to read.

Using standard punctuation and spelling and legible handwriting is a courtesy to your reader.

SKILL DEVELOPMENT IN CONTEXT

Supportive writing skills help the writer transfer oral communication into written communication. A comma indicates a brief pause that you would normally make when communicating orally. An exclamation mark serves to show your amazement, astonishment, or excitement—something that is naturally understood by the intonation of your voice when you speak.

Understanding the Importance of Supportive Writing Skills

We need to help children understand how the acquisition of writing skills is essential to their written communication. Too frequently students are asked to memorize isolated rules that they should apply to their writing such as, "Place a period at the end of a sentence which tells something." Rules learned out of context with little explanation for learning them in the first place are rarely remembered. Children are more apt to develop and use good writing skills when they understand why correct punctuation, capitalization, spelling, and handwriting are important.

To help students understand the relationship between effective written communication and the use of correct writing skills, experiences reading their own writing aloud and also having others read it are needed. When they try to read an unedited first draft, the children will quickly see the need for more conventional mechanics of writing, spelling, and more legible handwriting. You may even want to present material that illustrates the dependence of written language communication upon skills in spelling, handwriting, capitalization, and punctuation.

Using a Functional Approach to Teaching Writing Skills

If we view writing skills as tools that we use to make our written language more readable for others, then we must use a functional approach to teaching these skills. Skills taught in isolation from content or the composition process are meaningless. First, we must have the thoughts or ideas that we wish to express. These comprise our composition. We already know that young children have difficulty keeping more than one thought in mind. To ask them to express on paper ideas and thoughts while at the same time remembering commas, question marks, periods, and so on, is asking too much. Older children may experience the same difficulty, or they may have decided from what their teachers emphasize that spelling, handwriting, punctuation, and capitalization are more important than the ideas in the composition. Therefore, every word may be spelled correctly, periods are in their right places, and question marks appear at the end of questions, but the composition itself has suffered.

A functional approach allows both primary and upper elementary students to express themselves freely while attending to correct spelling, legible handwriting, proper punctuation, and capitalization. Neither the quality of the composition nor appropriate skills are slighted when the writing experience is done in several steps. Children are encouraged first to put down their thoughts and ideas on paper. The emphasis is upon the quality of content in the first draft, not correct writing mechanics. After a child is satisfied with the content and there is a need to edit, emphasis is then given to correct spelling and proper placement of punctuation or capitalization items in the composition. After making the necessary corrections, the final draft of the composition is prepared. This final writing is done in the student's most legible handwriting and is then shared with others.

Chris's poem illustrates this process. The student first wrote his thoughts and feelings, giving little attention to writing mechanics, poetry form, or spelling. Afterwards, he rewrote the poem to make

A young animal started eating
grass in the meadow
Looking straight down at the
fresh green grass.
His felt so steady with fresh
brown fur
He is listing for any movement
in case of danger.
A little crackle of a twig
breaking.
A split second it was off in
a come. flash
A hunter was coming out to a
bush. He fired.
It fell to the ground
It was a perfect eight point
buck. He got away in a flash

by Chris Gowan

it readable for others. (The revised poem is on page 262.) The poem became part of a growing collection of student poems that have been placed in the classroom library area.

When children recopy their writing, it should be done with a purpose in mind. If we stress the importance of making a paper "letter perfect" for others, then we need to provide a means for sharing the piece of writing. Here are a few ideas that may be used in a classroom situation.

1. Have mailboxes in the classroom where children can actually receive mail from one another. Names can be placed on the boxes and students can deliver their own letters or notes. To make sure that each child writes and receives mail, they may each have a pen pal within the classroom.
2. Children can write and illustrate their own stories. A film from

An animal eating grass in a
meadow,
Looking down at the fresh
green grass,
His feet so steady with fresh
brown fur.
He is listening for any movement
in case of danger,
A little crackle of a twig
breaking,
A split second later he was
off in a flash.
A hunter was coming out to
a bush.
He fired —
But he got away in a flash.

(deer)

by Chris Gowan

Weston Woods, *The Lively Art of the Picture Book,* may be
shown to students to demonstrate how an author / illustrator first
makes a dummy before producing a book in its final form.

3. Children who are interested in reading and writing poetry can
   be responsible for a "Poetry Bulletin Board." They can share
   their poetry by attractively displaying it, and some poems may be
   recorded on cassette tape to accompany the bulletin board. Information regarding poetry content, children's poets, or ideas
   about writing poetry can also be posted on the board.

4. Older children can be encouraged to have a pen pal in another
   part of the country. Or, you may be able to arrange pen pal assignments with another class.

5. Stories written by individual students may be collected and kept
   in a special book. This compilation of children's stories may be
   placed in the classroom library area for others to read. If some
   students wish, they can keep their own book of stories to share

with their parents and friends. (See directions in Chapter Thirteen for making a book.)

MECHANICS OF WRITING: PUNCTUATION AND CAPITALIZATION

Learning to Punctuate Written Material

To illustrate and help children understand how punctuation assists us in writing our language, a teacher may tape-record materials for students to punctuate. The recorded material may be typed on a ditto sheet without punctuation marks and then distributed to the students. As they listen to the tape they can hear a pause, the stress at the close of a question, and an exclamatory remark calling for an exclamation point. If you wish, a key may be provided for children to check what they have done at the end of the recording. Small group instruction may also take place using this method of punctuating material. For example, if a few children are having difficulty in remembering to place commas in a list, specific material may be recorded that contains a series of listed items. The teacher discusses the pause that occurs between each item and how a comma is used to indicate the pause. It is a way of separating one item from another.

Besides punctuating tape-recorded material, children may be taught to read their writing aloud to determine if punctuation is needed. When we read material orally, we frequently pause where it seems most natural. If a question mark is missing at the end of a question, reading the material aloud may call the error to our attention. Children can learn to listen for this when they are reading their own material.

In considering the punctuation items, or "rules" as they are frequently called, we certainly do not expect the child to learn and apply all of them during the first years in school. We need to teach those items that the children actually need to use, remembering that not all children need the same things. Perhaps we should look at the kinds of writing that children do at different levels to determine what punctuation items they need to know.

Preoperational (until about seven) In the early stages of writing, the preoperational child primarily uses uncomplicated sentences. These children begin writing their names, the date, the name of their school, etc. They may also compose or copy notes and invitations to take home to their parents. They are probably dictating

---

and writing experience stories that only require periods, question marks, and commas. We should consider teaching only what they need to use, for to ask children to do more than this may be expecting too much at their developmental level.

Concrete operational (about seven to eleven) This age child is writing more and more. The sentence structure becomes more complex as the child gets older, requiring more sophisticated mechanics of writing. According to research, dialog appears in children's compositions at about the age of nine. Older children are attending to more detail and their ability to use a variety of punctuation marks has increased. As they begin to use more complex structures and their writing becomes more detailed, children need instruction on the aspects of punctuation they are actually using and need for their writing.

Following are two lists of items of conventional punctuation that children in the elementary schools may need to use in their writing. Some of the more complex punctuation devices are not included because we feel they are more appropriate for later ages.

Simple Punctuation
Period at the end of a sentence that states something.
Period after abbreviations or initials.
Question mark at the end of a sentence that asks something.
Comma between day and year in writing a date.
Comma between city and state.
Comma after salutation and closing in a note or personal letter.
Comma to separate three or more items in a list.
Apostrophe in common contractions like *isn't* or *don't.*

More Complex Punctuation
Period after number when listing items. (e.g.: 1. a box
                                                 2. a couch)
Period after numerals or letters in an outline.
Comma with a conjunction such as *and* or *but* in a compound sentence.
Comma to set off an appositive or noun of direct address.
Comma after an introductory phrase or dependent clause.
Comma before a quotation within a sentence.
Apostrophe to show possession.
Apostrophe in less common contractions like *she'll, he's,* or *weren't.*
Exclamation mark at the end of a sentence requiring it.
Quotation marks before and after a direct quotation.
Quotation marks around titles of poems and stories or chapters within a book.

Underlining book titles.
Colon in writing time (1:25) or after salutation in a business letter.
Colon to set off a list that follows.
Hyphen when dividing a word at the end of a line.

Children need first to master those punctuation skills that are most needed in their writing. McKee[1] suggests that there are seven punctuation items that give children difficulty. Glancing at the list, you will notice that the first two items are basic to all written material:

No period at the end of a sentence
No question mark at the end of a question
Failure to use a colon
Lack of a period after abbreviations
Failure to set off nonrestrictive clause by commas
Failure to set off a series by commas
Lack of commas in setting off an appositive

Why are these particular items frequently not applied in children's writing? There may be a number of reasons: the method of instruction, the amount of practice or experience a student has in using these items, and when and how the item is introduced.

What can a teacher do to help children learn and use punctuation skills? We have already mentioned a few significant ideas, but the following list presents a range of possibilities.

1. Tape-record material for children to punctuate.
2. Have children read their writing aloud in order to hear intonations and pauses that indicate a need for punctuation.
3. Conduct instruction in small groups for children having similar difficulties in using particular punctuation items.
4. Teach punctuation inductively and let children see how it works and state their own rules.
5. Prepare written materials for children to punctuate or in which to find punctuation errors only after the rule is discovered inductively.
6. Use devices that will illustrate certain punctuation items:
   a. Show children that a series such as *the wet, cold, icy winter* is the same as saying *the wet and cold and icy winter*.
   b. When an appositive is taken out of a sentence, the sentence remains complete and meaningful: *Mary Smith, the girl next door, is waiting for you (Mary Smith is waiting for you);*

He sat in the chair, the one with the broken arm (He sat in the chair).

7. Prepare transparency materials to use on an overhead projector for children. These may be writing samples that require punctuation; or they may contain errors that can be identified and discussed.

Learning to Capitalize Written Material

The need to learn specific capitalization skills also parallels children's writing needs. The young child will be concerned only with the most frequently used skills such as capitalizing the first word of sentences. Older students, whose writing needs are more varied, will require a wider knowledge about capitalization.

The following suggests simple and more complex items your children may need.

Simple Capitalization
The first word of a sentence
The child's first and last names
The word I
The teacher's name
The month and day of the week
Other people's names
The name of the school
The name of the city and state

More Complex Capitalization
Proper names such as streets, cities, states, countries, oceans, common holidays, and trade names
The first word of the salutation and closing in notes or personal letters
Mother and Father when used in place of their name
Names or abbreviations of titles such as Mr., Reverend, Ms., and Dr.
Names of organizations to which the children may belong such as Grade Five, Girl Scouts, Level III
First and important words in titles of books, stories, poems, compositions
First word in a line of verse in poetry
Names of the Diety, the Bible
The first word of a sentence being quoted
Capitalization as used in outlines

Children can first become aware of the need to capitalize letters when the teacher is writing on the chalkboard or recording a child's dictated story. While writing, the teacher can mention words that should be capitalized. In this way, children can become acquainted with capitalization items before they do much independent writing. They also begin to understand that capitalization is a continual and necessary part of the writing process. If children are to copy their story, the teacher can point out that certain letters should be capitalized and why.

Initial instructions in capitalization can be an integral part of children's writing. Using a student's written work, the teacher can determine what capitalization items a child needs to learn. The student may be helped individually; or, if a number of children have similar capitalization needs, the teacher may group children for instruction.

Look at the following samples of children's written work. For what capitalization skills might you group these children? What kind of instruction might you give them?

> *i like to feed*
> *sam. he is a cute*
> *hamster.*

Jane

> *our class hamster*
> *is fat. he eats all*
> *the time. i like him.*

Susan

> *i like sam and he is*
> *brown and fat. he wiggles*
> *his nose.*

Jeff

All three children need help with the following items: capitalization of the word *I*, capitalization of the first word of a sentence, and capitalization of a proper name (in this instance, Sam). To help Jane, Susan, and Jeff with these capitalization items, the teacher might consider the following:

1. Assuming the children are completely unaware of their errors, beginning instruction is necessary. Using an overhead projector or chalkboard, the teacher may write several sets of sentences correctly capitalized to illustrate the three rules they need to

learn. After they see and can say the words that should be capitalized, other sentences may be written for the children to observe and correct, thus applying their newly acquired knowledge about capitalization. They may be asked to correct their own stories about Sam to be reviewed by the teacher.

2. Following small group instruction, the children may be given material to copy-edit that contains similar capitalization errors, for example, *morris is the name of a cat. he is big because he eats a lot. i like morris.* Or, the children may write their own group story which they will in turn copy and edit for mistakes.

3. a. Sentences for inducing capitalization of *I* might be: *Sue and I are going. I like cats. That is what I want.* These include *I* used in midsentence as well as at the beginning.

   b. Sentences for inducing capitalization of the first word in a sentence could be: *Sally is my friend. The dog chewed his bone. There are two boxes of pencils.*

   c. Sentences for inducing capitalizing a proper name could be: *I saw Benjie on television. My cat is named Fluffy. The new boy is Karl.*

The teacher's questions need to focus attention on the words illustrating correct use of the rule being taught.

Children's "Rule Books"

Children can make and keep their own punctuation and capitalization rule books. When a child is having difficulty in remembering to use a particular item of punctuation or capitalization, the rule for using the item may be written in a special book that is kept close at hand for quick and easy reference.

When the student feels that he is consistently applying the rule in his writing, the written rule may be checked off in the book. Figure 11 might be a page from Jeff's book.

SPELLING INSTRUCTION

The ability to spell correctly is necessary if we are to communicate effectively with others in writing. There is a steadily growing concern that too many students are graduating from high school and college who are poor spellers. Not only have complaints come from parents, but business and industrial management say they are being forced into providing educational programs for many of their employees because they lack basic skills.

Figure 11

Jeff's rule book

With the research evidence that is available today along with tried and proven teaching methods, an instructional program in spelling can be provided to help all students become spellers. For instance, research has established a list of 3,000 words that, when learned, give individuals the power to spell 95 percent of the words needed for normal writing activities. If children learn to spell these 3,000 words, they will have a very adequate writing vocabulary. It has been confirmed that the test-study-test procedure is more effective in teaching spelling than the study-test procedure; and self-correction after the testing situation is a proven aid in learning to spell a word. Our current knowledge about the teaching of spelling includes much more; if we apply this knowledge, we can have a successful spelling program.

Early Experiences with Spelling

Some new research and reports of classroom activities that involve beginning students in spelling are well worth considering. In an article entitled "Write Now, Read Later" Chomsky suggests that children ought to learn how to read by creating their own spelling of familiar words using sets of plastic letters or alphabet blocks. Instead of words resembling a secret code that only others can break, writing words becomes a way of expressing something that the child knows. She points out,

> If we concede that word recognition, or even just the sounding out of words, appears so much more difficult for children than composing words, why do our reading programs as a matter of course expect children to deal with it first? The natural order is writing first, then reading what you have written. To expect the child to read, as a first step, what someone else has written is backwards, an artificial imposition that denies the child an active role in the whole process.[2]

SUPPORTIVE WRITING SKILLS

In the beginning stages, when children are trying to represent words with letters, their spellings are not conventional. Instead, they reflect the children's knowledge of the sounds the letters stand for and the ways that children pronounce words. Many children start with their own names and change initial sounds. Mike put some plastic letters together to spell his name saying, "That's me, I'm Mike." When asked how he could change it to *like*, he quickly put an *l* at the beginning to replace the *m*. Another Michael, age 5, wrote I NO MI ABC WOT U PLY WF ME—his version of *I know my ABC, won't you play with me.*[3]

Montessori also used this method with children in Rome. She worked in a very directive manner, but the process was essentially the same. The children were given a box with all the consonants and vowels they knew; and while the directress pronounced a word, the child selected the letters to compose it. Montessori comments, "But the reading of the word which he has composed is not so easy. Indeed, he generally succeeds in reading it only after a certain effort. . . . But once he has understood the mechanism of the game, the child goes forward by himself, and becomes intensely interested."[4]

One concern might be that such prolonged exposure to highly individualistic spelling patterns might make children poorer spellers in the long run. Chomsky points out that standard spelling finds its way gradually into the children's writing from reading, dictionary use, and direct instruction.[5] She adds that a recent study in which the spelling subtest of the California Achievement Test was given to a group of children who had spelled inventively all through first grade showed grade-level scores in second grade and above-grade-level scores in third grade.

The results of this kind of early spelling instruction certainly fit with Piaget's view that children understand best what they have figured out for themselves. Once children have invented a system of spelling, the principle of how it works is theirs and converting to standardized spelling is quite easy.

Present Instructional Programs

In most schools you will find a spelling textbook series being used to teach spelling. Although commercial textbooks differ to some degree, the organization of the basic instructional program usually follows a similar pattern. The test-study-test plan is basic to these spellers and can be a very effective method of learning words,[6] provided that students correct their own tests after identifying their own mistakes.

The main problem with spelling textbooks for children is that they encourage all children to study the same words and therefore bypass the concept of individualization. It is very possible that a few words will be too difficult, others too easy, and some very appropriate for individual study. Further, texts suggest that each child should use the same procedure and the same amount of time to learn the words. There is also no provision in most spelling textbooks for relating spelling instruction to children's everyday reading and writing needs. The spelling text may be used, however, as a resource book. As you individualize the spelling program, you may want to choose appropriate words for study or some instructional material from the text.

Ease of Learning to Spell a Word

There are a number of factors to be considered in determining the difficulty of learning to spell a particular word. Whether or not the word is spelled with the most common grapheme representing the particular sound or phoneme is one big factor. The phoneme /f/ is most commonly spelled with the letter f, although it may be spelled with ff, ph, or gh. Sometimes the position in the word will determine which letters or graphemes will be used; for example, ph is more common in an initial position and gh will only represent /f/ in a final position in the word. The most regularly spelled are the consonants, the next most regular are short vowel sounds, and long vowels are the least regularly spelled.

Another factor that enters into the ease with which a word is learned is the child's interest in learning it. Had may appear to be simpler, but the word elephant may actually be easier to learn. Letting children have some choice in which words they study may help them become better spellers. Words that are often used may also be learned through seeing them time after time. Thus, some frequently used words may be learned without specific study.

Sources for Selecting Spelling Words

Several sources other than a spelling text need to be considered in selecting words to study. There may be words that children use frequently in their own writing that they have not yet mastered. There are also frequency lists of words that can supply words used very often in writing, and the study of a particular topic in another content area may provide some words that children should learn. Often teachers can use a particular phoneme/grapheme correspondence group such as /e/ *ey* as in gr*ey*, h*ey*, th*ey* for spelling study as well as part of reading instruction.

From children's own writing   Since the purpose of learning to spell words correctly is to communicate with others effectively in writing, children's writing is a logical source for spelling words. One method of keeping a record of words that individual children continually misspell is offered by Dunkeld and Hatch.[7] They suggest that the teacher prepare three envelopes for each student. The student's name is written in red on the first envelope, yellow on the second, and green on the third. Red indicates *stop,* these are words I need to learn. Yellow is for *caution,* these are words that I am in the process of learning or almost know. Green is for *go,* indicating these are words that I know how to spell. The envelopes may be attached to a bulletin board, kept by the student in some appropriate place, or attached in a special notebook with the words *stop, caution,* and *go* written on each. Figure 12 shows such a notebook. This can be a part of a child's writing book in which words are written and then studied. For example, as the teacher discovers words that are consistently misspelled in children's writing, he or she writes the words for study on strips of paper and then places them in the red envelope. When a student feels that a word is almost mastered, the strip containing that word is put in the caution envelope. When the spelling of a word is completely mastered, the word strip is placed in the go envelope. This method of recording and learning to spell words has several advantages: the students are learning to spell words that they frequently use when they write; consistently misspelled words are identified and receive special attention; and students can evaluate their spelling progress by actually seeing how many problem words have been mastered from week to week and are in the go envelope.

A writing component is essential to an effective spelling pro-

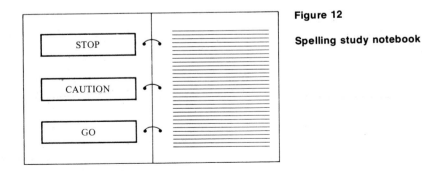

Figure 12

Spelling study notebook

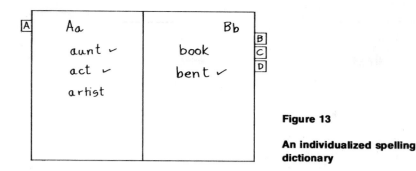

Figure 13

An individualized spelling dictionary

gram. By selecting and writing words, children develop the ability to spell words which are frequently used in their written compositions. As needs arise, new words are written, learned, and added to their growing spelling vocabularies.

To help students learn the spelling of words which they frequently use in their writing, individual dictionaries may be made and kept for quick and easy reference. Students will often ask the teacher to spell a word—"How do you spell . . . ?" is a common question in elementary school classrooms. If each child has a personal dictionary like the one in Figure 13, the teacher can write the word the student wants to know on the appropriate page or the student can write it. The children can then refer to their dictionaries each time they need to know how to spell a word. When a student feels that a word in the dictionary is mastered, it may be checked off. This method also allows the teacher to talk about the spelling of the word with a child and suggestions may be made about how the student can remember the correct spelling.

Word lists Frequency of use of words is another criterion for choosing words to learn to spell. Researchers have found that about 3,000 words make up 95 percent of all words most commonly used by individuals in their writing. A classic study conducted by Horn[8] revealed the basic words used by adults when engaged in everyday writing activities. Ten words account for 25 percent of all the running words in the writing of adults—*I, the, and, to, a, you, of, in, we,* and *for,* and one hundred words represent approximately 60 percent of all the words used in an average person's writing. If children can spell the hundred words shown to be the most frequently written, they will have a beginning basic writing vocabulary. Unfortunately these are sometimes difficult to learn because they have so little interest appeal and because too few represent concrete objects.

Horn's List of First 100 Words in Order of Frequency

I	if	which	come
the	all	some	were
and	so	has	no
to	me	or	how
a	was	there	did
you	very	us	think
of	my	good	say
in	had	know	please
we	our	just	him
for	from	by	his
it	am	up	got
that	one	day	over
is	time	much	make
your	he	out	may
have	get	her	received
will	do	order	before
be	been	yours	two
are	letter	now	send
not	can	well	after
as	would	an	work
at	she	here	could
this	when	them	dear
with	about	see	made
but	they	go	glad
on	any	what	like

Rinsland conducted a study similar to Horn's, but rather than surveying the writing of adults, he determined what words children most commonly use in their writing.[9] The list of words that he found most frequently used by children should prove helpful to the teacher of spelling.

Rinsland's List of First Words of Highest Frequency Use

a	am	asked	bed	boy	can
about	an	at	been	boys	car
after	and	away	before	bring	cat
again	another	baby	best	brother	children
all	any	back	better	but	Christmas
along	are	ball	big	by	close
also	around	be	black	called	cold
always	as	because	book	came	come

coming	give	last	now	sister	tree
could	glad	let	of	snow	two
country	go	letter	off	so	until
daddy	going	like	old	some	up
day	good	little	on	something	us
days	got	live	once	soon	very
dear	grade	long	one	started	want
did	great	look	only	summer	wanted
didn't	had	looked	or	sure	was
do	happy	lot	other	take	water
dog	has	lots	our	teacher	way
doll	have	love	out	tell	we
don't	he	made	over	than	week
door	heard	make	people	that	well
down	help	man	place	the	went
each	her	many	play	their	were
eat	here	me	played	them	what
every	him	men	please	then	when
father	his	milk	pretty	there	where
few	home	more	put	these	which
find	hope	morning	ran	they	while
first	house	most	read	thing	white
five	how	mother	red	things	who
for	I	much	right	think	why
found	if	must	room	thought	will
four	I'm	my	run	three	wish
friend	in	name	said	through	with
from	into	never	Santa Claus	time	work
fun	is	new	saw	to	would
gave	it	next	say	today	write
get	its	nice	school	told	year
getting	just	night	see	too	years
girl	know	no	she	took	you
girls	large	not	should	town	your

Spelling words taken from content areas Content areas, such as social studies and science, can be sources for spelling words. However, a word of caution is needed here. Words selected for study should be useful to children long after a given topic is completed in a subject area. Too frequently time is spent learning to spell words that will not be needed again for writing. If a child wants to learn some of the more unusual words, this is fine. But a required list of such words to commit to memory is unnecessary.

If your reading program includes work with phoneme/grapheme

correspondences, these groups of words could certainly be part of the spelling study words. In that way study in one area reinforces study in another related area. It also helps children organize words into groupings to be learned instead of a series of completely unrelated words. This would put together *fig, pig, dig,* and *wig* or a group such as *rain, grain, brain, drain, train,* and *strain.*

Methods of Studying and Learning Spelling

Although the letters we use in spelling a word represent sounds in our language, it is important to remember that spelling is primarily within the visual realm. Spelling is used in writing, not in speaking. In the past we have concentrated too much on asking children to sound out words, to study them by spelling aloud, and by conducting spelling bees. We should, instead, have children focus on whether or not words look right. If we do this, children's study will include close observation and writing of words; and spelling games will involve writing the words.

The steps that a child may take in studying a word are listed below.

1. Observe the word and pronounce it.
2. Close your eyes and mentally picture how the word looks.
3. Look at the word again and check the spelling with yours.
4. Write the word thinking about how it looks.
5. Check your written spelling of the word.
6. Try writing the word correctly one more time.

Notice that these study rules involve looking at the word, visualizing it, and checking it in written form.

We have all been amused or frustrated at one time or another by the apparent inconsistencies in the English spelling system. Although it does not have a perfect one-to-one phoneme (sound) and grapheme (letter or letter combinations) correspondence, it is more regular than we thought. This was made clear in an extensive computer study conducted by Hanna, Hanna, Hodges, and Rudorf. According to their findings, "there are patterns of consistency in the orthography which, based upon linguistic factors may be said to produce correspondences that are surprisingly consistent."[10] (Orthography refers to representation of the sounds by letters.) Three of the factors which were important in producing consistencies were: position of the phoneme in the syllable of a word, whether or not the syllable is stressed, and other internal constraints.

For years we have attempted to teach spelling rules or generalizations to help children learn to spell. A most revealing study by Davis[11] of the applicability of spelling generalizations to words in six major spelling programs suggests that we should be rather careful in teaching these. For example, one common generalization is: "When there are two vowels side by side, the long sound of the first one is heard and the second is usually silent." Davis found 1,893 words with two vowels side by side; 612 conformed to the rule and there were 1,281 exceptions. If you learn the rule and use it, you will be wrong more than two out of three times. There were some rules that worked 100 percent of the time, however. Two of these are "When *ght* is seen in a word, *gh* is silent," and "When a word begins *kn*, the *k* is silent." There are not a large number of words to which these apply—sixty-four for the first and twenty for the second—but the real question about them is how much help they are to the speller.

Using an arbitrary standard of 75 percent applicability or higher and a minimum of one hundred words or more to which it would apply, there are only ten spelling generalizations from Davis's study that may be helpful to children.

1. The *r* gives the preceding vowel a sound that is neither long nor short.
2. Words having double *e* usually have the long *e* sound.
3. When *y* is the final letter in a word, it usually has a vowel sound.
4. When *c* and *h* are next to each other, they make only one sound.
5. *Ch* is usually pronounced as it is in *kitchen*, *catch*, and *chair*, not like *sh*.
6. When *c* is followed by *e* or *i*, the sound of *s* is likely to be heard.
7. When the letter *c* is followed by *o* or *a*, the sound of *k* is likely to be heard.
8. The letter *g* often has a sound similar to that of *j* in *jump* when it precedes the letter *i* or *e*.
9. When two of the same consonants are side by side, only one is heard.
10. When there is one *e* in a word that ends in a consonant, the *e* usually has a short sound.

This list does not include generalizations having to do with syllabication or accents. Most of the generalizations listed are more helpful in checking a word after writing it than in helping you spell the word in the first place.

Morphology, the study of how words are formed, can also contribute to spelling success. Compounding is one way in which words are put together, and an understanding of this increases the number of words children can spell. Once students have mastered the spelling of *play* and *ground,* they should have no difficulty in mastering the compound form, *playground.* Lists of morphemes (a word or part of a word that bears meaning) along with corresponding compound forms can illustrate to students the usefulness of compounding when applied to spelling words.

Morpheme	+	Morpheme	=	Compound Word
play		ground		playground
some		thing		something
every		time		everytime
any		thing		anything
every		day		everyday
care		taker		caretaker

Affixation provides rules that, when understood, can be applied to the spelling of many words. An affix is a bound morpheme (a word part that carries meaning but cannot stand alone) that occurs before or after a base, i.e., *un____*, or *____ing.* Prefixes are affixes which occur before bases (*un____*) and suffixes are affixes that occur following bases (*____ing*). When children can associate the familiar phonemic sound of *ing* with the combination of letters that spell *ing,* just think how much their spelling power will have increased.

Factors Contributing to Poor Spelling

In order to diagnose what kinds of problems a particular student is having with spelling, it is important to look for patterns in the errors that the child makes. Some errors indicate less trouble with spelling than others. For example, although *afrade* is not the conventional way of spelling *afraid,* we can still recognize the word. Recognizing *thaitch* as *through* is almost impossible and indicates a far more difficult problem. The types of errors that children make can be classified into five main groups:

1. *Overdependence on sounding out words.* Although English phoneme/grapheme correspondences are fairly regular, there

are words with diacritic (silent) letters (We*d*nesday and C*h*rist-mas), and mispronunciation, faulty hearing, or dialectical pronunciation may cause errors.

2. *Using incorrect options.* In English there are usually several alternative ways of representing a sound in writing. Selecting the wrong option will cause a word to be misspelled (gra*f*eme for graph*eme, swi*m*ing for swi*mm*ing, or b*ai*r for b*a*re).

3. *Not using the English phoneme/grapheme system.* A child who does not use the system of phoneme/grapheme relationships shows no recognition that there is any system to spelling (*congth* for *country* and *pract* for *present* indicate that the child doesn't know the system or has given up on using it).

4. *Reversing letters.* This is a frequent error in spelling—perhaps from studying aloud—which indicates the child knows which letters are in the word but is unsure of their order (*gril* for *girl*). Proofreading for this may help those children who make this error frequently.

5. *Spelling the homonym or homophone.* Often children are not sure which spelling goes with the meaning they are using and therefore spell the wrong one (*to, too,* and *two,* or *hear* and *here*).

If students' spelling errors are analyzed, mistakes that consistently occur may be diagnosed and corrected. A card or notebook for each child is kept as a record of spelling errors. Misspellings are recorded from time to time by the teacher as the papers are read or other written work is checked. After a number of words are listed, the teacher can often pick up a pattern in the mistakes and help the child solve that problem. Look at the following lists of misspellings and see if you can find any pattern in the children's errors.

Sally	Bobby
street/sreet	America/Amercia
Christmas/Chrismas	know/no
cried/cryed	their/thier
on/own	really/realy

The errors recorded for Sally indicate that she is depending too much on sounding out the words since three of the four (all except *cryed*) indicate problems with pronunciation or dialect speech. The words on Bobby's list show two words with reversed letters—carelessness or lack of visual check—one word is a homonym often misused by children, and *realy* involves simply using the wrong option, *l* for *ll*.

Below is another list of a child's misspellings recorded from several pieces of writing.

John
friend/frend
does/dose
could/coud
because/becaus
heard/herd

A review of John's record of spelling errors indicates an inability to spell words that are commonly misspelled in children's writing. These are sometimes referred to as spelling "demons." Although Hanna et al.[12] found that only about 3 percent of a vocabulary of 17,000+ words can be considered demons, many of these difficult spelling words are in frequent written use. They are words that appear on highest frequency usage lists, such as Horn's and Rinsland's. What makes them demons? They are words in which there exists a high degree of irregularity between phoneme and grapheme. The written representation of one or more sounds is not the most commonly used one for that particular sound.

Words that are spelling demons require direct teaching. Emphasis upon word formation or visual impression is very important when teaching children to spell these words. Following is a list[13] of one hundred words most commonly misspelled by elementary school age children.

One Hundred Words Most Frequently Misspelled

their	February	something	running	its
too	once	named	believe	started
there	like	came	little	that's
they	they're	name	thing	would
then	cousin	tried	him	again
until	mother	here	all right	heard
our	another	many	happened	received
asked	threw	knew	didn't	coming
off	some	with	always	to
through	bought	together	surprise	said
wanted	getting	you're	before	swimming
hear	going	clothes	caught	first
from	course	looked	every	were
frightened	woman	people	different	than
for	animals	pretty	interesting	two

know	because	went	sometimes	jumped
decided	thought	where	friends	around
friend	and	stopped	children	dropped
when	beautiful	very	an	babies
let's	it's	morning	school	money

Spelling Games and Activities

Occasionally a spelling game or special activity will add motivation and interest to learning to spell. All games should meet two criteria: the spelling should be done in written form and all children should participate throughout the activity. This eliminates the spelling bee, at least in its traditional format. An acceptable spelling bee would allow teams to consult on the spelling of a word and the word would be written on the board instead of being spelled orally.

Some children enjoy word puzzles of various kinds, and for them crossword puzzles may prove enjoyable. These must be very simple at first as most children do not understand how they work. Early puzzles might have only two or three words.

Another old-fashioned game that still has a great deal of appeal for children is "Hangman." In playing this game the children try to find out what word the teacher or another student has selected by guessing what letters might be in it before they are "hung." Figure 14 shows what would be drawn for a five-letter word before the game begins. Each wrong guess allows another part of the person to be added to the noose. The children must guess the word before the figure is completely drawn. The teacher may vary the number of guesses allowed by varying the number of parts to the man being hung; that is, only the head, torso, arms, and legs may be used giving six incorrect guesses, or hands, feet, and so on may be added to the list.

Classroom versions of television game shows can be worked out to provide interesting spelling games. One such game calls for the contestant to locate words in a line of continuous letters. This is good practice in developing a visual set toward spelling. You can use

Figure 14

Spelling hangman

one line of letters or several rows depending on the children's age and ability. After you give the clue, the children must identify the word by giving its position and saying or writing it. An example of this is:

1	2	3	4	5	6	7
n	o	d	d	i	m	e

Clue	Answer: Position	Word
a. ten cents	4	*dime*
b. strange or peculiar	2	*odd*
c. word that means you	6	*me*
d. opposite of bright	4	*dim*
e. shake your head	1	*nod*

Another version of a television game requires a spinner on a wheel with varying numbers of points marked off around the circle. A preselected title, person's name, or object is shown with a dash for each letter. The players from each team alternate trying to guess which consonants might be in the mystery word. They may use some of the points they have accumulated to buy a vowel (they guess which one) or they may guess the word. If they make an incorrect guess, the next player takes over. The object is to get as many points as possible. If there are two or more repeated consonants in the word, they get the number of points spun multiplied by the number of times that consonant appears.

Team competitions may also be set up by asking children to alternate in listing words that have a particular prefix, suffix, or compound part. This could also include writing synonyms or antonyms. For example, use the prefix -*un:*

Team A	Team B
1. *unfriendly*	2. *unable*
3. *unhappy*	4. *unnecessary*
5. *unclean*	6.　？

Team A wins the first round and Team B starts the second round. This game is not only good practice in spelling, it is also good for vocabulary development.

The commercial game of Scrabble can also be an enjoyable spelling activity for children. To score points, players are required to think of a variety of word choices that contain letters or a specified number of letters. Children also use a dictionary to check word spellings as well as the existence of words.

Games for spelling practice are intended to develop interest in spelling and make spelling study more interesting. They are an excellent alternative to looking up the meaning of each word in the dictionary or to writing each word in a sentence week after week.

Testing in the Individualized Spelling Program

If the spelling words that children are learning are from completely individualized lists, then the testing must also be individualized. If you have an aide or teaching assistant, they may give the tests; otherwise the children may test one another. Some teachers prefer to individualize spelling study by reading groups with each child having a personal word list only every few weeks. If this is the case, the teacher may dictate the spelling tests for the various groups on the weeks when they are working on the same words. The test words and sample sentences may also be put on tape by the teacher or by each individual child, and the cassette tape can then be used to test whenever that child is ready. If it is possible to have a cassette for each student, there are many possibilities for reviewing words.

Perhaps this is an appropriate time to point out that it is not necessary to work with a new group of words each week; there is nothing sacred about Friday spelling tests. Some children may use a four-day study period; others a seven- or nine-day period. Having some variation in when children start a new list to study and when they are tested on the words may help you individualize their learning.

A Final Word

The discussion in this section has centered around a variety of methods and approaches that may be used to facilitate spelling instruction. We need to recognize that an effective spelling program does not adhere to a single approach. A method that helps one child spell better may not help another. And when all is said and done, it is not the method *per se* that makes good spellers, it is how well the method is implemented and children learn.

HANDWRITING INSTRUCTION

The manuscript style of writing often called *printing* first appeared in this country in the early 1920s. After its debut in suburban and private schools, the teaching of manuscript writing spread throughout the public schools. By 1950, this style of writing had become widely accepted in the primary grades, replacing the cursive style of writing which had been learned by young children for years and years.[14]

Teachers, who were concerned with teaching children to read, were delighted to see manuscript writing come into vogue. There was no longer a problem of teaching two styles of writing—cursive for the purpose of writing and manuscript for the purpose of reading. Now children could focus on one style of writing—print—when first learning to read and write.

Beginning Handwriting Instruction

It is widely accepted that young children should begin to write in manuscript or print. The rationale for initial instruction in manuscript is aptly stated by Herrick.[15] If we consider young children's eye-hand coordination and motor development, the straight lines and circles which are used to make manuscript letters are best. The first grade child is learning to read, and manuscript symbols correspond to the print children are asked to read. Finally, children's writing is more legible when they use manuscript.

Prewriting experiences Before formal instruction in manuscript writing, young children can benefit from prewriting experiences. The kindergarten child has not yet fully developed coordination of the smaller muscles in the hands and fingers. Experiences which consider children's physical development and help them prepare for writing can be an integral part of the learning environment.

The following activities illustrate the kind of prewriting experiences that might be provided for young children.

Painting: Children need frequent opportunities to paint, either at an easel or on the floor. Children consistently use strokes similar to those needed for manuscript writing when they paint their own pictures. You will readily find simple straight lines and circles, basic strokes in manuscript writing, in their paintings.

Making designs: Children can design their own book jackets, borders for bulletin boards or pictures, fabric for beanbags, and so on. Ideas for using designs that incorporate basic writing strokes are many.

Sand or salt trays: Sand or salt trays are easy to make and loads of fun for children. Using their fingers for drawing, children can make pictures and designs one after the other.

Finger painting: Finger painting offers children the oppor-

Figure 15
Overall design

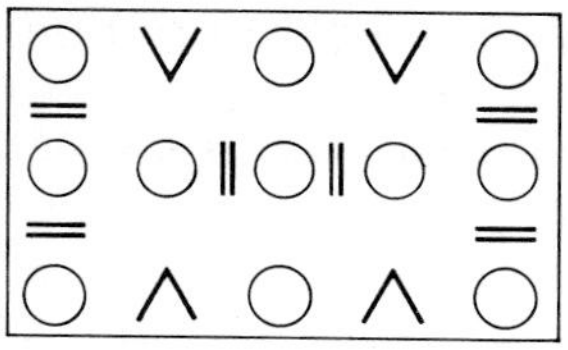

Figure 16
Border designs

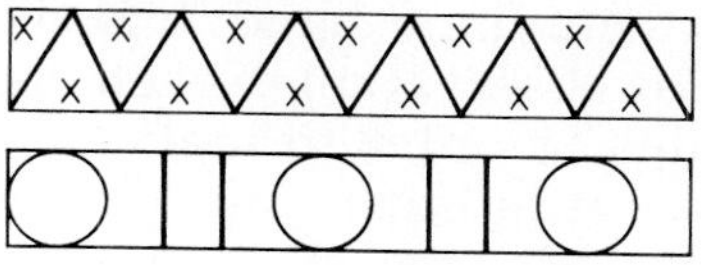

Figure 17
A design as a frame

Figure 18
Fabric design

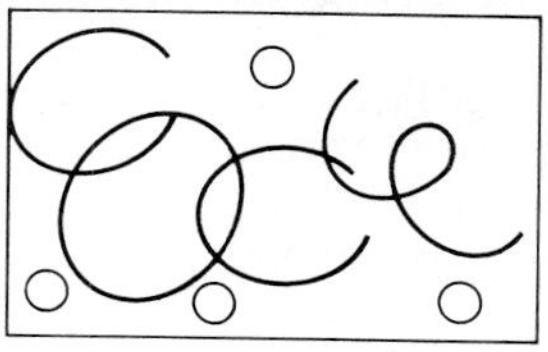

tunity to explore in a tactile manner lines, curves, ovals, squiggles, and so on.

Children's designs, paintings, or finger paintings can be used in a variety of ways. Those on heavy paper like Figure 15 may become book covers or placemats for lunch, snacks, or a party. Designs done on long strips like those in Figure 16 may form a border for a bulletin board or decorate a learning center. Basic writing strokes like those in Figure 17 may frame a story, a poem, or a picture. Designs on cloth as in Figure 18 may be sewn into a cushion, a beanbag, or even a pocket on a cover-up shirt. Experiences such as these should continue throughout kindergarten, and, for some children, during the first grade in school. Because young children physically develop at different rates, some students will not be ready for formal writing instruction when they enter first grade. They will need many more experiences that will get them ready to write.

The teacher who is concerned with initial writing instruction needs to determine which children are ready to learn manuscript. Berry[16] has developed a list that can be helpful in assessing writing readiness. She says children may be taught to write when: an interest is shown in writing their own names; they have developed facility in the use of scissors, crayons, the paintbrush, and the pencil in a variety of informal activities; they can copy simple geometric or letterlike characters with proper orientation; they have established a dominant hand; and they sense a personal need to write.

Close observation of each child's physical or motor development is needed in order to make an accurate evaluation of his or her abilities. It is important for a teacher to understand that certain children, because of their stage of development, cannot be expected to write as well as those children who are already well coordinated.

Appropriate Materials for the Beginning Writer

Paper. The beginning writer will perform best if he is given large sheets of unlined paper. Newsprint or butcher paper works very well because the young child needs the freedom to use his large muscles for writing. Small sheets of paper require the child to use small hand muscles, and may lead to fatigue and frustration. Because children's eye-hand coordination is still developing, unlined paper is recommended for use throughout grade one.

Easels and Chalkboards. Children can write on paper that is attached to an easel or practice manuscript strokes or letters on the chalkboard. Both provide the area that young children need when beginning to write.

Writing Instruments. Large crayons or primary pencils are frequently recommended as writing instruments for young children. The primary pencil or readiness crayons are approximately twice the thickness of a conventional no. 2 pencil and are intended to be easier for beginning writers to hold. However, research studies indicate that most young children do very well with a standard size writing instrument, and many children are already familiar with these because they have used them at home.

A Manuscript Alphabet. Sample alphabet cards are familiar in the elementary school classroom. You will frequently find them placed above the chalkboard in the front of the room. To make the manuscript alphabet easier for children to see and use, try taping a sheet containing the alphabet to the top of each student's desk or table. Looking up to the front of the room and back to one's paper is difficult. The alphabet sheets may be laminated or covered with clear contact paper for protection from wear and tear, and this way children can also trace over the letters as often as they wish.

Teaching Handwriting within a Meaningful Context

Instruction in handwriting should occur within a meaningful context. Practicing and mastering isolated strokes and letters before writing words belongs to the past. Young children can first learn to write their names, addresses, telephone numbers, the name of the school, and their teacher's name. They can keep their very own book or diary for recording each day's date along with something special to remember for the day. Meaningful writing experiences may also include writing notes to parents, labeling objects, recording observations of the classroom hamster or fish, writing messages to a pen pal within the class, or attaching captions to their drawings and paintings. Children may copy dictated experience stories or begin writing their own stories using their own spelling system.

Children may require special help with some letters. Research suggests that the manuscript letters *q, g, p, y,* and *j* are difficult letters for children to learn, and *m* is the most difficult. Children will reverse particular letters because of similarity. We frequently see children reverse the manuscript letters *b* and *d*. When children are beginning to learn the formation of either manuscript or cursive writing symbols, it is important that the teacher emphasize how letters are alike and different, giving special attention to those that cause children the most difficulty.

Preventive instruction in handwriting is far better than remedial instruction. It is much easier to teach children to write correctly in the beginning than it is to change poor writing habits later. For children to begin writing properly, the teacher needs to show them individually how to form the letters, where to start the letter, and what makes the letter different from others that are similar.

For initial instruction, letters should be grouped by similarity of formation starting with some of the most frequently used letters. That would suggest *a, c, e,* and *o* as the first group since these are all variations of a circle. A second group could be *d, g,* and *q* since these start with a circle and add a long line up or down. An alternative group is *i, l, t, k,* and *j* which is made almost entirely of straight lines, includes a vowel, and has some frequently used consonants. Another grouping is *b, h,* and *p* which should be contrasted to *d, g,* and *q*. The *b, h, p* group starts with a line instead of a circle and you make them by pushing up and around to the right instead of pulling down and around to the left. Thorough skill with one group before learning the other one—combined with careful instruction as to differences in formation—should help children avoid reversing these letters. This leads into the *m, n,* and *r* trio, leaving only those three letters that do not fit with a group—*f, u,* and *s*—and a group of seldom used letters made with diagonal lines—*v, w, x, y,* and *z*.

After children have gone through the initial stages of learning to form the letters in manuscript, the teacher needs to individualize handwriting instruction. Some children may be reversing letters, others may need help with spacing, and a few students simply may

---

be unable to write certain letters. Children who have similar writing problems can be grouped together for instruction. Using the overhead projector, chalkboard, or prepared worksheets, the teacher can easily give these children special help.

In order to diagnose writing problems, a teacher must observe children writing. Children too frequently develop poor writing habits because no one has observed them while they have formed letters. In both manuscript and cursive writing styles, letters are formed according to a sequence. For example, as in Figure 19, in the manuscript *a* the circular part of the letter is made first by moving the pencil in a counterclockwise direction. The straight line, moving the pencil from the top down, is formed second. Only by observing a child write, can a teacher really know if the student is correctly forming the letters. You cannot tell from finished copy. Correct order and direction in forming the letters is important for future development of speed and to make conversion into cursive style much easier.

Starting the Left-Handed Writer

Because most children in elementary school classrooms are right-handed, the few who are left-handed frequently get slighted. Without special guidance, the left-handed writer will naturally follow the instructions for right-handed writers. Too often, left-handed children develop the habit of hooking their wrist when they write because they have learned to slant their paper in the same direction as right-handed children.

It is the primary teacher who gives children their start in both manuscript and cursive writing. What must this teacher be concerned about when teaching the left-handed writer? According to Enstrom,[17] the left-handed student should be taught the following:

1. The paper for the left-handed writer should slant about 30 degrees to the *right* for both manuscript and cursive styles of

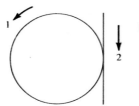

Figure 19

Forming an *a*

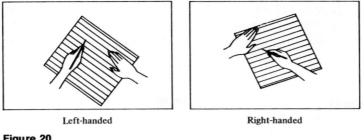

Left-handed   Right-handed

Figure 20
Writing paper positions

writing, or slightly more slanted than for a right-handed person and in the opposite direction. Getting the child to position the paper in the proper direction is the first step toward making a successful writer. See Figure 20.

2. The left-handed child should hold the pencil farther back from the point than the right-handed child.
3. The child's elbows should be kept rather close to the body.
4. The blunt end of the pencil or pen should be directed back over the shoulder.
5. The desk should be high enough for the child to see the pencil or pen as it touches the paper.

Teaching Cursive Writing

Although nearly all schools convert children from manuscript to cursive writing, there are several arguments for some children, if not all, to continue writing in manuscript style. Using research and theoretical evidence, those who favor continuing manuscript[18] point out:

There is no difference between manuscript and cursive writing speeds when children have had comparable practice.

Under pressure to write quickly, manuscript writing remains more legible.

A signature does not have to be done in cursive writing to be legal.

Children who develop slowly could benefit from continuing manuscript writing throughout the elementary school.

Time spent in instruction in cursive writing could be better spent in creating, composing, and expressing ideas in the writing style that children have already mastered.

The primary concern of secondary schools is legibility, and manuscript writing is more legible than cursive. Note the frequency of "PLEASE PRINT" on applications and other forms.

In spite of numerous logical reasons for continuing manuscript writing, it is difficult to break with tradition. Many parents want their children to learn cursive style; and many children look forward to the time when they will learn to write in "real writing." Certainly all students should be taught to read cursive writing and many would choose to learn to write it if they could. Since it is somewhat unrealistic to consider eliminating cursive writing from the elementary school curriculum, we are including suggestions for teaching it.

Suggestions for Teaching the Reading of Cursive Handwriting

Reading cursive should begin before formal instruction in this style of writing. The second- or third-grader will initially find cursive writing difficult to read and will need some special help. Several weeks prior to instruction in cursive, do the following:

Write the day's date on the chalkboard each morning in cursive:

Monday, April 1

If you are writing brief instructions on the chalkboard for children to read, write them in both manuscript and cursive:

Don't forget! Take the announcement about the P.T.A. meeting home to your parents.

Don't forget! Take the announcement about the P.T.A. meeting home to your parents.

Prepare ditto sheets that have sentences written in both manuscript and cursive writing styles. As a whole-class activity, read and discuss the sentences. A comparison may be made between the formation of corresponding manuscript and cursive letters.

As the children become adept at reading cursive writing, start writing more of your instructions or announcements entirely in this writing style.

Teaching Children to Write in Cursive Style

Most of the letters in cursive writing are very similar to their corresponding manuscript form except for the connecting strokes or loops which help join the letters within a word. Only five lower case letters are significantly different—s, r, f, e, and z. These five need to be taught separately. The only other group of letters that presents a particular problem are the lower case letters that start their connection to the following letter at a midpoint between the lines rather than at the base; these are b, o, v, and w.

Lower case letters should receive special attention since they comprise about 90 percent of our writing.[19] It is poor formation of lower case letters, not capital letters, that contributes most to illegible writing. Just as in teaching manuscript writing, the lower case letters should be grouped according to similarities to help children see what essential differences there are among them. One such grouping might be those letters that begin with a stroke similar to an *ℓ* :

ℓ f h k b

Capital letters may also be grouped and taught according to similarities and differences.[20]

O and *a* have similar beginning strokes. It is important for children to note that the slant of the letter is retraced.

In teaching *C* and *E* together, children can practice writing the letter *E* over the letter *C* : *E* . This gives the letter the proper slant!

S , *G* , and *L* begin with an undercurve and not a straight line.

D , *J* , and *F* are similar because the beginning strokes are compound curves. When considering the legibility factor, it is best to avoid connecting these letters.

The letters *P* , *B* , *R* begin with the same strokes.

The beginning strokes of *J* and *Q* should be stressed because they are important to good form.

The beginning strokes for *H* and *K* have frequently been called "cane strokes."

N and *M* evidence distinct similarities in how they are formed. Because they are similar, children often write one for the other.

The beginning stroke for $\mathcal{V}$, $\mathcal{U}$, $\mathcal{Y}$ is the same.

$\mathcal{W}$ and $\mathcal{X}$ have similar beginning strokes and are frequently difficult letters for children to form.

$\mathcal{Q}$ and $\mathcal{Z}$ have the same beginning stroke.

Children need to observe how letters are formed. A teacher may use both an overhead projector and the chalkboard to demonstrate such things as letter formation, uniformity of size, slant, or how particular letters are connected.

Practicing handwriting is not a very exciting task and anything the teacher can do to make it more interesting seems worthwhile. Children may use the chalkboard or an overhead projector to work on particular groups of letters. They also enjoy using colored felt tip pens and brightly colored paper. Even while they are learning to write in cursive style, they need opportunities to keep up some facility with manuscript writing. Making signs, labels for displays, or titles for bulletin boards helps keep them in practice.

Assessing Legibility in Writing

Early evaluators of handwriting emphasized its aesthetic qualities and instruction emphasized "beautiful" writing. Current methods emphasize teaching for legibility since the entire purpose of writing is its readability. What factors influence legibility? Four factors are the most important in determining legibility: proper formation of letters, regularity of slant, uniformity of size, and regular spacing within and between words. The first of these is especially worth noting since four letters account for 50 percent of the illegibilities in writing: *a*, *r*, *e*, and *t*. Two major problems that children have that affect legibility are failing to close letters such as *a* (which would look like *u* or *ci*) and *d* (which then looks like *cl*), and not looping letters that should be or looping those that should not be looped. The latter causes all kinds of problems with *e* and *i*, with *d*, and the *t* or *l* distinction.

Improving Handwriting

One of the main ways to improve handwriting is to improve the quality of instruction in the initial stages of writing. Developing legibility and speed is then an individual problem. Teacher conferences are helpful in getting children to see what particular problems they have and how they can make their handwriting more legible. Prior to such a conference, the teacher should actually observe the child writing. This helps in assessing handwriting speed and facility as well as helping to determine if that child is forming letters correctly. After such teacher-student conferences to determine what particular skills the children should work on, there is direction and purpose to their practice.

Handwriting scales such as the one available from Zaner-Bloser[21] can be used by students to evaluate their own handwriting. They simply compare a sample of their writing with the writing specimens given on the scale. When they find a specimen that closely resembles theirs, they read the corresponding rating score and evaluative comments. Children can help determine what factors, such as letter size and slant, can be improved in order to increase the quality or speed of their writing.

Children may also keep samples of their writing that can be used for evaluative purposes. It is best to begin a handwriting folder for each child at the first of the school year. From time to time, new handwriting samples are added to the folder. By dating each sample, students can compare papers written in September with those placed in the folder in October, November, December, and so on. The growing collection of handwriting samples can be used by students to assess their own handwriting progress. When later samples are compared with earlier written samples, students can determine if the quality of their handwriting is steadily improving. They also can diagnose problem areas that need further improvement. Individualization, allowing children to work on their own handwriting problems, is essential to an effective handwriting program.

PRELIMINARY LEARNING ACTIVITIES

1. Look at the excerpt from a child's story in Figure 21, in her own writing. List the words spelled correctly; then categorize the misspelled words according to the probable cause of the error.

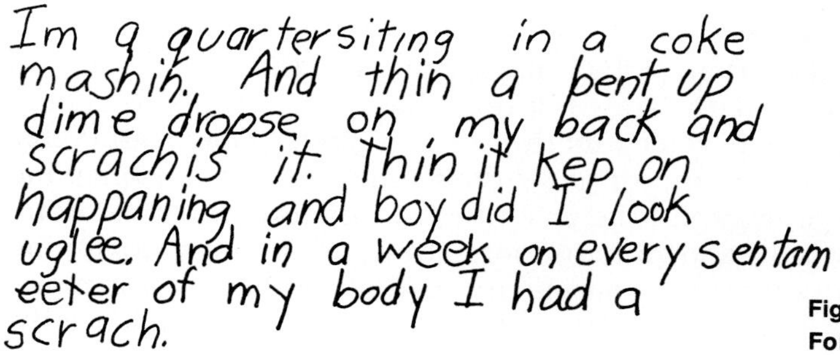

Im a quarter siting in a coke mashih., And thin a bent up dime dropse on my back and scrachis it. Thin it kep on happaning and boy did I look uglee. And in a week on every s entam eeter of my body I had a scrach.

Figure 21
For spelling analysis

a. Overdependence on sounding out .

d. Reversing letters

b. Using the incorrect options

e. Spelling the homophone or homonym

c. Not using the phoneme/ grapheme system

2. In Figure 22 are two samples of children's handwriting—one in manuscript and one in cursive style. Examine each sample carefully and list for each two major problems with legibility. You should consider spacing within and between words, letter formation, regularity of size, and slant. (Specify examples in the children's handwriting that illustrate these general problems.)

Figure 22

For handwriting analysis

3. Prepare a cassette tape of a series of short pieces of material involving punctuation skills appropriate for the age level you would use them with. The children who listen to the tape should be able to use your voice and timing as a guide. They could have a copy of the same material (without punctuation present) and add the appropriate marks or write the material down as dictation, both words and punctuation. (Start with one simple skill and gradually increase complexity and length.)

LANGUAGE SKILLS: SUBSTANCE AND STRATEGIES

PARTICIPATION ACTIVITIES

1. Select one of the spelling games or activities and try it out with a group of children. If you wish, you can devise a game or cross-word puzzle of your own. (Be sure it involves writing the words or seeing them in print and that all children can continue to participate and learn.)
2. Teach inductively some element of punctuation or capitalization that a group of children need to learn so that they discover the "rule" from the examples that you give.
3. Take some children who are having difficulty with handwriting and analyze their legibility problems. Keep a sample from before you start and then take another sample after working with them several times. See what progress they have made.

REFERENCES

[1] Paul McKee. *Language in the Elementary School.* Boston: Houghton Mifflin, 1934, p. 272.

[2] Carol Chomsky. "Write Now, Read Later," IN *Language in Early Childhood Education* (Courtney B. Cazden, ed.). Washington, D.C.: National Association for the Education of Young Children, 1972, p. 120.

[3] Carol Chomsky. "Invented Spelling in First Grade," Unpublished paper, Harvard Graduate School of Education, May 1974, pp. 1–2.

[4] Maria Montessori. *The Montessori Method.* Cambridge, Massachusetts: Robert Bently, 1967, p. 283.

[5] Carol Chomsky. "Invented Spelling." pp. 11–12.

[6] Thomas D. Horn. *The Effect of a Syllabic Presentation of Words upon Learning to Spell.* State University of Iowa, 1947.

[7] Colin Dunkeld and Lynda Hatch. "Building Spelling Confidence," *Elementary English*, vol. 52, no. 2, February 1975, p. 227.

[8] Ernest A. Horn. "A Basic Writing Vocabulary—10,000 Words Most Commonly Used in Writing," *University of Iowa Monographs in Education*, First Series, no. 4. Iowa City, Iowa: University of Iowa, 1926.

[9] Henry D. Rinsland. *A Basic Vocabulary of Elementary School Children.* New York: Macmillan, 1945.

[10] Paul R. Hanna and Jean S. Hanna. "The Teaching of Spelling," *The National Elementary Principal*, vol. 45, November 1965, pp. 19–28.

[11] Lillie Smith Davis. "The Applicability of Phonic Generalizations to Selected Spelling Programs," *Elementary English*, vol. 49, no. 5, May 1972, pp. 706–713.

[12] Paul R. Hanna, Richard E. Hodges, and Jean S. Hanna. *Spelling: Structure and Strategies*. Boston: Houghton Mifflin, 1971.

[13] Leslie W. Johnson. "One Hundred Words Most Often Misspelled by Children in the Elementary Grades," *Journal of Educational Research*, vol. 44, October 1950, pp. 154–155.

[14] Gertrude Hildreth. "Manuscript Writing after Sixty Years," *Elementary English*, vol. 37, no. 1, January 1960, pp. 3–13.

[15] Virgil E. Herrick. "Children's Experiences in Writing" IN *Children and the Language Arts* (Virgil E. Herrick and Leland B. Jacobs, eds.). Englewood Cliffs, New Jersey: Prentice-Hall, 1955, pp. 271–272.

[16] Althea Beery. "Readiness for Handwriting," *Readiness for Reading and Related Language Arts*. Champaign, Illinois: National Council of Teachers of English, 1950.

[17] Eric A. Enstrom. "The Extent of the Use of the Left Hand in Handwriting and the Determination of the Relative Efficiency of the Various Hand-Wrist-Wrist-Arm-Paper Adjustments," *Dissertation Abstracts*, vol. 27, no. 5, Ann Arbor, Michigan: University of Michigan, 1957.

[18] Modified list taken from Gertrude Hildreth. "Manuscript Writing after Sixty Years," pp. 3–13.

[19] E. A. Enstrom and Doris C. Enstrom. "It's a Family Affair," *Elementary English*, vol. 46, February 1969, p. 237.

[20] Ibid., pp. 240–241.

[21] *Guiding Growth in Handwriting Scale*. Columbus, Ohio: Zaner-Bloser Company.

RESOURCES FOR PART TWO

FOR FURTHER READING

Becker, George J. *Television and the Classroom Reading Program.* Newark, Delaware: International Reading Association, 1973.

Burrows, Alvina, Doris C. Jackson, and Dorothy O. Saunders. *They All Want to Write.* New York: Holt, 1964.

Chomsky, Noam. *Language and Mind.* New York: Harcourt Brace Jovanovich, 1968.

Elgin, Suzette Haden. *A Primer of Transformational Grammar for Rank Beginners.* Urbana, Illinois: National Council of Teachers of English, 1975.

Evertts, Eldonna L., ed. *Explorations in Children's Writing.* Urbana, Illinois: National Council of Teachers of English, 1970.

Fox, Robert P., ed. *Teaching English as a Second Language and as a Second Dialect.* Urbana, Illinois: National Council of Teachers of English, 1973.

Gerbrandt, Gary L. *An Idea Book for Acting Out and Writing Language K-8.* Urbana, Illinois: National Council of Teachers of English, 1974.

Henry, Mabel Wright. *Creative Experiences in Oral Language.* Urbana, Illinois: National Council of Teachers of English, 1967.

Hopkins, Lee Bennett. *Pass the Poetry, Please!* New York: Citation Press, n.d.

Jacobs, Roderick A., and Peter S. Rosenbaum. *Transformations: Style and Meaning.* Waltham, Massachusetts: Xerox College Publishing, 1971.

Kaye, Evelyn. *The Family Guide to Children's Television.* New York: Pantheon, 1974.

Lundsteen, Sara W. *Listening, Its Impact on Reading and the Other Language Arts.* Urbana, Illinois: National Council of Teachers of English, 1971.

May, Frank B. *Teaching Language As Communication*. Columbus, Ohio: Merrill, 1967.

Mearns, Hughes. *Creative Power: The Education of Youth in the Creative Arts*. New York: Dover, 1958.

Petty, Walter T., and Mary Bowen. *Slithery Snakes and Other Aids to Children's Writing*. New York: Appleton Century Crofts, 1967.

Ross, Ramon R. *Storyteller*. Columbus, Ohio: Merrill, 1972.

OTHER INSTRUCTIONAL MATERIALS

Cassette Tapes

O'Hare, Frank, and Enola Borgh. *Grammar Today*. Urbana, Illinois: National Council of Teachers of English, 1974.

Films

Creative Writing Skills, Oxford Films, 1136 N. Las Palmas Avenue, Hollywood, California 90038.

Heathcote, Dorothy. Teaching Series, Drama in Education, Northwestern University Film Library, P.O. Box 1665, Evanston, Illinois 60204.

Marceau, Marcel. *Pantomime: The Language of the Heart*, Encyclopedia Britannica Educational Corporation, 425 North Michigan Avenue, Chicago, Illinois 60611.

PART THREE

Components: A Comprehensive Language Arts Program

To have a comprehensive language arts program, children's literature and reading are fundamental components. However, because both are usually dealt with in separate and complete courses at the college level, the discussions presented in this text are primarily devoted to the relationship of language, literature, and reading.

There are strong indications that children who are surrounded with books and encouraged to read widely will develop broader vocabularies, will become more fluent speakers, and will be more proficient readers. If books can offer these advantages, then literature programs should be commonplace in elementary school classrooms. As suggested in Chapter Twelve, such programs would include reading books aloud, sharing poetry, listening to recorded stories and poems, participating in small group book discussions, and sharing favorite stories through various creative projects.

Reading instruction is often separated from the natural development of language skills. In Chapter Thirteen, the use of children's language is emphasized as a basis for reading instruction and a description of the reading process according to psycholinguistic theory is presented. The discussion describes the teaching of reading using the language experience approach. It outlines specific ways of helping children learn word attack skills since all too often teachers spend time eliciting stories from children for experience charts but devote very little time to using them in the instruction of basic reading skills.

The last chapter summarizes the linguistic and cognitive bases for the language arts program presented in the text. A guide which emphasizes the interrelatedness of all the language arts is included in Chapter Fourteen to help with the planning of a balanced and integrated program. Suggestions for involving parents and teacher aides are also an integral part of both this chapter and of the individualized instructional program developed within the text.

CHAPTER TWELVE

Literature in the Language Arts

PREVIEW QUESTIONS

1 In what ways does literature—both prose and poetry—relate to language development?

2 What special opportunities does poetry offer for speaking and writing creatively as well as personal enjoyment?

3 In what ways can poetry be shared with children?

4 What are some books that will contribute to growth in language?

5 How is a literature program developed and implemented?

Children enjoy hearing stories read aloud. "Read me a story. Read it again!" And after three times, "Just one more time, just one!" Their attention is just as rapt the fourth time as the first—and they may correct you on a misread word or a section accidentally omitted.

Children's interest in stories is good for them. Parents who respond to children's request to read aloud are helping their young children become verbally proficient. There is a strong chance that learning to read will be easier, vocabularies will be larger, and greater fluency in language usage will occur.

LANGUAGE DEVELOPMENT THROUGH LITERATURE

How can something as simple as reading aloud be so helpful to children? How can the language of books influence a child's development to that extent? Looking closely at literature, we see that the language may be as emotional as:

> "Go out and hold that mongrel if you don't want him shot." He held the door ajar the width of the boy's body and thrust him out. The boy fell on the back of the dog, whose snarling jaws had pushed into the light between the boy's legs. A heavy boot half pushed, half kicked the entangled feet of the sprawled boy and the nose of the dog and slammed the door. "Get that dog out of my way and hold him if you don't want him dead."[1]

The language may be as rhythmical as:

THE MODERN HIAWATHA

He killed the noble Mudjokovis,
With the skin he made him mittens,
Made them with the fur side inside,
Made them with the skin side outside,
He, to get the warm side inside,
Put the inside skin side outside:
He, to get the cold side outside,
Put the warm side fur side inside:
That's why he put the fur side inside,
Why he put the skin side outside,
Why he turned them inside outside.[2]

George A. Strong

The language may be as descriptive as:

> *In the city everything is squeezed together.*
> *The buildings are so close they have to stretch up*
> *into the sky to find enough room. . . . A city sky is*
> *caught between tall buildings, with only a little bit*
> *showing.*[3]

From literature, children learn the complexities of language, the diversity in its usage, the emotions of its tones, the softness of its beauty.

Related Research

There are several research studies that support the use of books to stimulate children's language and vocabulary development. Courtney Cazden[4] conducted an experimental study to determine if the finding of certain grammatical constructions in young children's oral language was related to parents' frequent expansion of their telegraphic speech. In reviewing her findings, she reported that children whose statements were extended by adult responses gained more than two other groups on six measures of language development. The significance of this finding, as it relates to literature, is that stories were read aloud to this group to stimulate conversation and discussion. The investigator, in citing implications of the research, suggests children be given extensive opportunities to discuss ideas out loud and that books are excellent for creating talk about the pictures or story content.

A related study was conducted at New York University. Over 500 black children, kindergarten through grade three, were involved in the year-long research effort. Approximately half the children (ten classrooms) assigned to the experimental group, "participated in a literature-based oral language program intended to expand experience, conceptual ability, control over the structure of language and the range of language used."[5] Selected books were read aloud each day, followed by activities emphasizing the use of children's oral language. The control group, comprised of the remaining half of the participating children, enjoyed a literature program, but the enrichment activities were intentionally not based on oral language. The results of the research indicated literature expanded language skills for both groups of children. The greatest gains, however, were evidenced by students in the experimental group, with the most significant increase in kindergarten. In view of these findings, director of the study, Bernice Cullinan, makes the recommendation that a literature-based oral language program begin early. She further states that emphasis on oral language enhances a child's mastery of standard dialect while maintaining facility in his own dialect.

From these two studies, we can conclude that reading books aloud—and then allowing time for plenty of conversation and discussion—stimulates children's oral language development. It would appear students also are given a greater opportunity to become proficient in a more socially acceptable dialect when participating in this kind of language environment. The earlier a literature-based oral language program is provided, the better.

As a second part of a linguistic study, Chomsky directed an investigation that involved children from six to ten. Extensive information was gathered about each child's exposure to reading. Specifically, data was compiled regarding the amount a child read and was read to, and the complexity of the reading material itself. Further information was obtained using Huck's *Taking Inventory of Children's Literary Background*,[6] a measure indicating a child's knowledge of the content of sixty well-known books for children. The primary purpose of the study was to determine the relationship between reading exposure and a child's rate of linguistic development. The investigator considered written language to be potentially of a more complex nature than oral speech. Therefore, the assumption was made that children who read and hear a variety of rich and complex materials receive greater linguistic benefits than children who are nonliterary. The study's findings on all reading measures were highly significant, resulting in the conclusion that reading exposure and linguistic stages of development are definitely related. The Huck inventory proved an excellent measure consistently showing a positive relationship between scores and linguistic stages. Chomsky's summary of the results and implications of research speaks profoundly to the classroom teacher:

> Our reading results indicate that exposure to the more complex language available from reading does seem to go hand in hand with increased knowledge of the language. This would imply that perhaps wider reading should find a place in the curriculum. The child could be read to, stimulated to read on his own, not restricted to material deemed 'at his level' but permitted access to books well 'above his level' to get out of them whatever he may. Perhaps he should be encouraged to skim when he reads, to skip uninteresting portions and get to the 'good parts' instead of concentrating at length on controlled texts. In general it may be that the effort should be towards providing

more and richer language exposure, rather than limiting the child with restrictive and carefully programmed materials.[7]

The last piece of research to be discussed in this section is related to literature and reading with a special emphasis on vocabulary development. Conducting an extensive study to determine the influence of literature on vocabulary and reading achievement, Cohen identified second grade classrooms containing children who were slow to learn to read. Each of the experimental classes received fifty books to be read aloud during the year, with some selections being read more than once. The books chosen for the study dealt with universal experiences, allowed for emotional identification with characters, and contained language that flowed smoothly and best conveyed the idea or image to the child. No limitation was placed on vocabulary when selecting the books. Throughout the academic year teachers read stories aloud, followed by a variety of activities, while the control group received no special attention. The results of the study showed the experimental group increased significantly over the control group in word knowledge, quality of vocabulary, and reading comprehension.[8]

Implications

The following implications for teaching in the elementary school classroom can be drawn from these four research studies.

1. A literature-based language arts program should begin in kindergarten and continue throughout the elementary grades.
2. A variety of rich and complex reading materials should be provided for children.
3. It is important that teachers consistently read books aloud to their children. Oral language activities—such as discussions of the story, role playing, or puppetry—should frequently be used as follow-ups to reading aloud.
4. Children should be encouraged and motivated to increase their independent reading.

SELECTING BOOKS FOR A LANGUAGE-BASED LANGUAGE ARTS PROGRAM

Realizing the significance of books and their language, selection becomes increasingly important. Approximately 2,000 books for children are published each year, and certainly not all are quality books containing quality language. The teacher must be able to distinguish between those books that are deserving of children's attention and those that are not. If a primary purpose is to select books for their language value, then it is incumbent upon teachers to become discriminating and knowledgeable about the language offered in books for children.

Metaphorical Language in Books

Metaphorical language is found frequently throughout books for children. Authors creatively turn the familiar into the unusual by comparing unlike objects or personifying the inanimate. The Caldecott Award Winner, *White Snow, Bright Snow*, is an excellent example of such creativity with language. In describing the effects of a heavy snowfall, Alvin Tresselt writes in metaphorical language.

> *In the morning a clear blue sky was overhead*
> *and blue shadows hid in all the corners.*
> *Automobiles looked like big fat raisins*
> *buried in snowdrifts.*
> *Houses crouched together, their windows*
> *peeking out from under great white*
> *eyebrows.*
> *Even the church steeple wore a pointed*
> *cap on its top.*[9]

Hearing and discussing language that is used in an interesting manner contributes to a child's own use of language. Merely exposing children to creative language by reading various books may not be enough. To become aware of how an author has used language, a certain amount of discussion needs to take place. The imagery Tresselt creates may not be overtly noticed or appreciated unless attention is somehow drawn to it. Rewriting the passage in a reporting style and then comparing it with the original is one method of helping children understand the importance of using language creatively. However, paraphrasing a creative effort such as this should only be done to emphasize the effectiveness of such language. It should not be a technique that becomes a part of the daily classroom routine. The passage rewritten might be:

The morning sky was clear and blue with some
shadows.
Automobiles were buried in snowdrifts.
Houses were covered in snow and their
windows could hardly be seen.
Even the church steeple was snow-
covered.

Older students may be asked to rewrite the passage and then
make the comparison by responding to certain questions. An effective method for doing this is to pair students, having them read their
piece of writing and then the original from the book. To bring these
differences out in the discussion, the following questions might be
asked: "How would you describe the language that author Alvin
Tresselt chose to use?" "How does this compare with the way you
used language in your writing?" "If you want to visualize the scene
in your mind, which piece of writing helps you the most?" "What
is it about metaphorical writing that creates images?" As a follow-
up to this discussion, students may wish to try changing the language of a recently written piece of their own writing. Or, using
the reporting of some event in a news article, they may want to try
their hand at writing it more creatively.

A considerable number of books for children are available that
offer the kind of creative language we have been talking about here.
The following is a beginning list to help you become acquainted
with a few of them. As you review and read other books that belong
with these, extend the list. More importantly, however, read them to
your students, encourage your students to read them, and intervene
at appropriate times to call attention to the interesting ways language is used.

Bourne, Miriam. *Emilio's Summer Day*. New York: Harper & Row, 1966.
McCloskey, Robert. *Time of Wonder*. New York: Viking, 1957.
Tresselt, Alvin. *A Thousand Lights and Fireflies*. New York: Parents'
    Magazine Press, 1968.

Repetition in Books

Young children enjoy repetition. They enjoy the rhythm of language
when words are creatively strung together and repeated. They like
saying and hearing rhythmical patterns of words over and over
again, much as they enjoy repeating nursery rhymes. Actually, the
activity of repeating refrains or rhythms can be described as lan-

guage play. Children like the way particular words sound when they are put together. For example, "I'm in the milk and the milk's in me. God bless the milk and God bless me."[10] from Maurice Sendak's book *In the Night Kitchen,* is learned and said repeatedly by children because they enjoy the sound of the language. The refrain is adopted by the child and hence becomes very personal. It is taken out of its original context and added to a storehouse of rhymes, jingles, and enjoyable word patterns to be conjured up during an evening meal, at bedtime, or on the school playground.

Books are excellent sources for providing the repetition children find so enjoyable. *Chicken Soup With Rice,* by Maurice Sendak, is a favorite among young children. Written in rhyme and ending with similar refrains, each month is described as delightful when eating chicken soup with rice.

In January
it's so nice
while slipping
on the sliding ice
to sip hot chicken soup
with rice.
Sipping once
sipping twice
sipping chicken soup
with rice.

In February
it will be
my snowman's
anniversary
with cake for him
and soup for me!
Happy once
happy twice
happy chicken soup
with rice.[11]

Numerous books for children contain repetition and refrain Become acquainted with some of the more outstanding ones, and be prepared to read them more than once to young children. When you come to the refrain in a book, encourage children's participation. Let them say the refrain along with you. Let them enjoy the sounds of language. You may want to start with the following list:

Brown, Margaret Wise. *Goodnight Moon*. New York: Harper & Row, 1947.

Gag, Wanda. *Millions of Cats*. New York: Coward-McCann, 1927.

Lindgren, Astrid. *The Tomten*. New York: Coward-McCann, 1961.

Piper, Watty. *The Little Engine That Could*. New York: Platt, 1954.

Preston, Margaret Mitchell. *Monkey in the Jungle*. New York: Viking, 1968.

Smith, Mary and R. A. *Long Ago Elf*. Chicago: Follett, 1968.

Vipong, Elfrida, and Raymond Briggs. *The Elephant and the Bad Baby*. London: Hamish Hamilton, 1969.

The Language of the Accumulative Tale

The language of the accumulative tale is closely related to the kind of language found in books containing repetition and refrain. Children enjoy the built-in rhythm created by the plot structure of such a tale. Specifically, a pattern is established and repeated each time an event or character is added to the developing story. This continues until the climax or end of the tale. In *The Great Big Enormous Turnip* by Alex Tolstoy, the old man finds the turnip he planted has grown so big and strong that he cannot pull it out of the ground by himself. He first asks the old woman to help him.

> *The old woman pulled the old man.*
> *The old man pulled the turnip.*
> *And they pulled and pulled again,*
> *but they could not pull it up.*

Next, the granddaughter is called to help the old man and woman.

> *The granddaughter pulled the old woman,*
> *The old woman pulled the old man,*
> *The old man pulled the turnip.*
> *And they pulled and pulled again,*
> *but they could not pull it up.*[12]

When the three are not successful in pulling it up, others, one by one, lend a hand until the turnip comes up at last.

Accumulative tales are excellent for getting children involved in the language. Students can repeat the refrain together, "And they pulled and pulled again, but they could not pull it up." Accumulative stories may also be role played by children or retold using felt characters and a flannel board.

To become more familiar with the language and enjoyment of the accumulative tale, the following books should be helpful:

Frasconi, Antonio. *The House That Jack Built.* New York: Harcourt Brace, 1958.

Burningham, John. *Mr. Gumpy's Outing.* London: Jonathan Cape Ltd., 1970.

Zemach, Harve. *The Judge.* New York: Farrar, Straus, 1969.

Aardema, Verna. *Why Mosquitos Buzz in People's Ears: A West African Tale.* New York: Dial, 1975.

Books Lending Themselves to Conversation and Discussion

We have already talked to some extent about the value of discussion. Verbal interaction among children or between children and their teacher fosters the development of language, concepts, and ideas. Certain books for children invite conversation and discussion. In fact, an experience with books of this nature is incomplete if, after they are read, no conversation about them takes place. Books demanding discussion can be categorized in the following three ways: books requiring close observation and attention to detail; books having surprise endings; and books having several layers of meaning.

Books requiring close observation and attention to detail   An amusing book by Ellen Raskin, *Nothing Ever Happens on My Block,*[13] is an outstanding example of a book in this category. Chester Filbert claims he lives in an unexciting place, yet while he sits and ponders this, innumerable events are occurring all around him: a house catches fire, is rebuilt, and then struck by lightning; a thief is caught in the neighborhood; and a parachutist falls to the ground landing almost directly on top of Chester. Happening after happening takes place, all completely unnoticed by Chester Filbert. The illustrations are a myriad of discoveries and demand more than one glance through the book. Asking the question, "What do you notice on this page that Chester doesn't?" can stimulate closer observation and loads of enjoyable conversation that develops and extends children's language and thinking.

Books requiring close observation demand a keen eye and are few in number when we consider the quantity of books available for children. Therefore, you may want to become acquainted with the following:

Raskin, Ellen. *Spectacles*. New York: Atheneum, 1968.
Sendak, Maurice. *Where the Wild Things Are*. New York: Harper, 1963.
Wildsmith, Brian. *Puzzles*. London: Oxford University Press, 1970.
Sheer, Julian. *Rain Makes Applesauce*. New York: Holiday, 1964.
Brown, Marcia. *Once a Mouse*. New York: Scribner, 1961.
Burton, Virginia Lee. *The Little House*. Boston: Houghton Mifflin, 1942.
Sendak, Maurice. *In the Night Kitchen*. New York: Harper & Row, 1972.
Hoban, Tana. *Look Again*. New York: Macmillan, 1971.
Kraus, Robert. *Owliver*. New York: Dutton, 1974.

Books containing surprise endings   Have you read a book and been completely surprised by its ending? Or, can you remember a movie with an unexpected ending and your total surprise at the finish? How do you feel when this happens? If you are like most of us, you immediately want to share the experience with another person. The same thought occurs to young children when they hear stories having surprise endings. Conversation about what has happened is spontaneous and natural. For example, reading aloud the book *One Monday Morning*,[14] children are surprised and delighted when they discover a boy's daydream about a royal family coming to visit him was all started while playing with a deck of cards. The chatter that begins at the end of reading such a book can be guided and extended by asking questions.

Other books with surprise endings:

Holl, Adelaide. *The Runaway Giant*. New York: Lothrop, 1967.
Mahy, Margaret. *The Dragon of the Ordinary Family*. London: William Heinemann, Ltd., 1968.
Tworkov, Jack. *The Camel Who Took a Walk*. New York: Dutton, 1951.
Charlip, Remy, and Supree Burton. *Harlequin and the Gift of Many Colors*. New York: Parents' Magazine Press, 1973.

Books having several layers of meaning   Some books for children have several layers of meaning and consequently different levels of interpretation. *The Velveteen Rabbit*, a long-standing favorite, is enjoyed by all age groups. Young adults recently adopted the book and have made it a popular gift item for close friends. The theme of the story has far-reaching implications, making it possible for varying age groups to enjoy and discuss the book. The following excerpt illustrates the point being made here. The sawdust-stuffed Rabbit asks the Skin Horse:

> "What is REAL?" asked the Rabbit one day, ... "Does it mean having things that buzz inside you and a stick-out handle?"
> "Real isn't how you are made," said the Skin Horse. "It's a thing that happens to you. When a child loves you for a long, long time, not just to play with, but REALLY loves you, then you become Real."

"Does it hurt?" asked the Rabbit.

"Sometimes," said the Skin Horse, for he was always truthful. "When you are Real you don't mind being hurt."

"Does it happen all at once, like being wound up," he asked, "or bit by bit?"

"It doesn't happen all at once," said the Skin Horse. "You become. It takes a long time. That's why it doesn't often happen to people who break easily, or have sharp edges, or who have to be carefully kept."[15]

Another book having several layers of meaning is *Crow Boy*,[16] a story frequently recommended for second-grade children that appears in a basal reading series at the fourth grade level. It is that kind of story—enjoyable and appropriate for more than one age group. Chibi, a small frightened Japanese boy, is not accepted by other children in his class. He gradually withdraws into his own world, and it is not until sixth grade and Mr. Isobe that Chibi is viewed by others as someone worthwhile with something to contribute in life. The book ends with Chibi being called Crow Boy, the change in name depicting the change and growth in Chibi. He is no longer the scared, withdrawn little boy who hid under the school. Huck[17] says this is one of the few picture books for children that shows character development.

Books such as *The Velveteen Rabbit* and *Crow Boy* stimulate provocative, sensitive discussions. They allow the reader or listener to confront the content of the story at a personal level and talk about it. The sensitive message and theme conveyed in each book makes it beg to be discussed. These books and others like them can make a significant contribution to the rich language environment of your classroom. If you are not yet acquainted with Leo Lionni's *Frederick*[18] and *Swimmy*,[19] you may want to get to know them, too.

ESTABLISHING A LITERATURE PROGRAM IN THE ELEMENTARY SCHOOL

The daily curriculum already seems to bulge at the seams with content and skill requirements. Teachers frequently complain about the amount of material that has to be covered and the short amount of time for doing it. Somehow, when the priorities get weighed, reading books aloud or independently falls at the bottom of the day's list.

How can a teacher be certain that time is provided to make books and language an integral part of the daily learning environment? The best insurance is to plan a literature program at the very beginning of the academic year. In broad terms, such a program means surrounding children with books and providing a wide variety of activities that make reading an enjoyable experience. In more specific terms, however, the following plan might be used as a guideline and source for establishing a successful literature program in the classroom.

Components of a Literature Program

Establish a relaxed and comfortable atmosphere for reading An attractive library center in the classroom can create an environment conducive to reading books for enjoyment. A rug, soft pillows, or maybe a comfortable chair or rocker turns the traditional reading area into a warm, cozy place for pleasurable reading. Think about the kind of comfort you want when you decide to spend an evening reading the most recent best seller. You certainly do not select a straight-back chair behind a desk. Many children have been discouraged because they have never found reading an enjoyable experience. Establishing a relaxed atmosphere that invites children to read just for the sheer fun of it is one step toward making readers out of them.

Make books freely and constantly accessible to children Within such a library center there should be a wide variety of books available to children. The size of the collection will vary. However, a minimum of three or four books per child seems essential if children are to have a reasonable choice. New books should be talked about and continually added to the existing collection. Research shows that if a teacher introduces a book to children, interest in reading it is stimulated. If certain books, time and time again, appear uninteresting to youngsters, remove them from the shelves and replace them with books you feel will be more appealing. The most important thing to remember is to have books that children want to read. To do this and keep children's interest high, you will more than likely need to change the entire collection several times during the year. If there is not a library within the school, public libraries are usually willing to lend a number of books to teachers for their classrooms.

Provide time for children to read books As an elementary student, did you ever have a book taken away from you because you were reading it during a lesson in math, social studies, science, and so on? If it did not happen to you, do you remember it happening to

Provide time for all children to read and enjoy books in the classroom. (*Photograph by Thomas England*)

another student? Still reflecting on your days in elementary school, were you ever given time to simply sit and read that book you were so engrossed in? Frequently, the only reading children are allowed to do in school is related to content subjects and the basal reader. Children rarely discover that reading can be enjoyable, and many teachers seldom discover that their best readers are those who constantly enjoy reading. It may well be worth considering that children learn to read by reading, and children learn to enjoy reading by reading. This being the case, time allotted to reading books for pleasure is never wasted.

One method that offers possibilities for providing time in the classroom for reading is an Uninterrupted Sustained Silent Reading Program. What is it? It means you set aside a certain thirty- or forty-minute time period each day for pleasurable reading. Children and teachers alike read books of their own choosing—or magazines, comic books, and newspapers can be brought in to give a choice of reading material. The point is that everyone reads! What about reluctant readers—children who refuse to read during this time? Give them a variety of books you think they can read easily and will enjoy. Some children may refuse for a while, but if everyone else is reading, they will join in before long. These children may first begin by browsing but will eventually be captured by material that they have found interesting.

Read books aloud to children Children throughout the elementary grades benefit from hearing books read aloud. We know children's language is developing at least through age ten. Consistently hearing quality and complex language contributes to this development. Reading stories aloud not only enhances language facility but also stimulates children's interest in reading books independently. Many will want to reread a book that has been read aloud to the class or may be inspired to read another book written by the same author.

A read-aloud program can be planned at the beginning of the year. First, a time needs to be set aside each day for reading aloud. Many teachers seem to read to children after the lunch or recess break before other work or activities are started. Secondly, books for reading aloud must be carefully chosen. Certain books for children simply lend themselves to being read aloud where others do not. Considerations as to appropriate age level and interest appeal of the book enter into the selection process. The size and quality of illustrations would apply to picture books. The following questions may be useful when choosing books to read aloud: Will the story interest your children, both boys and girls? Is the sequence of the story easy to follow? Is the language enjoyable? Does it flow smoothly for reading aloud? Does the book avoid stereotyping? If it is a picture book, can the illustrations be readily seen and shared with children as you read the story? Do the illustrations enhance the enjoyment of the book? Before reading a book aloud to children, it is crucial that a teacher read the book first and decide if it is suitable for the class. Familiarity with a book promotes a smooth, enjoyable reading and prevents stumbling over words or phrases. An excellent book can be ruined when it is read aloud poorly.

Conduct small group book discussions Children who are not ego-centric can readily become involved in small group book discussions. Paperback books are numerous and inexpensive. Several copies of the same book may be purchased for the classroom and read by interested students. A discussion of a book that has been enjoyed by four or five children can often be provocative and stimulating. For such a discussion to be productive, however, it is necessary that the teacher or students have prepared questions about the plot, characters, specific incidents, or even the ending of the book. For example, an excellent book for small group discussion is Armstrong Sperry's *Call It Courage*,[20] a Newbery Award winner. The main character of the story, Mafatu, leaves his native island to prove his courage to his father and to himself. The author develops the character in many different ways by the end of the first chapter. The reader gets to know and understand Mafatu by hearing his friends talk about him, through comments made by his father, and certain thoughts and perceptions are revealed by Mafatu himself. Children, when asked, "How did you get to know Mafatu?" can identify an author's technique in developing a central character. Questions directed toward interesting discoveries in books can enhance the enjoyment and quality of a discussion; however, questions that consistently probe for recall answers about a story may create a test situation and destroy both the discussion and the book for children.

Make books memorable for children   Enjoyable activities following the reading of a book can be effective in making books memorable to children. Formal written book reports are *passé*, and hopefully have seen their last days in the classroom. Required book reports probably have done more to turn children away from reading than any other single source. Art activities such as the creation of a wall hanging, mobile, box movie, diorama (three-dimensional scene), or a series of puppets relating to the story or characters heighten children's enjoyment of the book. Much constructive, enjoyable learning takes place while doing such activities. Children must plan and develop a creative work—decisions have to be made about materials that will be used, how things will be put together or displayed—and throughout it all, language is a vital, living part of the process. Role playing a story is still another way of sharing and making a book memorable. Tape-recording book reviews or retelling the story from one character's point of view may be interesting activities for some students. A more extensive discussion of ways to share and interpret books can be found in Chapter 8.

Make records, cassette tapes, and film strips available when possible
Many schools provide listening centers for teachers to use in their classrooms. If not, a tape recorder placed in a corner of the room will suffice. Having such a center means several children can hear a particular recording at the same time. You can make a recording of a story for children to listen to while looking at the book. More and more literature for children is being offered commercially on

record or cassette tape—some with accompanying film strips. School libraries frequently order and store such materials for teachers' use. However, if you are interested in brochures, catalogs, or purchasing literature-based materials for yourself, the following are some major companies which produce these.

Miller Brody Productions
342 Madison Avenue
New York, New York 10017

Scholastic Book Services
50 West 44th Street
New York, New York 10036

The Viking Press, Inc.
625 Madison Avenue
New York, New York 10022

Weston Woods Studios
Weston Woods, Connecticut 06880

Poetry in a Rich Language Environment

Poetry, perhaps better than any other type of literature, presents the very essence of creative language. According to Huck, "Poetry is language in its most connotative and concentrated form. Each word must be chosen with care, both for its sound and meaning."[21] It is a poet's thoughtful and imaginative use of words that creates a poem. Reading aloud and sharing poetry offers children an opportunity to hear creative language at its very finest.

If we want children to enjoy poetry and the language of poetry, then we must first select poems that will interest them. In the past, required memorization has dulled children's enthusiasm for poetry. However, an inappropriate or poor selection of poems can be just as deadly. Reading condescending or sentimental poems to students may cause them to reject poetry. Choosing only the older more traditional poems to share with children may also hinder a developing interest in poetry.

If teachers begin poetry at the level of the children's interest, they have a better opportunity of sustaining children's enthusiasm for poetry. The first task is to have students wanting to read, write, and hear poetry. After this accomplishment, a teacher can gradually introduce poems that raise the quality of children's tastes and appreciation. But first, get them to like poetry.

Sharing Poetry in the Elementary School Classroom

Poetry may be shared in a variety of ways in the elementary classroom. Children can listen to poems on record or cassette tape, certain poems may be compared and discussed, or some children may wish to put poems to music. A teacher has the opportunity to be creative in how poetry is presented and enjoyed in the classroom. A few suggestions follow to illustrate the kind of diversity that is possible when sharing poetry.

Reading poetry aloud   Poetry is meant to be read aloud, and poems containing the qualities of rhythm and sound are particularly enjoyable. The appeal of such poetic characteristics are well illustrated in David McCord's "Song of the Train."

> *SONG OF THE TRAIN*
> *Clickety-clack,*
> *Wheels on the track,*
> *This is the way*
> *They begin the attack:*
> *Click-ety-clack,*
> *Click-ety-clack,*
> *Click-ety,* clack-*ety*
> *Click-ety*
> *Clack.*
>
> *Clickety-clack,*
> *Over the crack,*
> *Faster and faster*
> *The song of the track:*
> *Clickety-clack,*
> *Clickety-clack,*
> *Clickety, clackety,*
> *Clackety*
> *Clack.*
>
> *Riding in front,*
> *Riding in back,*
> Everyone *hears*
> *The song of the track:*
> *Clickety-clack,*
> *Clickety-clack,*
> *Clickety,* clickety,
> *Clackety*
> Clack.[22]
> David McCord

Humorous poems are fun and children like them. Reading poems that bring laughter into the classroom not only enhances the enjoyment of poetry but also promotes a wholesome atmosphere. School should be a pleasant place where learning is an enjoyable rather than painful experience for children. Poems such as John Ciardi's "Mummy Slept Late and Daddy Fixed Breakfast" and the limerick "There Was an Old Man of Blackheath" will certainly contribute to this kind of learning environment.

MUMMY SLEPT LATE AND DADDY FIXED BREAKFAST

Daddy fixed breakfast.
He made us each a waffle.
It looked like gravel pudding.
It tasted something awful.

"Ha, ha," he said, "I'll try again.
This time I'll get it right."
But what I got was in between
Bituminous and anthracite.

"A little too well done? Oh well,
I'll have to start all over."
That time what landed on my plate
Looked like a manhole cover.

I tried to cut it with a fork:
The fork gave off a spark.
I tried a knife and twisted it
Into a question mark.

I tried it with a hack-saw.
I tried it with a torch.
It didn't even make a dent.
It didn't even scorch.

The next time Dad gets breakfast
When Mummy's sleeping late,
I think I'll skip the waffles.
I'd sooner eat the plate![23]

John Ciardi

THERE WAS AN OLD MAN OF BLACKHEATH

There was an old man of Blackheath,
Who sat on his set of false teeth.
Said he, with a start,
"Oh, Lord, bless my heart!
I've bitten myself underneath!"[24]

Unknown

Listening to poetry on cassette tapes or records As mentioned earlier, a variety of commercial recordings of literature for children are now available; poetry seems to have received greater emphasis in the last few years. Therefore, not only is there choice but the quality of such presentations is usually excellent. For example, a recording of "Over in the Meadow" may be obtained from Scholastic Book Services with an accompanying paperback book illustrated by Ezra Jack Keats. The poem is set to music and by the third stanza, everyone who is listening is nodding to the beat. The first few stanzas of the poem will give you an idea of its rhythmical qualities.

OVER IN THE MEADOW

Over in the meadow, in the sand, in the sun,
Lived an old mother turtle and her little turtle one.

"Dig!" said the mother.
"I dig," said the one.
So he dug all day,
In the sand, in the sun.

Over in the meadow, where the stream runs blue,
Lived an old mother fish and her little fishes two.

"Swim!" said the mother.
"We swim," said the two.
So they swam and they leaped,
Where the stream runs blue.

Over in the meadow, in a hole in a tree,
Lived a mother bluebird and her little birdies three.

"Sing!" said the mother.
"We sing," said the three.
So they sang and were glad,
In the hole in the tree.[25]

All recordings of poetry for your classroom do not have to be commercially produced. You can record poems on cassette tapes for children to hear in a listening center, and children can record favorite poems for others to hear. Poetry can also be read and recorded with a musical background that contributes to the tone, mood, or rhythm of a poem.

Poetry interpreted through art   Poetry is personal. What one person pictures in his mind when reading the poem may not be exactly what another pictures. Therefore, interpretation of a poem through art is individualistic. Children may illustrate particular poems using a variety of media. When art materials are limited, creative work is limited. Supply children with a choice of materials: tempera and an assortment of brushes, water colors, materials for collage, pastels, oil-based crayons, to name a few. Poems containing imagery or picturesque descriptions lend themselves to interpretation through art. For example, how might *you* illustrate the following poem? What media would best picture what you see in this poem?

FAR AND NEAR

Farther away than a house is a lawn
  A field and a fence and a rocky hill
  With a tree on top, and farther still
  The sky with a cloud in it gold at dawn.
Closer than dawn in the sky is a tree
  On a hill, and a fence and a field and a green
  Lawn and a house and window screen
  With a nose pressed against it—and then me.[26]

Harry Behn

Poetry and popular music lyrics   Many older children, for one reason or another, have become disenchanted with poetry. Haviland and Smith comment, "How natural and harmonious it all is at the beginning; and yet what happens along the way later to make poetry to many children the dullest and least enjoyable of literary expressions? It is usually about fifth grade in our schools that children decide poetry is not for them."[27]

Because popular music lyrics appeal to this age child, they may be used to stimulate or renew an interest in poetry. Lyrics from folksongs or popular rock music may be selected and typed copies given to students. Playing a recording while seeing the lyrics to a particular piece of music is helpful in making the experience more enjoyable. Students can be led to see how songwriters in actuality are poets. Content of some of our more contemporary poems for children often parallels that of contemporary songs. Both poets and songwriters frequently address the problems of society through their creative endeavors. By gaining an interest in poetry through musical lyrics, students may be encouraged to write their own poetry and set it to music.

Many other ways of bringing poetry into the classroom exist. The poetry discussions in Chapters Eight and Ten on choral reading and writing poetry should add to your growing collection of ideas. And as a creative, imaginative teacher, you will think of many more on your own.

REFERENCES

¹ William H. Armstrong. *Sounder.* New York: Harper & Row, 1969.

² George A. Strong. "The Modern Hiawatha" IN *Favorite Poems Old and New* (Helen Ferris, comp.). Garden City, New York: Doubleday, 1957, p. 337.

³ Alvin Tresselt. *A Thousand Lights and Fireflies.* Parents' Magazine Press, New York, 1965.

⁴ Courtney B. Cazden. *Child Language and Education.* New York: Holt, 1972, pp. 121–125.

⁵ B. E. Cullinan, A. Jagger, and D. Strickland. "Language Expansion for Black Children in the Primary Grades: A Research Report." *Young Children,* January 1974, vol. 29, pp. 98–112.

⁶ Charlotte S. Huck. *Taking Inventory of Children's Literary Background.* Glenview, Illinois: Scott, Foresman, 1966.

⁷ Carol Chomsky. "Stages in Language Development and Reading Exposure." *Harvard Educational Review,* vol. 42, February 1972.

⁸ Dorothy H. Cohen. "The Effect of Literature on Vocabulary and Reading Achievement." *Elementary English,* vol. 45, February 1968, pp. 209–213, 217.

⁹ Alvin Tresselt. *White Snow, Bright Snow.* New York: Lothrop, 1947.

¹⁰ Maurice Sendak. *In the Night Kitchen.* New York: Harper & Row, 1972.

¹¹ Maurice Sendak. *Chicken Soup with Rice.* New York: Harper & Row, 1962.

¹² Alex Tolstoy. *The Great Big Enormous Turnip.* New York: F. Watts, 1968.

¹³ Ellen Raskin. *Nothing Ever Happens on My Block.* New York: Atheneum, 1968.

¹⁴ Uri Shulevitz. *One Monday Morning.* New York: Harper & Row, 1967.

¹⁵ Margery Williams. *The Velveteen Rabbit.* New York: Doubleday, 1926.

¹⁶ Taro Yashima. *Crow Boy.* New York: Viking, 1955.

¹⁷ Charlotte S. Huck and Doris Y. Kuhn. *Children's Literature in the Elementary School.* New York: Holt, 1968.

¹⁸ Leo Lionni. *Frederick.* New York: Pantheon, 1967.

[19] Leo Lionni. *Swimmy*. New York: Pantheon, 1963.

[20] Armstrong Sperry. *Call It Courage*. New York: MacMillan, 1941.

[21] Huck and Kuhn. *Children's Literature*. p. 386.

[22] David McCord. "Song of the Train," *Far and Few*. Boston: Little, Brown, 1952, p. 87.

[23] John Ciardi. "Mummy Slept Late and Daddy Fixed Breakfast." *You Read to Me and I'll Read to You*. Philadelphia: Lippincott, 1962.

[24] Unknown. "There Was an Old Man of Blackheath," IN *Laughable Limericks* (Sara and John E. Brewton, comp.). New York: Thomas Y. Crowell, 1965.

[25] Ezra Jack Keats. *Over in the Meadow*. New York: Four Winds, 1971.

[26] Harry Behn. "Far and Near," *The Wizard in the Well*. New York: Harcourt, 1956.

[27] Virginia Haviland and William Jay Smith. *Children and Poetry*. Washington, D.C.: Library of Congress, 1969, p. v.

CHAPTER THIRTEEN

Language-based Development in Reading

PREVIEW QUESTIONS

1 How does a child's own language fit into reading instruction?

2 In what ways does reading relate to the other language arts?

3 How is instruction in word attack skills and comprehension handled within a language experience approach?

4 How can some language experience be included with a basal reading program?

Recent research in the area of reading has given us a new perspective on the reading process. We know, more than ever before, the importance of recognizing the relationship between reading, language, and thought. Evidence from psycholinguistic research demonstrates how thought and language interact as part of the reading process. Certain basic tenets comprise the psycholinguistic view of reading.

Reading is language: Goodman states that reading is language, in fact, that it is one of the four language processes.[1] How we use oral and written language may vary, but the purpose is the same—communication. While speaking and writing are productive processes, listening and reading are receptive language processes. And in reading, as in listening, the primary aim is the comprehension of meaning.

Readers are competent language users: The beginning reader comes to school an able language user. The child is already an effective listener and speaker, demonstrating real skill in language. When confronted with learning to read, this same child brings to the task an ability to use and understand language. Goodman explains that children "can process an aural language sequence, get to its underlying structures, and construct meaning. They are limited in doing so successfully only to the extent that cognitive development and relative lack of experience limit them. They have mastered the system of language, its symbols, rules and patterns. If they lack vocabulary it is more a result of limited experience and cognitive development than a cause of lack of comprehension."[2] The child's language strength cannot be ignored in the teaching of reading; rather, language competence, if understood and encouraged by teachers, becomes a primary means of helping children become proficient readers of their language.

Language communicates meaning: The purpose of both oral and written language is to communicate meaning. If children are to make effective use of their own linguistic ability when learning to read, their reading material must contain relevant and meaningful language. "Any attempt to reduce the complexity of language in reading by sorting out letters or word parts increases the complexity of the learning since it substitutes abstract language elements for meaningful language."[3] Any sorting out or categorizing must be done by children as they work out a systematic approach to the problems they encounter.

THE PSYCHOLINGUISTIC VIEWPOINT AND
THE TEACHING OF READING

If we adhere to the basic psycholinguistic principles regarding the relationship between language, thought, and the teaching of reading, our elementary school reading programs may need some alterations. In evaluating a reading program, we need to ask several questions.

Does the program respect and make use of children's language competence? Does the reading material contain natural sentence patterns that you would expect a child to use? Young children use sentence patterns that show a knowledge of language. Their use of syntax is not as complex as that of an older child or an adult, but they do not speak or write entirely in simple sentences. For example, a group of kindergarten children were involved in sand play. As you examine a transcription of their conversations, you can identify a variety of complex sentence patterns—sentences that are structurally similar to mature adult speech.

> I've got two sets of people and they all live in one house.
> Yeah, if we get more water in it, it will be soaked.
> If I had a bucket, I could make a sand castle.
> Dale and me and my friend in Richmond has the toad and it belongs to us.
> I know how he feels because my sister and I had a toad before.

Young children's written compositions also illustrate knowledge and control of their language. A first-grade class enjoyed writing "I wish . . ." poems that were later compiled in a book and placed in the classroom library area. Kim's poem, taken from this source, reveals not only her ability to use language but also some of her private and inner feelings.

> *I wish I had a guitar to play—*
> *I love the way it sounds.*
> *I wish I could go to my Grandmother's house.*
> *I wish, I wish I was 23 years old*
> *Because I would be able to live my own life—go where I wanted*
> *   to go.*
> *I wish my older sister was here.*
> *But now she can live her own life.*

Commercially-produced reading programs sometimes ignore children's ability to use language effectively by presenting material with unnatural language patterns in an attempt to simplify word recognition. The story below is a representative sample of what you might find young children reading at the beginning of formal reading instruction.

I see Skip.
See Skip, Father.
See Skip,
Oh, Skip!
See Skip, Father.
I see Skip.
Oh, oh, Skip!
Run, Skip.
See Skip jump, Father.
Jump, Skip, jump.

Children bring much more mature language to the reading process. Their reading material should more closely reflect their natural language patterns.

Does the reading program consider children's background of experience? Children's past experiences and their understanding of concepts are significant considerations when we teach reading. To give a child who has never been to the ocean a story containing such words as *jellyfish, starfish, evening tide, sand crabs, pier,* and *sandbar,* may create some unnecessary reading difficulties. Both children and adults apply knowledge of past experiences to the reading process. An engineer has no difficulty in reading material concerned with her profession; but the average layman, who has had very little experience in the engineering field, will find the same reading material difficult to comprehend. Even *sand* or *tide*— two relatively simple regular words—are difficult if there is no match with conceptual development.

Does the reading program consider how children acquire and use language when teaching word attack skills? Piaget's studies suggest that "The line of development of language is from the whole to the part."[4] And psycholinguistic theory says that the teaching of reading must deal with whole natural meaningful language. Goodman points out that "the actual importance of any letter, letter part, word or word part at any point in reading is totally dependent on all other elements and on the grammar and meaning of the language sequence."[5] Any reading program strictly adhering to a decoding approach that requires children to first learn sounds, then lists of words, and finally the reading of sentences violates everything we know about children's acquisition and knowledge about language.

(A) An experience story begins with an experience—here a walk through a nearby wooded area.

(B) The teacher answers questions and points out things to observe.

COMPONENTS: A COMPREHENSIVE LANGUAGE ARTS PROGRAM

(C) Eating outside is also part of the experience.

(D) After returning to the classroom, the teacher meets with small groups to discuss the walk.

(E) The experience story is begun as the children dictate to their teacher what they want to say.

(F) After the story is completed, the children take turns reading it. The teacher uses words and sentences in their story for practicing reading skills. Then the story is hung up to be reread later.

THE LANGUAGE EXPERIENCE APPROACH TO READING

Of all the many approaches to teaching reading, language experience offers many advantages in capitalizing on children's oral language skills and in developing a well-integrated language arts-reading program. Language experience may be the basis for reading instruction or a supplement to the regular reading program. Why?

1. *The content is meaningful.* Children dictate and write about experiences that are meaningful to them. Suppose a class is having a cooking experience like baking cookies for a classroom party. The recipe is first written on a chart for everyone to read. The children and teacher discuss the necessary steps in preparing the cookie dough. These are then written below the recipe for everyone to read. Finally, while the cookies are baking, the children dictate a group story about the experience. This is copied by each child and placed along with other experience stories in a special book. The stories may be read to the teacher, a reading partner, or perhaps taken home and read to a parent. The content of experience stories is meaningful to children. This is very important to note since past experience is so much a part of the reading process. Children are writing and reading about things they know and understand; and because the concepts and vocabulary are familiar, they can easily comprehend their own written language.

2. *Children read their own language.* Because the reading material is dictated or written by the children themselves, the written language is their own. A student dictates a story or experience to the teacher and it is recorded exactly as it is said. If the student says, "He be going to the store," the teacher writes "He be going to the store." If a child says, however, "I'm goin' to the stowe in the mornin'," the teacher would write the dictated sentence using the correct spellings. Children need to see their words as they will actually appear in printed reading material. Children's linguistic ability is recognized and used in teaching them to read. Children experience success at the very beginning of reading instruction. Because they use their language and their experiences, children can immediately read what has been written. They realize that reading is not some esoteric process only adults know about; they can actually see how language and reading are related.

3. *The language experience approach involves all the language arts.* Hall states, "the language experience approach is based on the interrelatedness of language and reading. Pupils learn to

---

read in a communication context where reading occurs in conjunction with talking, listening, and writing."[6] When using language experience in the classroom, a teacher naturally integrates all four of the language arts areas and each contributes to the development of the other.

4. *Reading is an active process.* The language experience approach makes reading an active process. Children become personally and actively involved in reading. The students participate in a wide variety of direct experiences, conservations, and discussions as a part of this approach; and they have many opportunities to write about those things that interest them. They find in their own individual stories and in group compositions that meaning is the essential element of reading. They formulate their own rules, seek out their own patterns, develop their own ways to identify unfamiliar words.

Research on the Language Experience Approach

As part of the National First Grade Studies, a number of investigators chose to compare the effectiveness of the language experience and basal reading approaches. Findings reported by Stauffer and Hammond show language experience to be an effective reading approach in grade one, and children taught with this method excel in written communication over those taught with a basal reader.[7] An extension of their study suggests that it is also an effective method in both second and third grades.[8] Studies conducted by Hahn[9] and Kendrick and Bennett[10] also favored the language experience approach.

Language experience has its limitations, and a teacher must guard against some of the inherent pitfalls. There is no manual or teacher's guide to follow. A teacher must rely on a knowledge and understanding of the reading process. It is certainly not an easy way to teach reading. A teacher needs to provide for individualized instruction, grouping children for needed skills, personalized record keeping, and continual diagnosis and evaluation of each student's reading capabilities.

A second pitfall is that learning to read may become incidental. If a teacher has children read and reread the same experience charts or stories expecting the sheer repetition of words to teach students to read, it will not work. There is more to the language experience approach than the mere reading of experience stories.

COMPONENTS: A COMPREHENSIVE LANGUAGE ARTS PROGRAM

Teaching Reading Using Language Experience

Basic to this approach is the writing of experience stories. At first, young children can dictate their stories to the teacher, a teacher's aide, or a parent who has volunteered to help in the classroom. An experience story may be dictated by a small group of children or by an individual child. As children mature, they can begin writing their own experience stories.

You can help children become independent writers if you provide special individual word boards and encourage their use each day. Printed on one side of the board is a list of basic sight words. Small cards containing the same words are slipped into a pocket below the printed words on the board. On the other side of the board, there are pockets and blank cards for children to write their own words. These are special words which they need in their individual writing. The small cards are taken from the board and strung together to construct sentences for the child's story. After a sentence is completed, the child writes it in a special storybook. The cards

Word boards are easy and inexpensive to make. Children can use them to build and write sentences for their language experience stories. (Photograph by Charles Jones)

are then returned to the pockets as children prepare to build and write the next sentence for their story. As this process continues, children learn to use configuration clues, recognize that words and sentences are read from left to right, and find that language is related to reading.

Word boards are very similar to the word banks that are usually associated with the language experience approach. Both help the beginning reader establish a sight vocabulary. Either method of collecting words, if consistently used, will contribute toward children's vocabulary development and ability to spell words correctly.

Basic sight words for children's word boards may be obtained from a variety of sources. You may want to choose words appearing frequently in children's group experience stories or words from their basal reader. The Dolch Basic Sight Word List[11] of 220 words has long been used and recommended by most reading authorities. It is still a useful list of words, but there are others that have been published more recently. The American Heritage List[12] is a highly recommended source since the 500 words included in the list are those that appear most frequently in printed materials for children. Another good list, developed by Kucera and Francis,[13] contains 220 high frequency words, 82 of which are not included in the Dolch Basic Sight Word List. It is shown here as one possible source that you may use in selecting words for individual children to learn.

220 Words of Greatest Frequency in the Kucera-Francis Study

the	at	her	so	two	after
of	by	all	said	may	also
and	I	she	what	then	did
to	this	there	up	do	many
a	had	would	its	first	before
in	not	their	about	any	must
that	are	we	into	my	through
is	but	him	than	now	back
was	from	been	them	such	years
he	or	has	can	like	where
for	have	when	only	our	much
it	an	who	other	over	your
with	they	will	new	man	way
as	which	more	some	me	well
his	one	no	could	even	down
on	you	if	time	most	should
be	were	out	these	made	because

each	being	states	school	took
just	under	himself	every	head
those	never	few	don't	yet
people	day	house	got	government
Mr.	same	use	united	system
how	another	during	left	better
too	know	without	number	set
little	while	again	course	told
state	last	place	war	nothing
good	might	American	until	night
very	us	around	always	end
make	great	however	away	why
world	old	home	something	called
still	year	small	fact	didn't
own	off	found	though	eyes
see	come	Mrs.	water	find
men	since	thought	less	going
work	against	went	public	look
long	go	say	put	asked
get	came	part	thing	later
here	right	once	almost	knew
between	used	general	hand	does
both	take	high	enough	
life	three	upon	far	

Children's experience stories can be written on large sheets of chart paper. They can then be taped to coat hangers and hung on a special rod in the classroom. Children can select their favorite stories, spread them out on the floor, and read them to partners or friends.

Students enjoy reading and collecting their own stories. Individual books can be made for each child's compilation of experience stories, or a teacher may choose to compile a book of classroom stories or poems. Each child submits a piece of writing to be placed in a large bound book. Books may be kept in the classroom library area for everyone in the class to read and enjoy.

Making Books

Books are easy to bind and children feel they are very special. They can also provide a purpose for children's writing. To make a book, fold the paper in half for the pages as in Figure 23 (A). Then sew along the fold with a needle and thread or with a sewing machine. If sewing the pages is not possible, they may be stapled

Children can make and enjoy their own books.

together along the folded line. See Figure 23 (B). Next cut cloth or wallpaper one inch larger on all sides than the book pages. Lay the pages open and flat to measure as in Figure 23 (C). Heavy wrapping paper or contact paper may also be used for the cover. Then cut two pieces of cardboard about the weight of a shirt cardboard a little larger than the pages as in Figure 23 (D). Two pieces of drymount are cut to fit and placed between the cardboard and the cloth cover material. If you prefer, glue works well also and may be spread evenly with a damp sponge. See Figure 23 (E). There should be some space between the two pieces of cardboard to allow the book to open and close easily. If you are using drymount, press with an iron in a few places to hold the cardboard in place. Then, fold the corners of the outer covering in, fold the top down and in, then fold the bottom up and the sides in and iron or glue as in Figure 23 (F). The final step is to glue or use drymount and iron the first and last pages to the cover, as shown in Figure 23 (G).

Using Wordless Books

Wordless books or books with very few words are excellent sources for stimulating children's oral and written language. A number of years ago wordless books for children were rare. Today, however, there are quantities available, both in hardcover and paperback.

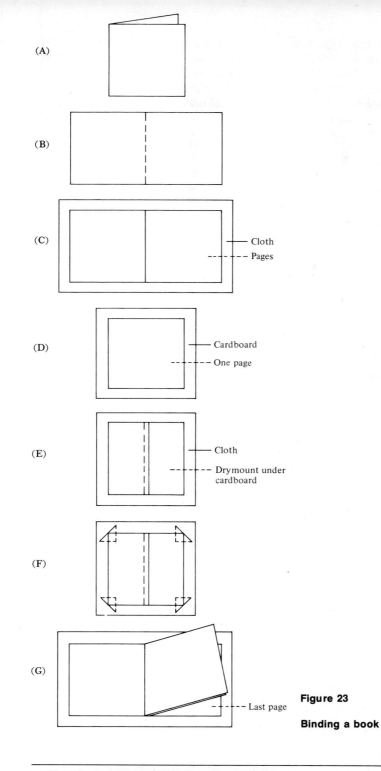

(A)

(B)

(C) —— Cloth
----- Pages

(D) —— Cardboard
----- One page

(E) —— Cloth
----- Drymount under cardboard

(F)

(G) ----- Last page

Figure 23

Binding a book

As part of language experience, children may dictate or write their own text to accompany the pictures of a wordless book. As you read your students' story texts, you will notice variations. Children can look at the same book, yet see and write about it in original ways. You may find that some students observe more closely and that their stories contain many details. Children's word choices will not always be the same, and certain portions of the story may even be interpreted differently by some pupils. You may also be aware of variations in sentence structure as well as differences in text originality.

To illustrate how children can look at the same book and write their own unique text, let's examine the following dictated stories about *Shrewbettina's Birthday.*[14]

A BIRTHDAY PARTY

Shrewbettina went to sleep.
And then she wakes up when the clock says cuckoo.
Her washing her face.
Her inviting the people to her birthday party.
The mean mouse is going to take her purse.
He's reaching for her purse.
He snatched her purse and ran.
The good mouse caught the bad mouse.
He is taking the mean mouse to the police.
He gave her back her purse and the police is taking him to jail.
They going in a grocery store.
She's talking to the grocery store man.
Her reading the note.
Her bought her groceries and came out of the store.
Her went back home.
Her wave at him good-bye.
Shrewbettina locking her door.
Her open the door and went in the kitchen.
Her cleaning up for the party.
Shrewbettina is cooking dinner.
Shrewbettina getting dressed up.
They brung Shrewbettina some presents.
They getting ready to eat.
They starting eating the food.
They getting ready to dance.
They dancing with their boyfriend.
They getting ready to leave.
Shrewbettina wave good-bye to her boyfriend.
They left all the plates on the table.
And then she went to bed.

Lemon Ellis   Age 10

SHREWBETTINA AND ANOTHER MOUSE

Shrewbettina is asleep and watches the clock.
She is washing her face.
She is reading her letter.
She is going out to the store and another mouse is going after her.
The mouse almost caught her.
He is going to get her purse.
He took her purse and she is going after him. She dropped her basket.
Tim is going to get the purse.
And he is crying and he is sad.
And Tim is holding him.
And he gave her the purse.
Him and her are going to the store.
She is walking up to the counter to tell the man what she wants.
She is getting her groceries.
She is going out the store and Tim is going with her.
She is going with him.
And she is by her door and she is going in the door.
She is unlocking her door.
She is in her cave house in the kitchen.
She is sweeping her floor cleaning up for her party.
She is cooking cake and her dinner.
She is dressing up for her party, looking in the mirror and putting on her jewelry.
Tim walked in with his present and so did his family with a present.
They is having a party dinner.
They is having cake, ice cream, cookies, and they is having a good time.
He is blowing the horn for the mices.
And they is dancing.
They is going to leave.
Tim is going up the steps waving bye-bye.
She is holding the candle and cleaning up.
And she is gone back to bed.

Greta Pines   Age 10

Stories such as these provide excellent opportunities for teacher evaluation. For example, considering language complexity, what can you say about a child's language development? Looking at various word choices, what do you know about a child's vocabulary development? Does a child's story text demonstrate creativity or originality? Answers to these questions and others will enable you to plan additional needed experiences to improve the quality of a child's written and oral language.

Picture Books with Few or No Words

The following is a compilation of picture books containing few or no words. Consider this merely a representative list, and plan to add other children's books that you find.

Anno, Mitsumasa. *Topsy-Turvies*. New York: Walker, 1970.
Aruego, Jose. *Look What I Can Do*. New York: Scribner, 1971.
Barton, Byron. *Elephant*. New York: Seabury, 1971.
Bolliger-Savelli, Antonella. *The Knitted Cat*. New York: Macmillan, 1971.
Carroll, Ruth. *What Whiskers Did*. New York: Henry Z. Walck, Inc., 1965.
Goodall, John S. *Paddy's Evening Out*. New York: Atheneum, 1973.
Goodall, John S. *Shrewbettina's Birthday*. New York: Harcourt Brace, 1970.
Hoban, Tina. *Circles, Triangles and Squares*. New York: Macmillan, 1974.
Hoban, Tana. *Count and See*. New York: Macmillan, 1972.
Hoban, Tana. *Look Again*. New York: Macmillan, 1971.
Hoban, Tana. *Over, Under and Through*. New York: Macmillan, 1973.
Hoban, Tana. *Push-Pull, Empty-Full*. New York: Macmillan, 1972.
Hoban, Tana. *Shapes and Things*. New York: Macmillan, 1970.
Hogrogian, Nonny. *Apples*. New York: Macmillan, 1972.
Hutchins, Pat. *Rosie's Walk*. New York: Macmillan, 1968.
Krahn, Fernando. *April Fools*. New York: Dutton, 1974.
Lisker, Sonia. *The Attic Witch*. New York: Four Winds, 1973.
Mayer, Mercer. *A Boy, a Dog and a Frog*. Eau Claire, Wisconsin: E. M. Hale, 1972.
Mayer, Mercer, and Marianna Mayer. *Mine*. New York: Simon & Schuster, 1970.
Meyer, Renate. *Vicki*. New York: Atheneum, 1969.
Shulevitz, Uri. *Oh What A Noise!* New York: Macmillan, 1971.
Wezel, Peter. *The Good Bird*. New York: Harper & Row, 1964.
Wildsmith, Brian. *Birds*. New York: F. Watts, 1967.
Wildsmith, Brian. *The Circus*. London: Oxford University Press, 1970.
Wildsmith, Brian. *Fishes*. New York: F. Watts, 1968.
Wildsmith, Brian. *Wild Animals*. New York: F. Watts, 1967.

Teaching Recognition Skills

The beginning reader needs to develop a sight vocabulary. Repetition of basic sight words needs to be provided for the young reader. Word boards with experience stories read over and over again will help, but experience charts may be cut up and individual word cards created. Children can practice reading the words to partners and, finally, the words may be used to reconstruct the original story.

The beginning reader also needs to develop the concept that words are made up of letters and each letter has a name. What better way is there to learn this than by seeing your dictated words written letter by letter on paper? A teacher can easily discuss letters that spell various words in a child's experience story. Children's ABC books, such as *Helen Oxenbury's ABC of Things*,[15] *John Burningham's ABC*,[16] or *Brian Wildsmith's ABC*,[17] can be provided for both learning and enjoyment.

Phonics Phonic instruction can coincide with the writing of experience stories. For example, children can look for words within a story which have the same beginning, middle, or ending sounds. If phonic generalizations are taught, only those which have high utility value should be considered (see research by Bailey,[18] Clymer,[19] and Emans[20]). A teacher should recognize that not all children will require the help of all phonic generalizations—the instruction should be personalized.

An inductive approach is best if teaching phonic generalizations. Have children look at a representative group of words that follow particular generalizations. After a discussion of the words, children can state their own generalizations.

For example, a teacher might say, look at the following words that begin with the letters *kn*. Let's read each of the words. What do you notice about the *k* in each of the words?

What rule might we follow when reading these words that begin with the letters *kn*?

knee	*knit*	*knew*
know	*known*	*knight*
knife	*knock*	*knack*

Context clues Children need to be helped to recognize how context clues can be used to "unlock" strange or unfamiliar words. If a child does not recognize a word, the entire sentence should be read leaving out the unknown word. Using the context of the sentence, the student should be encouraged to *predict* the unknown word. The number of contextual clues appearing within a given sentence influences how accurate a child may be in making predictions. For example, consider the following sentences. The same word is missing in each. Why is it difficult to predict the missing word in the first two sentences? Why is it easy to predict the missing word in the third sentence?

I'm going to buy some _____ at the store.
She makes her own Christmas _____.
The _____ he drew were both aces.

Therefore, in the sentence below, for the child who is unfamiliar with the word *camel*, the context of the sentence tells the child the word is a name of an animal that lives on a hot, dry desert.

The *camel* lives on a hot, dry desert.

The child should be encouraged to make predictions about the word. A teacher might say, "What animals live on a desert? What animal might this be living on a hot, dry desert?"

A form of the cloze procedure may help children understand the usefulness of context clues. Exercises, such as the following, may be given to children, or you may type their own experience stories leaving out key words for them to write in using the context of their own sentences. Students may be asked: What words tell you the missing word? Why are these words helpful clues?

Sue was _____ about going to Mary's birthday _____. She could hardly wait until Saturday. What should she _____ Mary for her birthday? Perhaps some _____ for her _____. Or maybe the _____ that she had been wanting to read.

COMBINING LANGUAGE EXPERIENCE WITH A BASAL READING PROGRAM

Reading in many schools today is taught using primarily a basal reading approach. If you are interested in language experience but expect to use a basal reader, there are effective ways of combining the two methods. Two are mentioned here, and you may explore other possibilities.

The Basal Reader as a Resource

It is possible to use basal readers as resource books along with the language experience approach. For example, children can read a story from their basal reader and then retell it in their own words. This may be done by having students dictate the retelling or write it themselves. Children may enjoy writing new episodes or adventures for stories. The following are examples of individual children's telling of a new episode after reading a basal reader story. In this particular case, the teacher read the story aloud to a group of beginning readers. Then after discussing the story, they each dictated their very own. (If you are not working with beginning readers, you may want your students to read the story silently and then dictate or write their stories.)

GOING TO THE COUNTRY

In the morning Ting-a-ling and Soo Ling were going to see their cousins, but first they must get a good night's sleep.

Finally, it was morning and they were on the way. When they arrived at their cousins, it was time to go trick or treating. After that they spent the night with their cousins. The next day they all went to church.

While they were in church, Ting-a-ling ran away. Everyone chased around looking for Ting-a-ling. They found Ting-a-ling and chased her all the way home. They stayed for dinner. After dinner they talked. Ting-a-ling ran away again. The children cried and cried.

Teresa Fisher

SOO LING GOES TO THE SEA

Today Grandfather and Soo Ling were going to the sea. They were so happy they decided to sing some songs on the way. Suddenly the car ran out of gas. It was a good thing they were on a hill. They went down the hill so fast that Grandfather lost all his hair.

Mike Kohlman

Each child's story was typed and placed in a special booklet. The teacher also included a few questions about each story on the second page of the booklets. The following day, the children were handed their booklets and encouraged to share their stories with one another. When the last reader had finished, the children asked if they could illustrate the front cover of their booklets. The reply was "yes" and they went immediately to get a variety of art materials for their project. Later, as they cut, glued, and painted, the teacher moved from child to child discussing the questions on the second page of each booklet.

That evening the teacher read through the reading skills section of the basal reading manual and selected several exercises and activities that would be useful to these children. The next day the students found new pages in their booklets. One showed their original story with several missing words, as in the example below.

IN THE COUNTRY

Ting-a-ling was supposed to go to school tomorrow. He was not happy about going to _____. Ting-a-ling decided to _____ away. He thought the country would be a good place to hide.

It was 1:00 a.m. and Ting-a-ling _____ the house. He walked and walked. At last he saw the country. Ting-a-ling was very _____ and hungry. He didn't have any _____. Ting-a-ling sat by a _____ and looked around. Ting-a-ling wished he was home. Just then he saw Soo Ling. He ran to her. Soo Ling smiled and took him _____.

The children read the stories silently filling in the missing words. They were instructed to read each sentence and then predict the missing word based on the context of the sentence.

Using Language Experience in Addition to a Basal Reader

A second way of combining the two approaches is to use a basal reading series supplemented with language experiences. For example, children can dictate or write experience stories about baking cookies, art projects, classroom visitors, handcraft demonstrations, model constructions, group dramatizations—the list is infinite. The stories may be read or shared, placed in special books for the library area, or written on large sheets of chart paper and displayed in the classroom. Students may also have their own writing books and word boards.

There are many ways to use components of the language experience approach while teaching in a basal reading program. As you reread portions of this chapter and also learn more about language experience through additional readings, other ideas will come to you.

REFERENCES

¹ Kenneth S. Goodman, ed., *Miscue Analysis.* Urbana, Illinois: Eric Clearinghouse on Reading and Communication Skills, 1973.

² Kenneth S. Goodman. "Effective Teachers of Reading Know Language and Children," *Elementary English*, vol. 51, September 1974, p. 824.

³ Ibid., p. 835.

⁴ Jean Piaget. *The Language and Thought of the Child.* New York: Harcourt Brace, 1926, p. 133.

⁵ Kenneth S. Goodman. "Effective Teachers of Reading Know Language and Children." P. 825.

⁶ Mary Anne Hall. *Teaching Reading As a Language Experience.* Columbus, Ohio: Merrill, 1970, p. 1.

⁷ Russell G. Stauffer and W. Dorsey Hammond. "The Effectiveness of Language Arts and Basic Reader Approaches to First Grade Reading

Instruction—Extended into Second Grade," *Reading Teacher*, vol. 20, May 1967, pp. 740–746.

⁸ Russell G. Stauffer and W. Dorsey Hammond. "The Effectiveness of Language Arts and Basic Reader Approaches to First Grade Reading Instruction—Extended into the Third Grade," *Reading Research Quarterly*, vol. 4, Summer 1969.

⁹ Harry T. Hahn, "Three Approaches to Beginning Reading Instruction—ITA, Language Experience and Basic Readers—Extended into Second Grade," *Reading Teacher*, vol. 20, May 1967, pp. 711–715.

¹⁰ William M. Kendrick and Clayton L. Bennett. "A Comparative Study of Two First Grade Language Arts Programs—Extended into Second Grade," *Reading Teacher*, vol. 20, May 1967, pp. 747–755.

¹¹ E. W. Dolch. *Teaching Primary Reading*. Champaign, Illinois: Gerrard Press, 1941, pp. 196–215.

¹² Wayne Otto and Robert Chester. "Sight Words for Beginning Readers," *The Journal of Educational Research*, vol. 65, no. 10, July–August, 1972, pp. 435–443.

¹³ Henry Kucera and W. Nelson Francis. *Computational Analysis of Present-Day American English*. Providence, Rhode Island: Brown University Press, 1967.

¹⁴ John S. Goodall. *Shrewbettina's Birthday*. New York: Harcourt, 1970.

¹⁵ Helen Oxenbury. *Helen Oxenbury's ABC of Things*. New York: F. Watts, 1971.

¹⁶ John Burningham. *John Burningham's ABC*. London: Jonathan Cape, 1964.

¹⁷ Brian Wildsmith. *Brian Wildsmith's ABC*. New York: F. Watts, 1963.

¹⁸ Mildred Hart Bailey. "The Utility of Phonic Generalizations in Grades One through Six," *Reading Teacher*, vol. 20, February 1967, pp. 413–418.

¹⁹ Theodore Clymer. "The Utility of Phonic Generalizations in the Primary Grades," *Reading Teacher*, vol. 16, January 1963, pp. 252–258.

²⁰ Robert Emans. "The Usefulness of Phonic Generalizations above the Primary Grades," *Reading Teacher*, vol. 20, February 1967, pp. 419–425.

CHAPTER FOURTEEN

Integrating the Language Arts

PREVIEW QUESTIONS

1 What bases are there for planning a language arts program?

2 How can parents or other adults help the teacher in individualizing and enriching language arts instruction for children?

3 How do you decide which kinds of activities to include in providing a well-balanced program?

4 How can a teacher extend one experience to include a variety of activities?

Throughout this text we have emphasized the importance of considering what we know about how children acquire language and how they learn cognitively as a basis for planning classroom activities and structuring the classroom environment. The language arts involve certain skills that children need to learn and offer many possibilities for expressing individuality. The language arts also provide the basis for learning in a wide range of other content areas such as mathematics, social studies, and science. The ability to read, compose, and express ideas orally can be satisfying ends within themselves as well as means of acquiring and expressing knowledge in other areas.

The various aspects of the language arts are so interrelated that it is essential for teachers at each age level to plan a language arts program that is balanced. Over-emphasizing one area at the expense of another often results in failing to accomplish one's first goal. We see this happening, for example, in reading programs which emphasize word attack skills at the expense of language development. Children may learn to sound out words rather well, but their comprehension skills are restricted by their limited vocabulary and sentence structures. They do not become avid readers—readers who enjoy reading and good literature; rather, frequently they remain word callers. In a balanced program oral expression, written expression, and reading all have an important part. There is time for skills development and time for imaginative uses of language.

THE BASES FOR LANGUAGE ARTS

This text and the activities suggested in the various areas of the language arts are based on two areas of developmental theory: linguistic and cognitive. We have attempted to draw from these two theories implications for practice in the language arts. Thus, the language activities suggested are those that should help children further develop their language, and they should be appropriate to the children's levels of cognitive development.

Linguistic Bases

Research and study by psycholinguists suggest three implications that relate to planning language arts activities. One of these is the need for children to have a rich language environment throughout their elementary school experience. Although most basic language structures are known by children when they enter school, there are others still being acquired. The child's vocabulary is constantly increasing and becoming more and more refined. It is through exposure to rich and varied language that children acquire new structures and new vocabulary. The language of books and poetry is one rich source, but children also need to hear adults using language. Tapes, records, and personal interviews add to their contacts with mature adult language.

Another important implication from linguistic theory is the need for children to use language in a variety of ways. This suggests that children be given opportunities to compare and contrast things, to play with words and sounds, to categorize, describe, explain, and give directions. They must use language orally and in its written forms. Only through direct experiences with language can students learn about the changes one makes to fit certain situations. The teacher, knowledgeable about linguistic theory, helps children use language to express their own views to satisfy themselves and to communicate effectively with others. Situations in the classroom that call for using language in many different ways are very important and can influence all areas of learning.

The third important language concept is that language develops in a particular sequence although there may be great variations in the rate of development. Although differences in language ability are obvious to kindergarten and early primary grade teachers, they become even more obvious in the later grades. This suggests that teachers should provide a wide range of activities for children so that each child is challenged without being given tasks which are impossible to accomplish.

Cognitive Bases

The psychological bases for language arts activities are almost exclusively cognitive in nature. Our understanding of how children learn cognitively indicates three major needs for teachers to keep in mind when planning for language arts. The first is that children should be actively and physically involved in what they are learning, working with real, concrete, touchable materials. The more removed from direct firsthand experience the learning is, the more difficult or even impossible a task becomes. Children throughout most of the elementary grades do not learn well from reading about things secondhand. Their thinking and learning are best facilitated by direct, concrete experiences. Touching, observing, and active involvement are all components of this environment.

The second implication is for children to have a variety of experiences. These experiences should lead to divergent ends—not those that have some predetermined answer. These experiences should also present a real problem to be solved. Sometimes the teacher may ask a question or suggest, "What if . . . ?" The classroom environment and the things that the teacher puts in this environment may structure the learning that goes on there. Children also should encounter experiences that are appropriate to their level of cognitive development. There will be many variations in the level of development within the same age group, and there must be experiences that will challenge each child at each level.

The third need is for children to make mistakes without feeling they have failed. Children, like adults, need to feel successful. This paradox presents a difficult but important problem for the teacher to handle. The key is that *trying* is the most important thing for children to do. Praise and encourage children for pursuing a reasonable approach, whether or not the approach works.

INVOLVING PARENTS AND OTHER ADULTS IN THE LANGUAGE ARTS PROGRAM

In such a highly individualized language arts program as the one we have suggested, it is often desirable to have additional help for the teacher. Parents, paid aides, volunteer adults in the community, college and high school students may all help the teacher give more individualized attention to children. Each may help in a very special way because of the unique skills they possess and the way each can relate to particular children.

Parent Involvement

It is particularly important that parents become involved in their children's education—because of the effect on the children's attitude toward learning, because of the implied positive value of learning, and for the help provided the teacher. A child's learning is not restricted to the five days a week or the approximately six hours in school on each of those days. Children learn all year round and during all their waking hours. This learning may be enriched by

Parents can become involved in their children's education. This parent is assisting the teacher during a fieldtrip to a nearby woods. (*Photograph by Charles Jones*)

the kinds of activities they do with their parents or older sisters and brothers, and the talk that accompanies such activities. Most parents are willing to help their children if they have some idea of what to do or how to do it. If you can give parents a choice of activities with which they are comfortable, they will work with their children. The following suggestions should indicate the kinds of things you might ask of parents:

Games to play developing word recognition skill or spelling
Book kits—one or several paperback books with some suggested areas for discussion or related things to do together
Simple experiments to try with ice cubes or seeds or baking powder
Things to cook or bake—a recipe to follow which requires reading or listening to directions
Things to make—beanbags or aprons or cover-ups for painting and other "messy" work
Observations to make at the grocery store, filling station, or park

COMPONENTS: A COMPREHENSIVE LANGUAGE ARTS PROGRAM

Magazine cutouts from several magazines sent home with specific
things to find and discuss

Tasks Utilizing Parents and Other Adult Assistance

There are so many kinds of assistance that parents and other adult
volunteers may give to help the classroom teacher in the language
arts program that each individual should find something valuable
to contribute. The following suggestions indicate some of the activities other adults may fulfill. As you develop your own ways of working with children, you may want to add to the lists or change items
to correspond more closely to your needs and ways of working with
your students.

Individualizing learning

Listen to a child read.
Read to a child or a small group.
Take dictation of children's compositions.
Read words or sentences for spelling practice or testing.
Help a child or small group of children with handwriting practice.
Assist child or children who are writing on their own with words
they can't spell, or provide other help as requested.
Go with a small group to an area on the school grounds for observations or experiments.
Work at a learning center.

Special instruction or enrichment There are numerous activities
that can be used as bases for listening, talking, writing, and reading. Almost everyone has some special ability or information they
can share with elementary school children. Some possible enrichment activities might be woodworking and construction; arts and
crafts activities; musical instruments; puppetry; film making;
photography; knitting, crocheting, embroidery, appliqué, quilting;
spinning and weaving; sharing special hobbies or collections;
cooking; storytelling; bookbinding.

Clerical assistance Not all adults want to work directly with children; they may be more comfortable in lending assistance to the
teacher in another capacity. There are numerous noninstructional

jobs, and having someone else help with them frees the teacher to spend more time with students. Some require working at the school, but many can be done at home. The following are examples of possible clerical tasks: typing, printing or writing out materials, lists, and so on; collating and stapling; checking work and keeping records; preparing materials or supplies; making games and puzzles; mixing paint, clay, and so on; collecting scrap materials or picking up supplies; cutting out pictures or letters or mounting children's work to be displayed; and making booklets for writing.

Consider very carefully what kinds of additional adult help you may need and how you have organized your ways of working with your students. Then find out what parent or other adult assistance is available in your area and how it is arranged in your school. Plan very carefully how your students can best benefit from more individualization, an increased base of enrichment experiences, and help at home. Identify useful clerical tasks and how they might be efficiently done with someone's help. Make your plans with all these ideas in mind.

PLANNING LANGUAGE ARTS ACTIVITIES

The needs of children, both linguistic and cognitive, must be the basis for planning in the language arts. Upon this basis the various components of a balanced program should include aspects of skills development and imaginative development in each of the major areas of oral expression, written expression, and reading.

The chart that follows has been helpful to a number of teachers in planning language arts activities to provide a program that is balanced among all the various areas. Not every area will be included every day and perhaps not even every week. Within a given block of time, however, each will be represented.

The activities suggested within each of the areas are not intended to be all-inclusive, but rather indicate the kinds of items that might be planned for each particular category. Some of the activities listed under "imaginative development" may also involve a considerable amount of "skill development."

The chart takes in all of the various areas of language arts: drama and discussion, composition skills of all kinds, supportive writing skills, listening, children's literature, and reading. The actual activities may be set up in a learning center approach or

LANGUAGE ARTS ACTIVITIES

	Imaginative Development	Skills Development
Oral Expression	Storytelling Choral reading Dramatic play Listening to stories or poems Improvised drama	Discussing Planning Reporting Introductions, messages and so on Critical listening
Written Expression	Writing stories Writing poetry Letter writing Personal writing	Note-taking Recording and reporting Spelling Handwriting Mechanics of writing
Reading	Reading for pleasure Literary elements Affective response to literature	Word recognition skills Comprehension skills Critical reading skills

worked out with the various groups if reading-language arts are being taught in that fashion. Some activities may be appropriate for the whole class, some for just a few children.

AN INTEGRATED EXPERIENCE IN LANGUAGE ARTS

A single experience often leads to many activities in the language arts reading area. The description or chart of what one class did after a visit to an historical home in their area may give you an idea of how interrelated the various aspects of language arts are and how one experience may be extended into oral and written language skills and imaginative work.

Some of the oral activities in this experience were specific speaking and listening skill development while others involved more imaginative uses of oral language. There were also many activities in written language—both reading and writing experiences. Some of these worked on skills such as letter writing and note-taking skills; others included more imaginative uses of the

LANGUAGE ARTS EXPERIENCES AND THE FIELDTRIP

	Listening	Speaking	Writing	Reading
Visit to a Local Historical Home				
Making arrangements for the visit		✓	✓	
Previsit research and information with a discussion of highlights	✓	✓	✓	✓
Introducing the guide to the group	✓	✓		
Recording information in individual booklets—sketches and information and writings	✓		✓	
Expressing appreciation—to guide, parents, or others involved			✓	
Additional information—speaker and film	✓			
Follow-up activities				
Stories and poems about the house, the time period, the people, and so on			✓	
Making display model—of the home, of a single room, or of an interesting piece	✓	✓		
Mini-biographies of famous local people			✓	✓
Improvised dramatization of events in the home, town, or area	✓	✓		
Reading stories or events in that time period or of people from the area				✓
Choral readings	✓	✓		✓
Mock news reports of people or events in local area			✓	
Informational reports on objects, costumes, or events related to visit			✓	✓

language such as writing mock news reports and reading stories of the time period.

The activities done in relation to this fieldtrip show a variety of planning and follow-up work in a meaningful setting. There are choices provided so that children may pursue their own individual interests, and there are enough options so that each child may be challenged and still find activities that are manageable.

RESOURCES FOR PART THREE

FOR FURTHER READING

Ashton-Warner, Sylvia. *Teacher*. Simon & Schuster, New York, 1963.

Goodman, Kenneth S., ed. *Miscue Analysis*. National Council of Teachers of English, Urbana, Illinois, 1973.

Hall, Mary Anne. *Teaching Reading as a Language Experience*. Merrill, Columbus, Ohio, 1970.

Haviland, Virginia. *Children and Literature*, Views and Reviews. Scott, Foresman, Glenview, Illinois, 1973.

Herrick, Virgil E., and Marcella Nerbovig. *Using Experience Charts with Children*. Merrill, Columbus, Ohio, 1964.

Huck, Charlotte S. *Children's Literature in the Elementary School*. Holt, New York, 1976.

Lee, Doris M., and Roach Van Allen. *Learning to Read through Experience*. Appleton Century Crofts, New York, 1963.

Sebesta, Sam Leaton, and William J. Iverson. *Literature for Thursday's Child*. Science Research, Chicago, Illinois, 1975.

Stauffer, Russell G. *The Language-Experience Approach to the Teaching of Reading*. Harper & Row, New York, 1970.

OTHER INSTRUCTIONAL MATERIALS

Filmstrips with Cassettes

Language Experience in Reading: An Overview, Encyclopedia Britannica Educational Corporation, 425 N. Michigan Avenue, Chicago, Illinois 60611.

The Learning Environment for LEIR, Encyclopedia Britannica Educational Corporation, 425 N. Michigan Avenue, Chicago, Illinois 60611.

Cassettes

Bonder, Barbara, Kenneth S. Goodman, and Jean Malmstrom. *Psycholinguistics and Reading.* National Council of Teachers of English, Urbana, Illinois, 1973.

Groff, Patrick. *Personalizing Reading Skills.* The set of five, one-hour cassettes may be obtained from Listener Educational Enterprises, 6777 Hollywood Boulevard, Hollywood, California 90028.

Films

Reading as Part of Life, Media Five Film Distributors, 1011 North Cole Avenue, Hollywood, California 90038.

Kohl, Herbert, Jerry Schmidt, and Dorothy Strickland, *et al., Building on What Children Know*, Media Five Film Distributors, 1011 North Cole Avenue, Hollywood, California 90038.

ACKNOWLEDGMENTS

William Armstrong, from *Sounder*. Copyright 1969 by William H. Armstrong. Reprinted by permission of Harper & Row, Publishers, Inc.

Harry Behn, "Far and Near," from *The Wizard in the Well*. Copyright 1956 by Harry Behn. Reprinted by permission of Harcourt Brace Jovanovich, Inc.

Althea, Berry, from "Readiness for Handwriting," in *Readiness for Reading and Related Language Arts*. A Research Bulletin of the National Council of Teachers of English, 1950. Reprinted by permission of NCTE.

Ruth Carlson, "Carlson Analytical Originality Scale," from "An Originality Story Scale," in *The Elementary Journal*, April 1965, Reprinted by permission of The University of Chicago Press.

Doris J. Chaconas, from *The Way the Tiger Walked*. Copyright 1970 by Doris J. Chaconas. Reprinted by permission of Simon & Schuster, Inc., Children's Book Division.

Carol Chomsky, "Write Now, Read Later," from *Language in Early Childhood Education*, Courtney B. Cazden (ed.), 1972. Reprinted by permission of National Association for the Education of Young Children.

Carol Chomsky, from "Stages in Language Development and Reading Exposure." *Harvard Educational Review*, **42**, February, 1972. Reprinted by permission of Harvard Educational Review.

John Ciardi, "Summer Song," from *The Man Who Sang the Sillies*. Copyright 1961 by John Ciardi. Reprinted by permission of J. B. Lippincott Company.

John Ciardi, "Mummy Slept Late and Daddy Fixed Breakfast," from *You Read to Me, I'll Read to You*. Copyright 1962 by John Ciardi. Reprinted by permission of J. B. Lippincott Company.

E. Clark, from "What's in a Word? On the Child's Acquisition of Semantics in His First Language," unpublished paper, August 1971.

Edgar Dale, et al., from *Techniques of Teaching Vocabulary*, 1971. Reprinted by permission of Cummings Publishing Co., Inc.

Lillie S. Davis, from "The Applicability of Phonic Generalizations to Selected Spelling Programs," in *Elementary English*, **49**, May 1972. Reprinted by permission of NCTE.

Robert H. Ennis, from "A Concept of Critical Thinking," in *Educational Leadership*, **21**, October 1963. Reprinted by permission of NCTE.

Aileen Fisher, "Skins," from *That's Why*. Copyright 1946 by Thomas Nelson, Inc.; renewal copyright 1974 by Aileen Fisher. Reprinted by permission of Aileen Fisher.

Kenneth S. Goodman, from "Effective Teachers of Reading Know Language and Children," in *Elementary English*, **51**, September 1974. Reprinted by permission of NCTE.

Marjorie Hart, from "Language Immunity: A Preschool View," in *Elementary English*, April 1973. Reprinted by permission of NCTE.

William F. Herrnkind, from "Strange March of the Spiny Lobster," in *National Geographic*, June 1975. Reprinted by permission of *National Geographic*.

Ernest Horn, from *A Basic Writing Vocabulary—10,000 Words Most Commonly Used in Writing*. University of Iowa Monographs in Education, First Series, No. 4, 1926. Reprinted by permission of The University of Iowa.

Mollie Hunter, from *The Ghosts of Glencoe*. Copyright 1966 by Evans Brothers, Ltd. Reprinted by permission of Funk & Wagnalls Publishing Company.

Leslie Johnson, from "One Hundred Words Most Often Misspelled by Children in the Elementary Grades," in *Journal of Educational Research*, **44**, October 1950. Reprinted by permission of Dembar Educational Research Services.

Henry Kucera & W. Nelson Francis, from *Computational Analysis of Present-Day American English*. Copyright 1967 Brown University Press. Reprinted by permission of publisher.

Melvin Walker La Follette, "The Ballad of Red Fox," in *New Poets of England and America*, Donald Hall & Robert Pack, Editors, 1962. Reprinted by permission; © 1952, The New Yorker Magazine, Inc.

S. M. Lane & M. Kemp, from *An Approach to Creative Writing in the Primary School*. Copyright 1967 by Blackie & Sons Limited. Reprinted by permission of publisher.

Alfred M. Lee & Elizabeth B. Lee (eds.), from *The Fine Art of Propaganda*. 1939 Harcourt Brace Jovanovich. Reprinted by permission of authors.

E. H. Lennenberg, chart adaptation from "Motor and Language Development: Selected Milestones," in *Biological Functions of Language*. 1967 by John Wiley & Sons, Inc. Reprinted by permission of publisher.

Leo Lionni, from *Alexander and the Wind-up Mouse*. Copyright 1969 by Leo Lionni. Reprinted by permission of Pantheon Books, a Division of Random House, Inc.

Leo Lionni, illustration from *Fish Is Fish*. Copyright 1970 by Leo Lionni. Reprinted by permission of Pantheon Books, a Division of Random House, Inc.

David McCord, "The Pickety Fence," from *Far and Few*. Copyright 1952 by David McCord. Reprinted by permission of Little, Brown and Co.

David McCord, "Song of the Train," from *Far and Few*. Copyright 1952 by David McCord. Reprinted by permission of Little, Brown and Co.

David McNeill, from *The Acquisition of Language*. 1970, Harper & Row. Reprinted by permission of publisher.

Eve Merriam, "Spaghetti," in *Finding a Poem*. Copyright 1970 by Eve Merriam. Reprinted by permission of Atheneum Publishers Inc.

Scott O'Dell, from *Sing Down the Moon*. Copyright 1970 by Scott O'Dell. Reprinted by permission of Houghton Mifflin Company, publisher.

"One, Two," from *Poems for the Children's Hour* by Josephine Bouton (Comp.). Garden City Publishing Company 1927.

Henry Rinsland, from *A Basic Vocabulary of Elementary School Children*. Macmillan Publishing Company, 1945. Reprinted by permission of Dr. Martha Rinsland.

John F. Savage, from *Linguistics for Teachers: Selected Readings*. Copyright 1973 by John F. Savage. Reprinted by permission of Science Research Associates, publishers.

Helen Schneeberg & Marciene Mattleman, from "The Listen-Read Project: Motivating Students Through Dual Modalities," in *Elementary English*, **50**, September 1973. Reprinted by permission of NCTE.

Maurice Sendak, "January," from *Chicken Soup with Rice* from *The Nutshell Library*. Copyright 1962 by Maurice Sendak. Reprinted by permission of Harper & Row, Publishers, Inc.

Kaye Starbird, "Speaking of Cows," from *Speaking of Cows*. J. B. Lippincott Company 1960. Reprinted by permission of author.

George Strong, "The Modern Hiawatha," from *Favorite Poems Old and New*, Helen Ferris (Comp.). Doubleday & Company 1957.

Geoffrey Summerfield, from "About Drama in England," in *Elementary English*, **47**, January 1970.

"There Once Was an Old Man of Blackheath," (unknown) from *Laughable Limericks*, Sara & John E. Brewton (Comps.). Thomas Y. Crowell 1965.

"There Was an Old Woman," from *Junior Voices, The First Book* by Geoffrey Summerfield. Penguin Books, 1970.

"This Old Hammer," from *Junior Voices, The Second Book*, by Geoffrey Summerfield. Penguin Books, 1970.

Alex Tolstoy, from *The Great Big Enormous Turnip*. Copyright 1968 by Alex Tolstoy. Reprinted by permission of Franklin Watts, Inc.

Alvin Tresselt, from *White Snow Bright Snow*. Copyright 1947 by Lothrop, Lee & Shepard. Reprinted by permission Lothrop, Lee & Shepard.

Alvin Tresselt, from *A Thousand Lights and Fireflies*. Copyright 1965 by Alvin Tresselt. Reprinted by permission of Parents' Magazine Press.

Andrew Wilkinson, from "Oracy in English Teaching," in *Elementary English*, **45**, October 1968. Reprinted by permission of NCTE.

Margery Williams, from The Velveteen Rabbit. Doubleday & Company, Inc. 1926. Reprinted by permission of publisher.

Evelyn Wright, from "Wishes, Lies and Dreams: Pedagogical Prescriptions," in *Elementary English*, **51**, April 1974. Reprinted by permission of NCTE.

Index